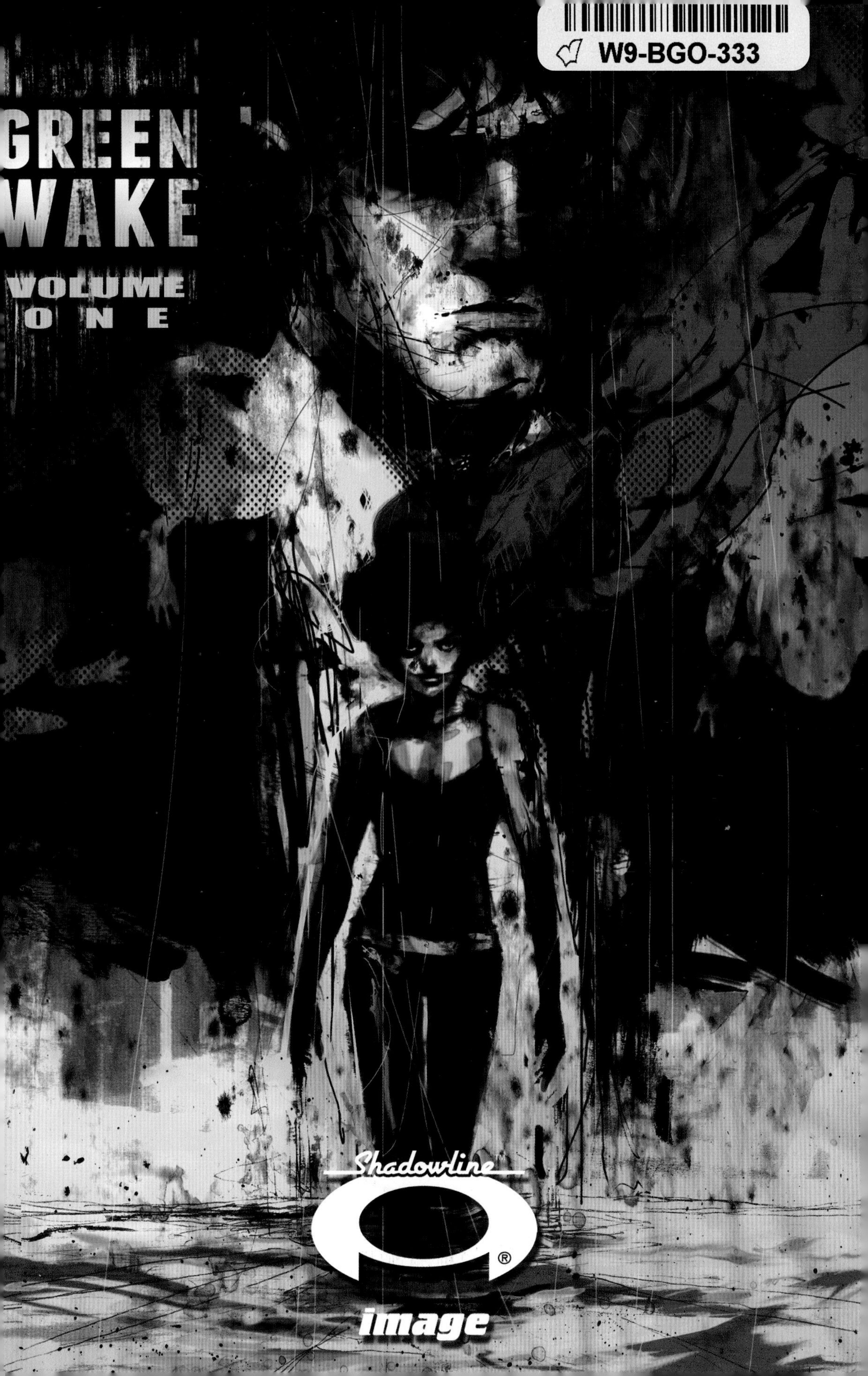
GREEN
WAKE
VOLUME
ONE
Shadowline
image

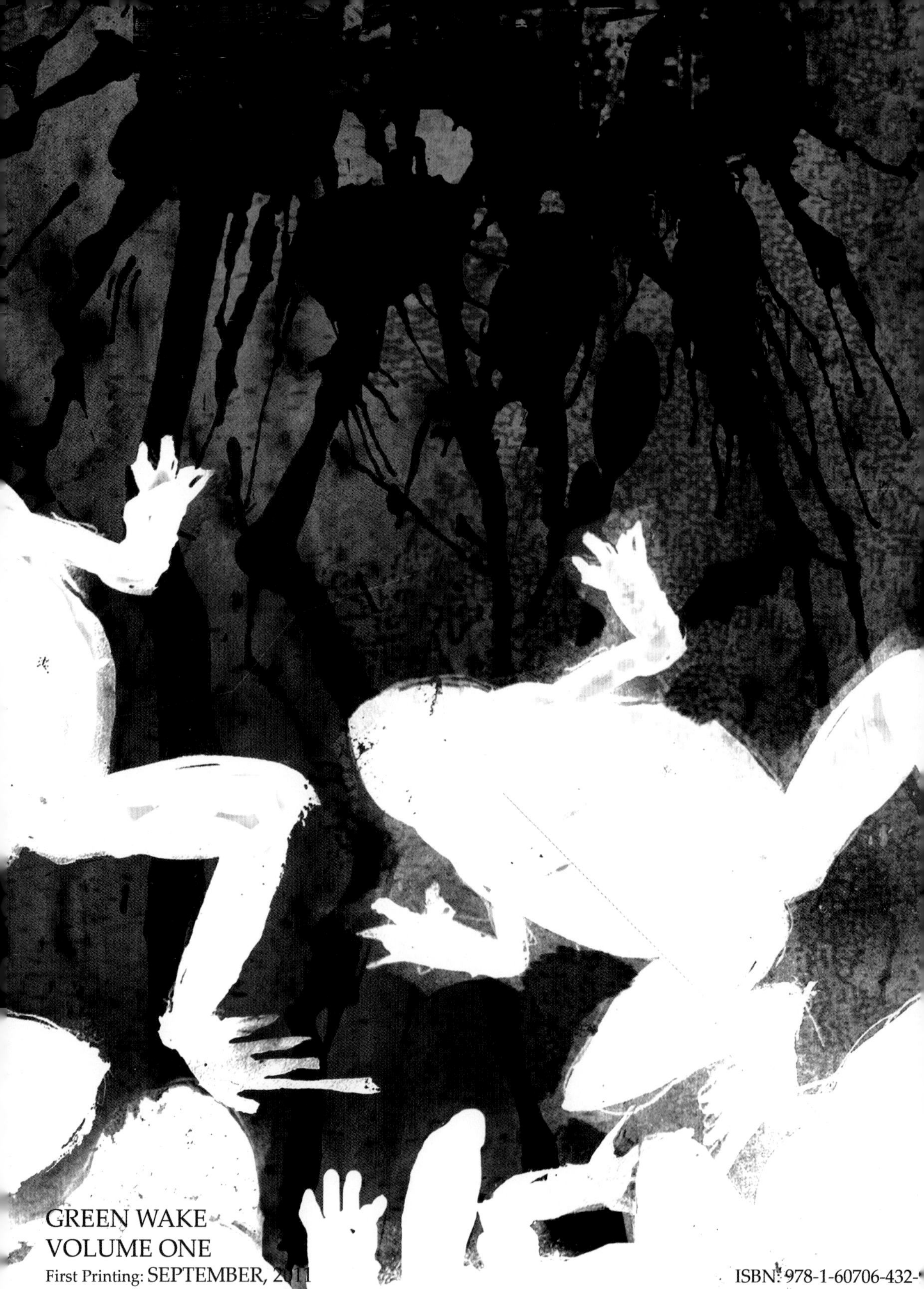

GREEN WAKE
VOLUME ONE

First Printing: SEPTEMBER, 2011

ISBN: 978-1-60706-432-

Published by Image Comics, Inc. Office of publication: 2134 Allston Way, Second Floor, Berkeley, California 94704. PRINTED IN KOREA. International Rights Representative: Christine Jensen (christine@gfloystudio.com).

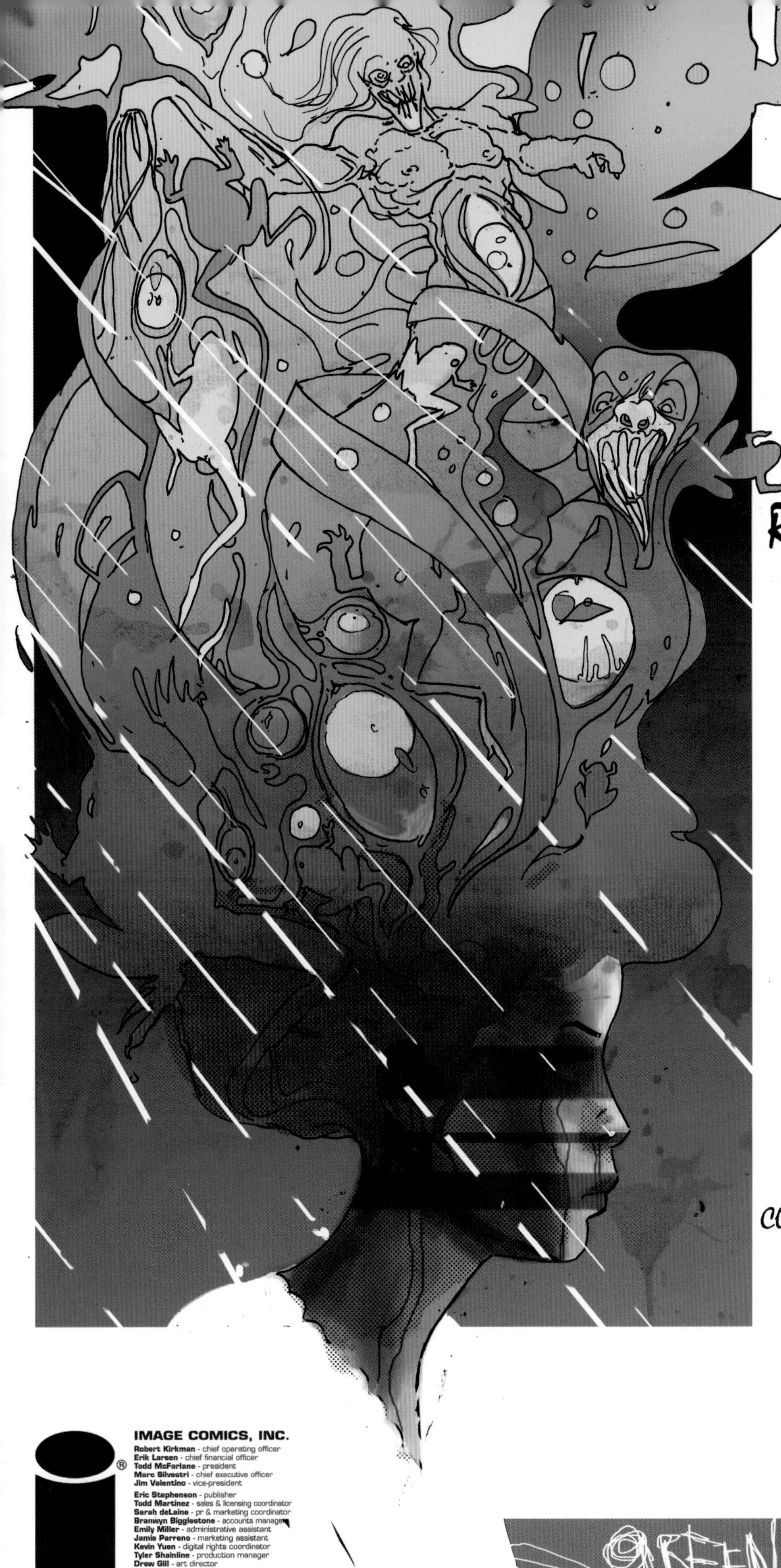

KURTIS WIEBE
STORY

RILEY ROSSMO
ART
and COLORS

KELLY TINDALL
LETTERS

JADE DODGE
EDITS

MARC LOMBARDI
COMMUNICATIONS

JIM VALENTINO
BOOK DESIGN
PUBLISHER

IMAGE COMICS, INC.

Robert Kirkman - chief operating officer
Erik Larsen - chief financial officer
Todd McFarlane - president
Marc Silvestri - chief executive officer
Jim Valentino - vice-president

Eric Stephenson - publisher
Todd Martinez - sales & licensing coordinator
Sarah deLaine - pr & marketing coordinator
Branwyn Bigglestone - accounts manager
Emily Miller - administrative assistant
Jamie Parreno - marketing assistant
Kevin Yuen - digital rights coordinator
Tyler Shainline - production manager
Drew Gill - art director
Jonathan Chan - senior production artist
Monica Garcia - production artist
Vincent Kukua - production artist
Jana Cook - production artist

www.imagecomics.com

GREEN WAKE

Dedication...

...to Jess for showing a clear path to the conclusion
when my gut said every other option just wouldn't suffice.
Kurtis J. Wiebe

...to Robin, Kelly, Noah, John, Theo, Dallas, Jammy, Geo,
Ryan, C-mac, Sean, the folks at AD and everyone in Saskatoon.
Riley Rossmo

Green Wake #1 cover

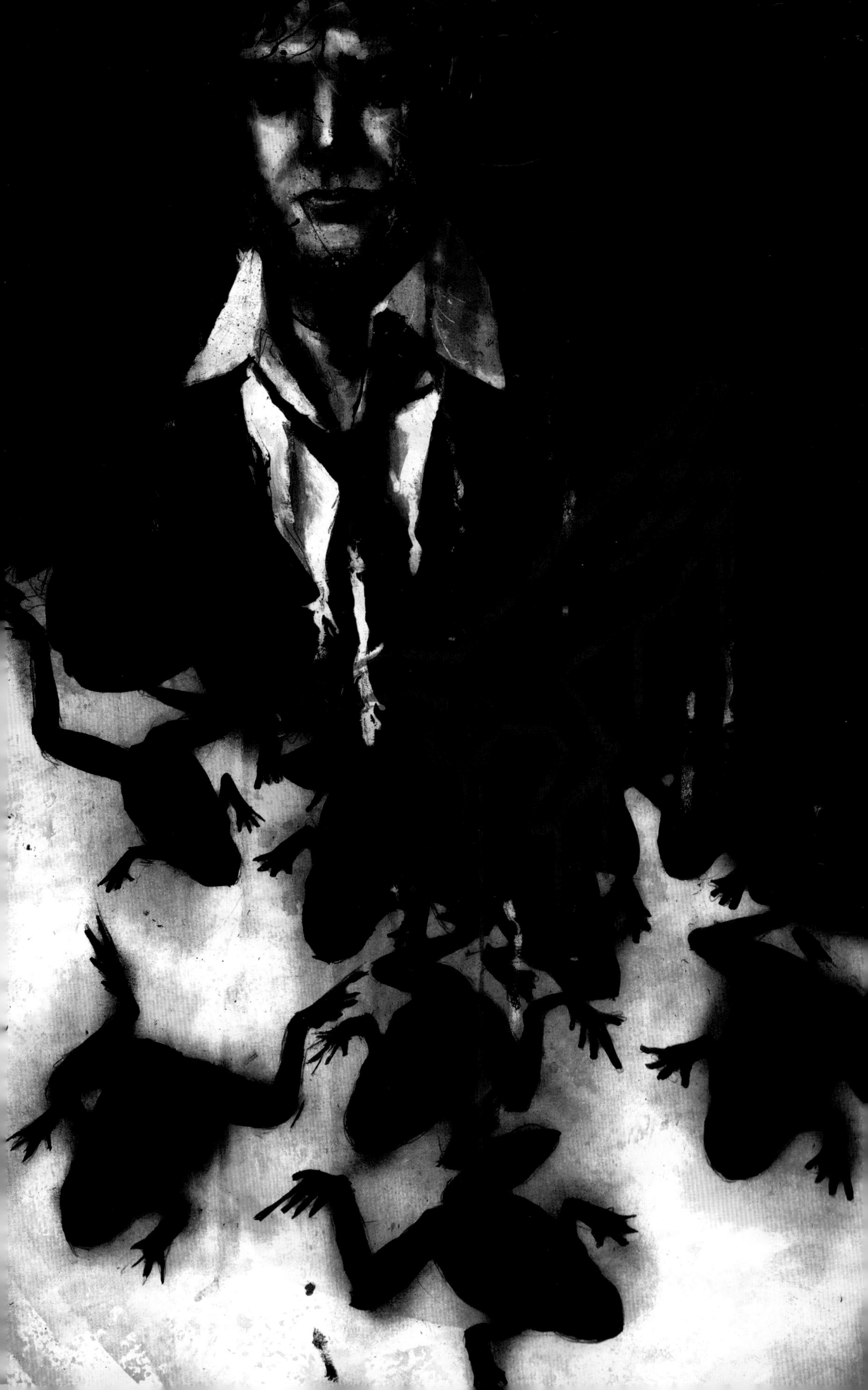

Green Wake #1-second printing cover

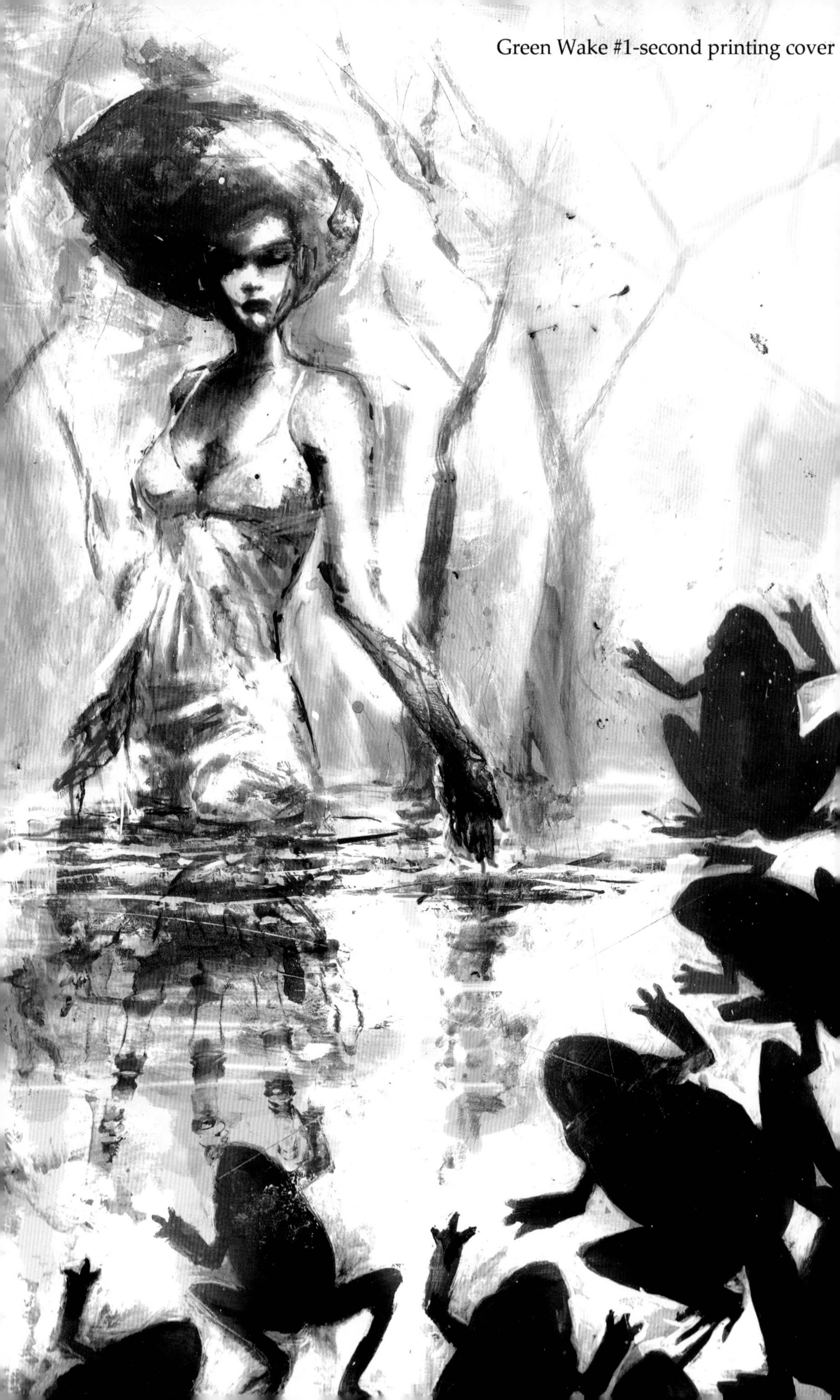

There's a moment in a man's life when he questions every decision he's ever made.

He believes that by going back, weighing each fork in the road and comparing the possible outcomes, he can actually change his fate.

Or desperately wishes he could.

ANNA?

But when reality shows its goddamn terrifying face, he realizes that there never was a fork in the road.

ANNA? SPEAK TO ME, SWEETHEART.

He drove down the one road he was always meant to.

Fate.

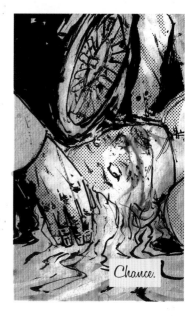

Chance.

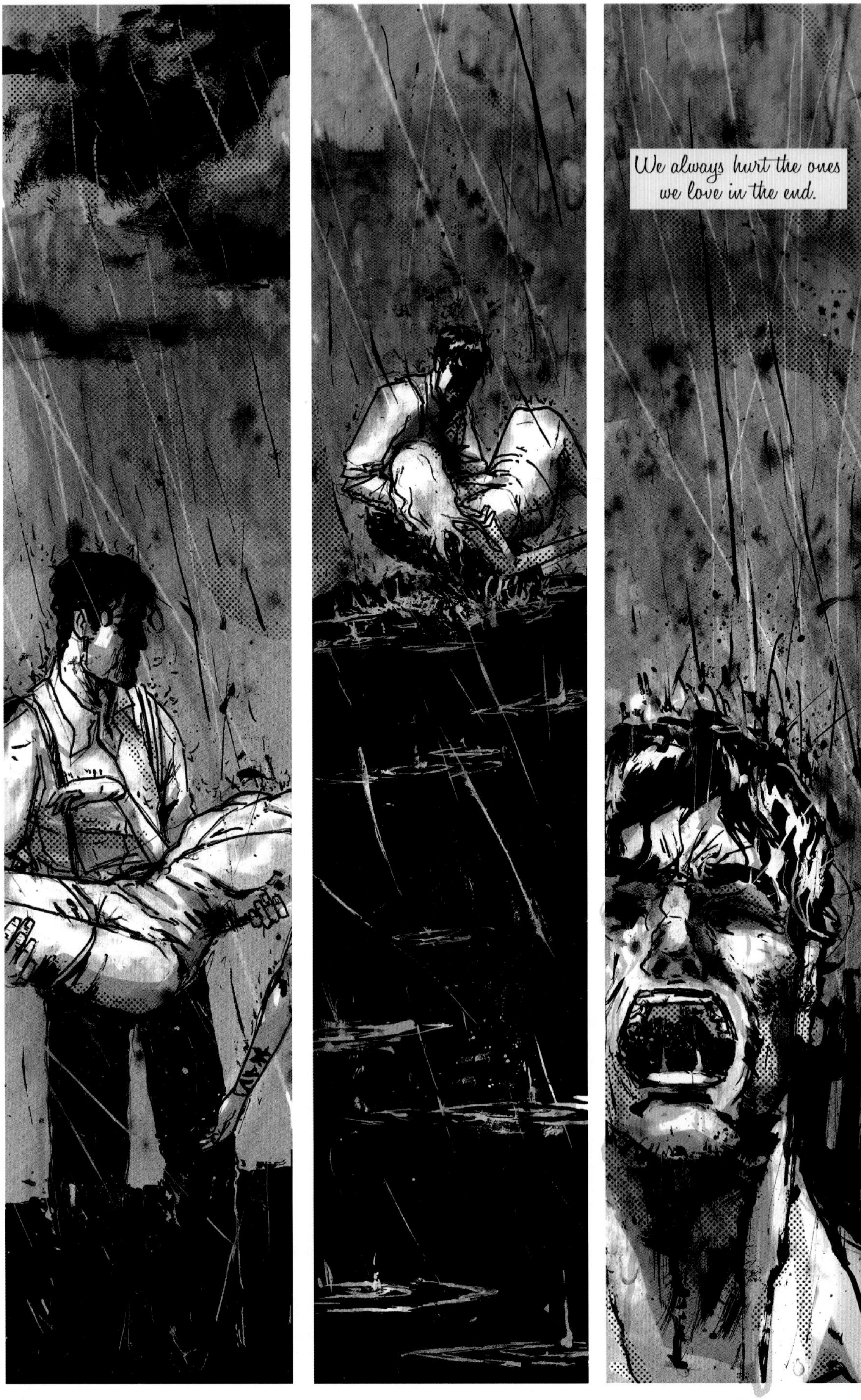
We always hurt the ones we love in the end.

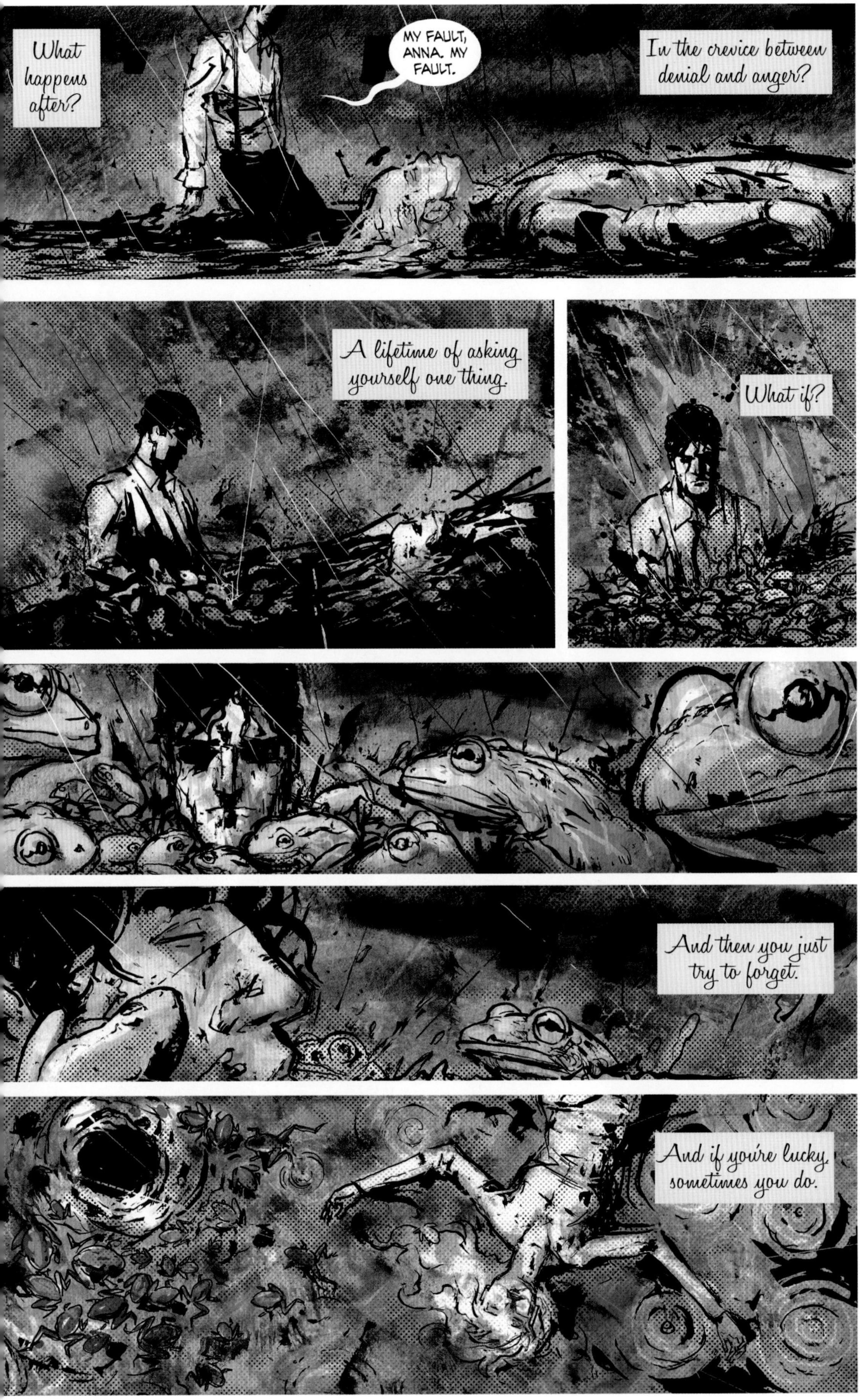

What happens after?
MY FAULT, ANNA. MY FAULT.
In the crevice between denial and anger?
A lifetime of asking yourself one thing.
What if?
And then you just try to forget.
And if you're lucky, sometimes you do.

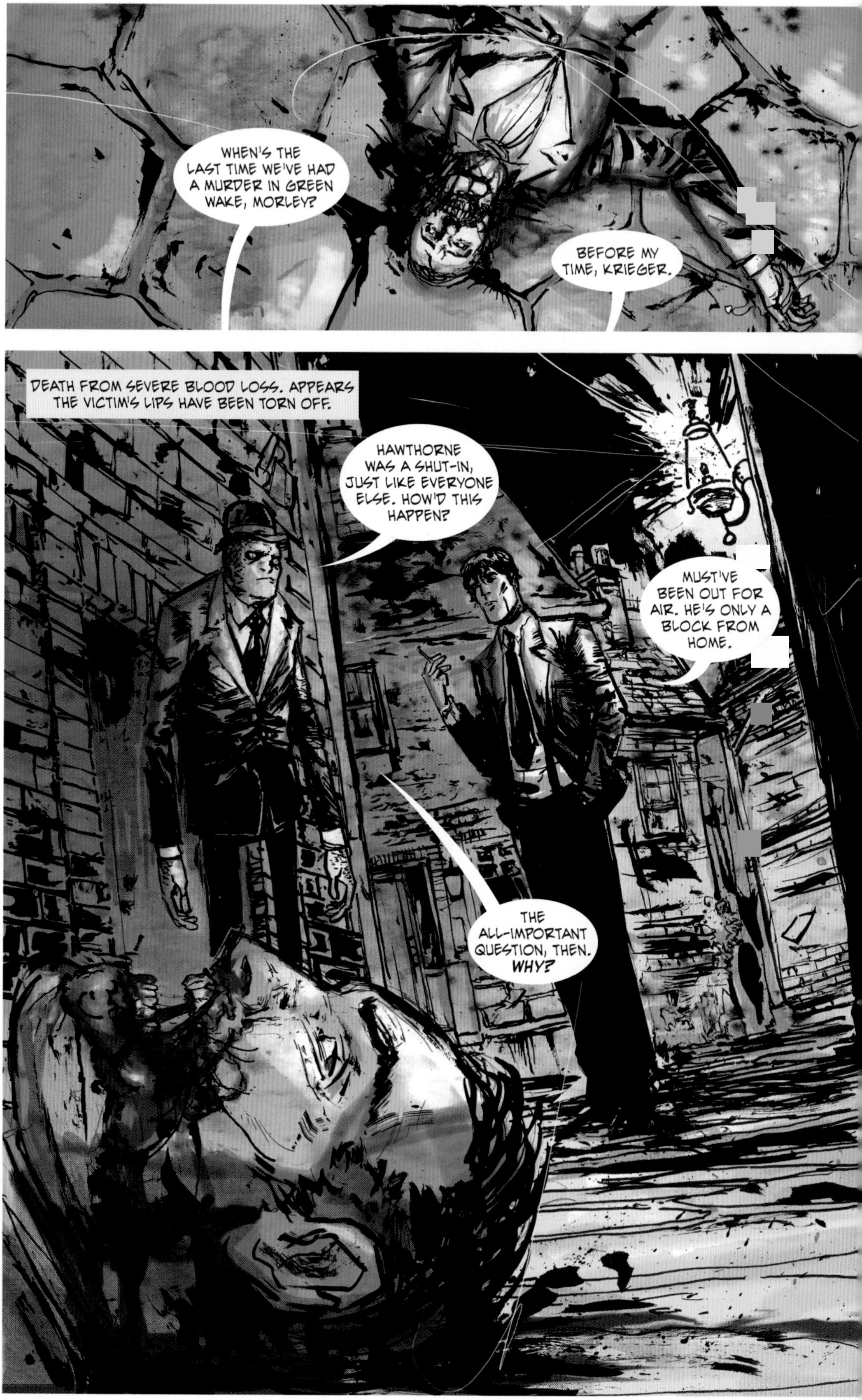
WHEN'S THE LAST TIME WE'VE HAD A MURDER IN GREEN WAKE, MORLEY?
BEFORE MY TIME, KRIEGER.
DEATH FROM SEVERE BLOOD LOSS. APPEARS THE VICTIM'S LIPS HAVE BEEN TORN OFF.
HAWTHORNE WAS A SHUT-IN, JUST LIKE EVERYONE ELSE. HOW'D THIS HAPPEN?
MUST'VE BEEN OUT FOR AIR. HE'S ONLY A BLOCK FROM HOME.
THE ALL-IMPORTANT QUESTION, THEN. *WHY?*

I'D HATE TO SAY IT'S CONNECTED, BUT I SPOKE WITH CARSON, AND HE SAID ARIEL FLED THE AREA IN AN AWFUL HURRY THIS MORNING.

SHE'S A SWEET GIRL, YOU THINK SHE'S THE CULPRIT?

DON'T HAVE THAT ANSWER, YET. I WANT TO SEE HER PLACE.

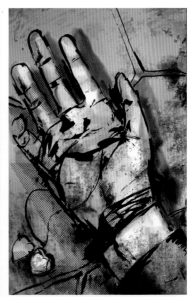

BUT THIS CERTAINLY ISN'T GOING TO HELP HER CASE.

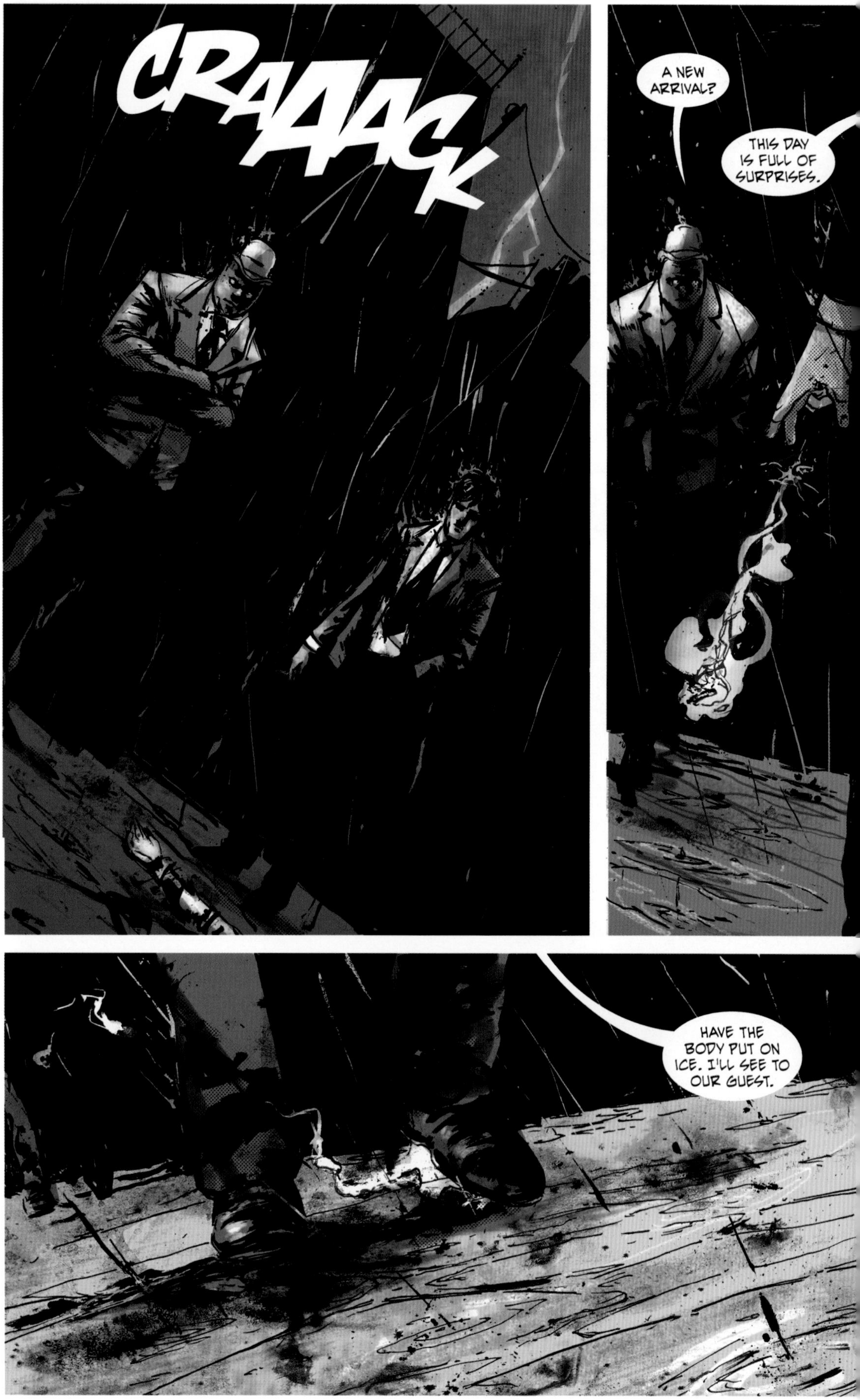
CRAAAACK
A NEW ARRIVAL?
THIS DAY IS FULL OF SURPRISES.
HAVE THE BODY PUT ON ICE. I'LL SEE TO OUR GUEST.

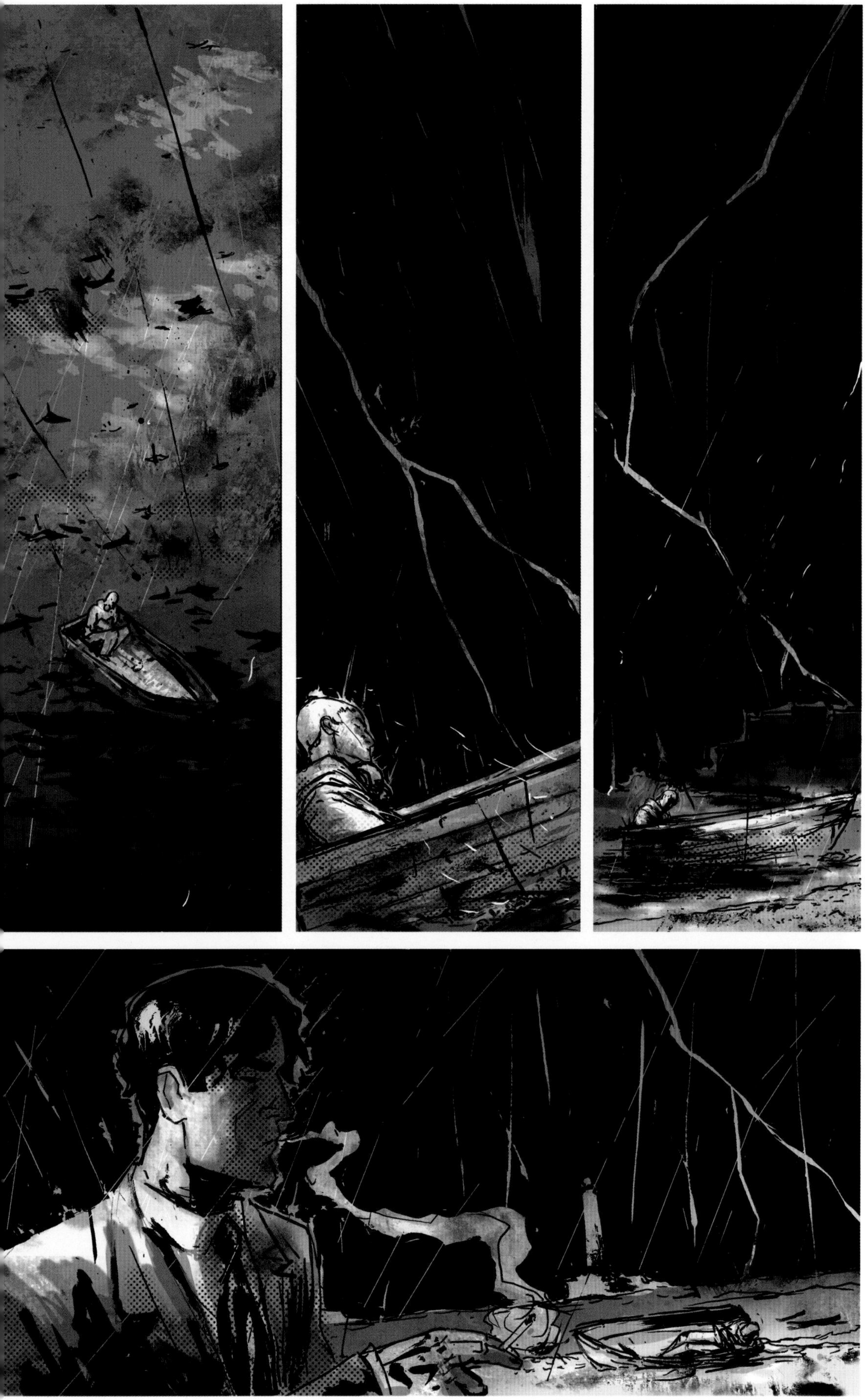

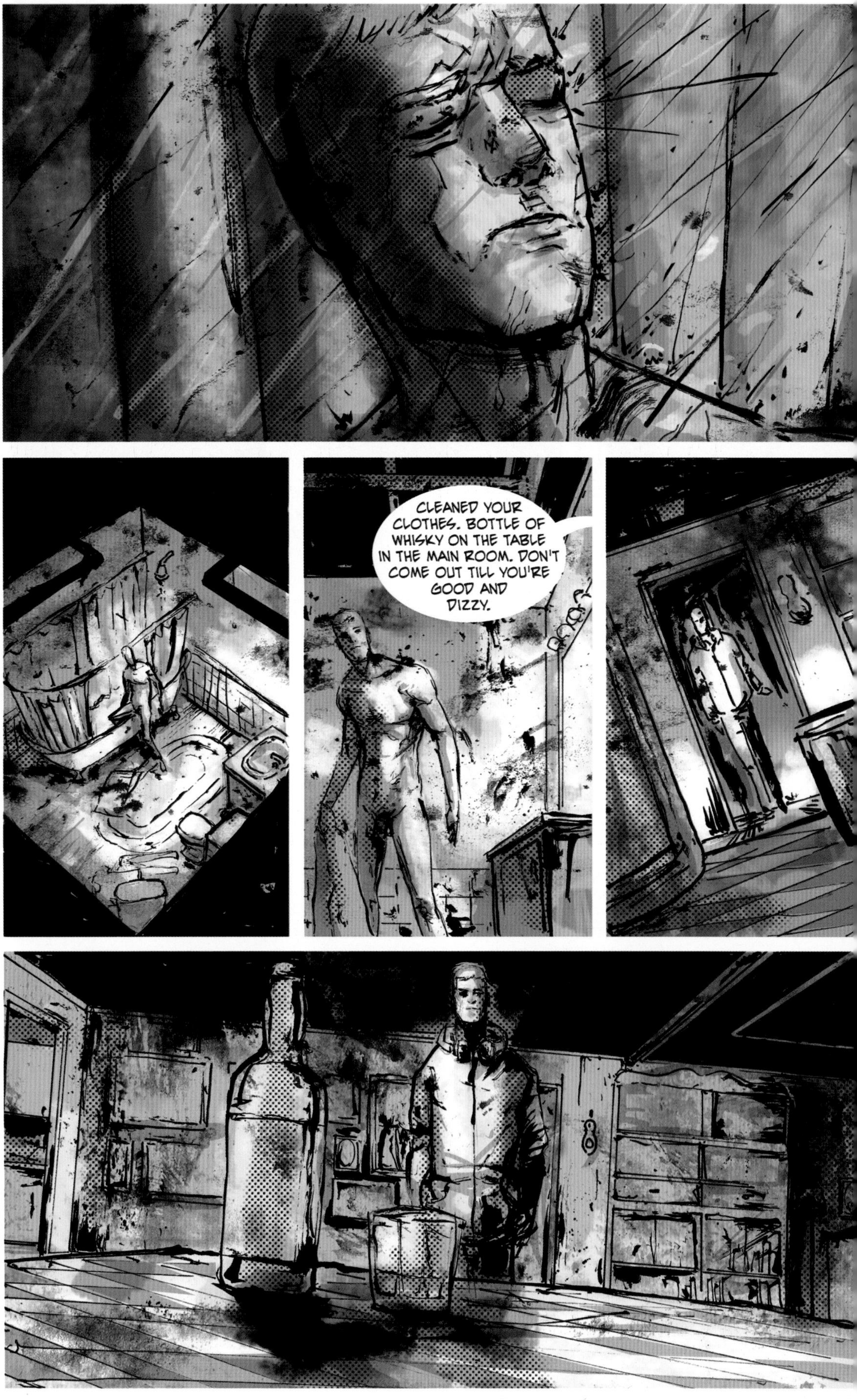
CLEANED YOUR CLOTHES. BOTTLE OF WHISKY ON THE TABLE IN THE MAIN ROOM. DON'T COME OUT TILL YOU'RE GOOD AND DIZZY.

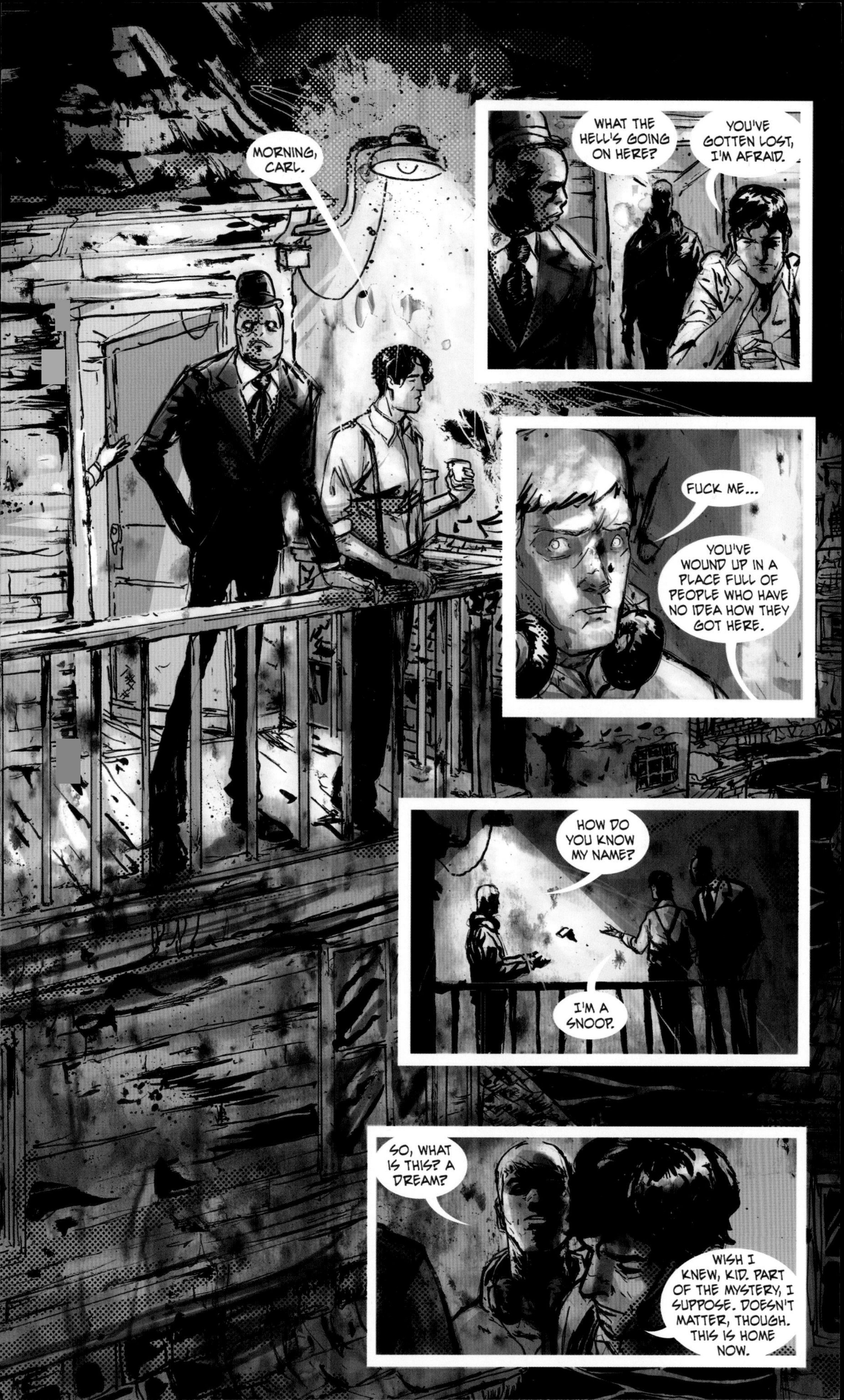
MORNING, CARL.
WHAT THE HELL'S GOING ON HERE?
YOU'VE GOTTEN LOST, I'M AFRAID.
FUCK ME...
YOU'VE WOUND UP IN A PLACE FULL OF PEOPLE WHO HAVE NO IDEA HOW THEY GOT HERE.
HOW DO YOU KNOW MY NAME?
I'M A SNOOP.
SO, WHAT IS THIS? A DREAM?
WISH I KNEW, KID. PART OF THE MYSTERY, I SUPPOSE. DOESN'T MATTER, THOUGH. THIS IS HOME NOW.

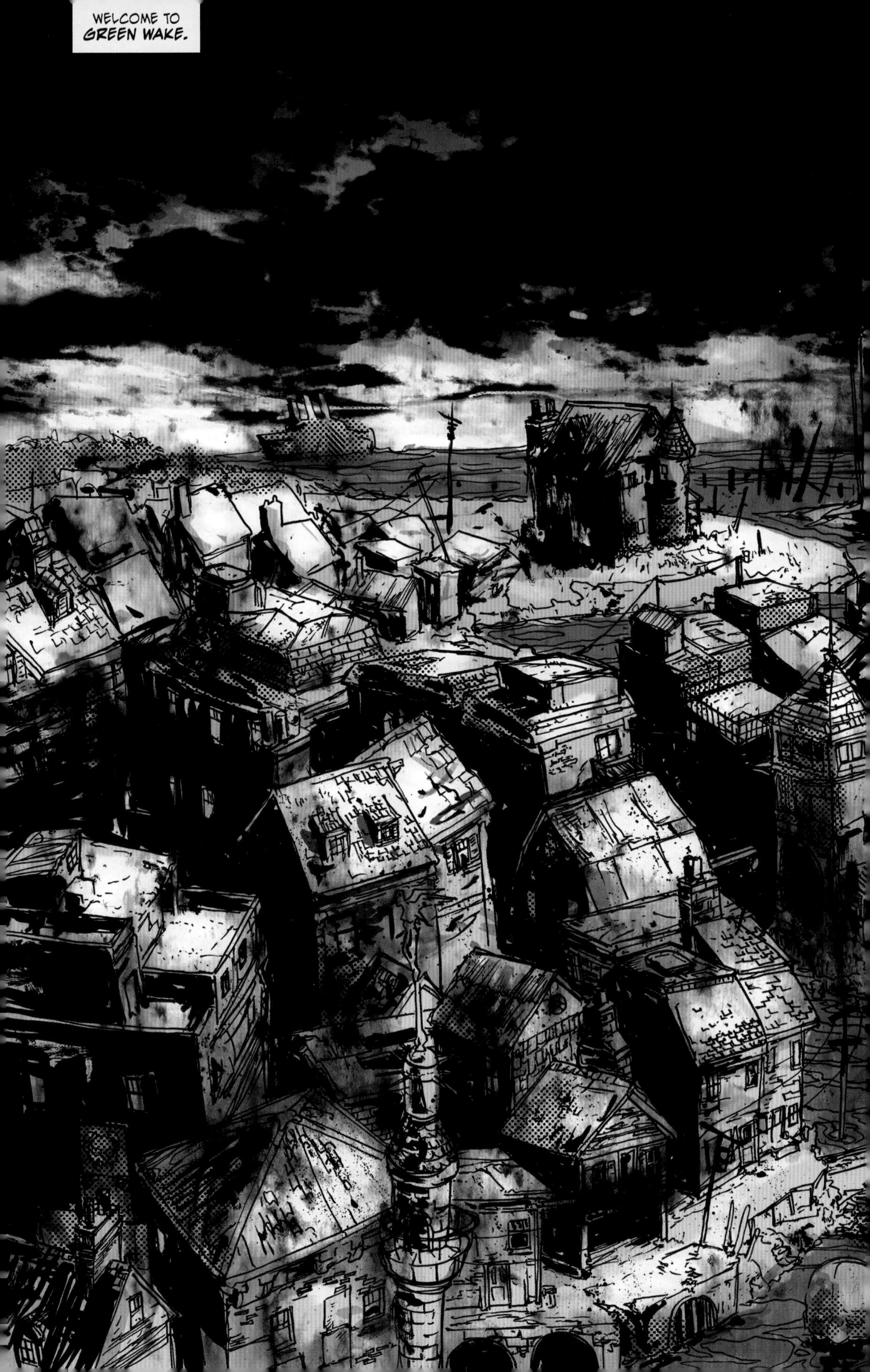
WELCOME TO GREEN WAKE.

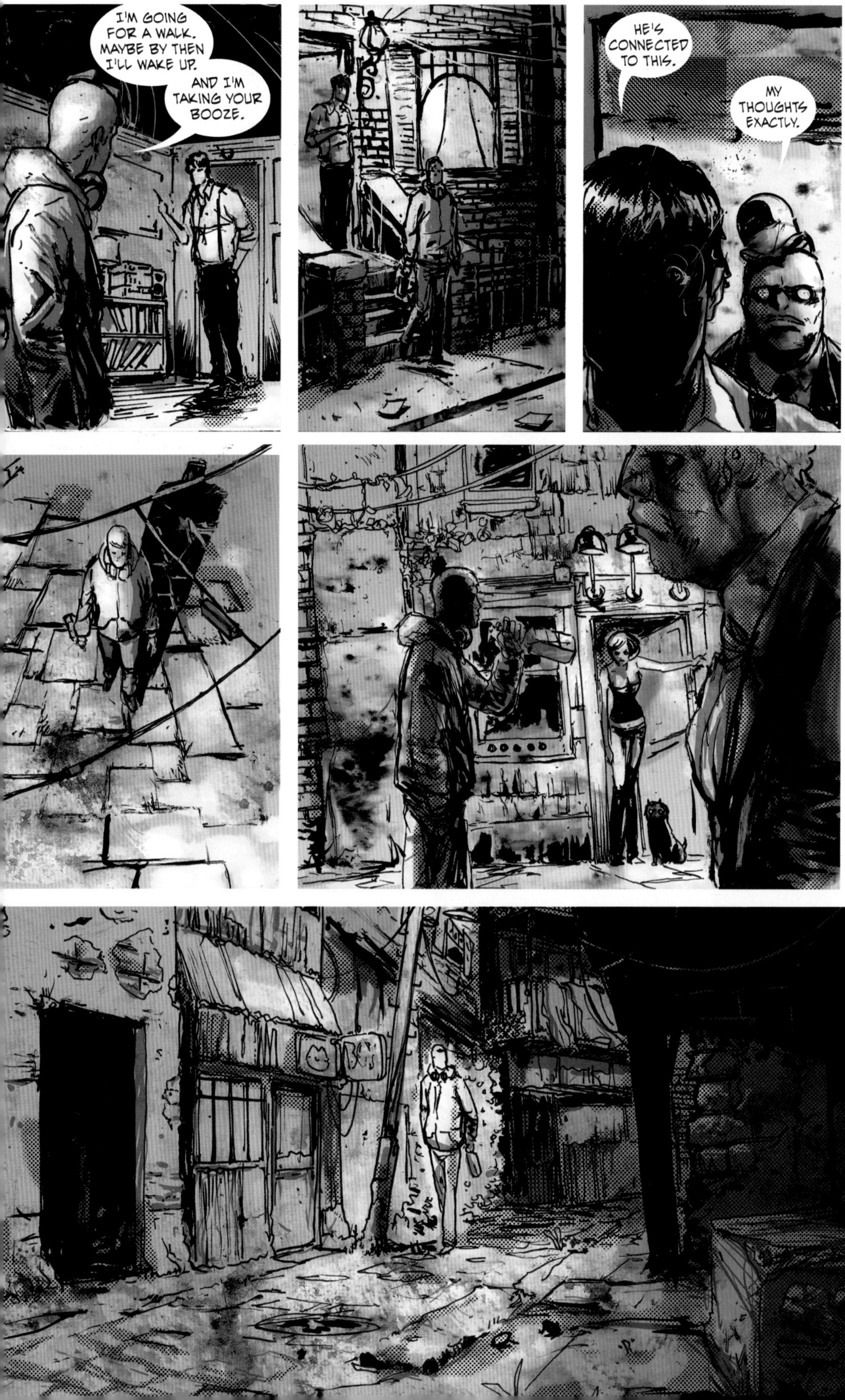
I'M GOING FOR A WALK. MAYBE BY THEN I'LL WAKE UP.
AND I'M TAKING YOUR BOOZE.
HE'S CONNECTED TO THIS.
MY THOUGHTS EXACTLY.

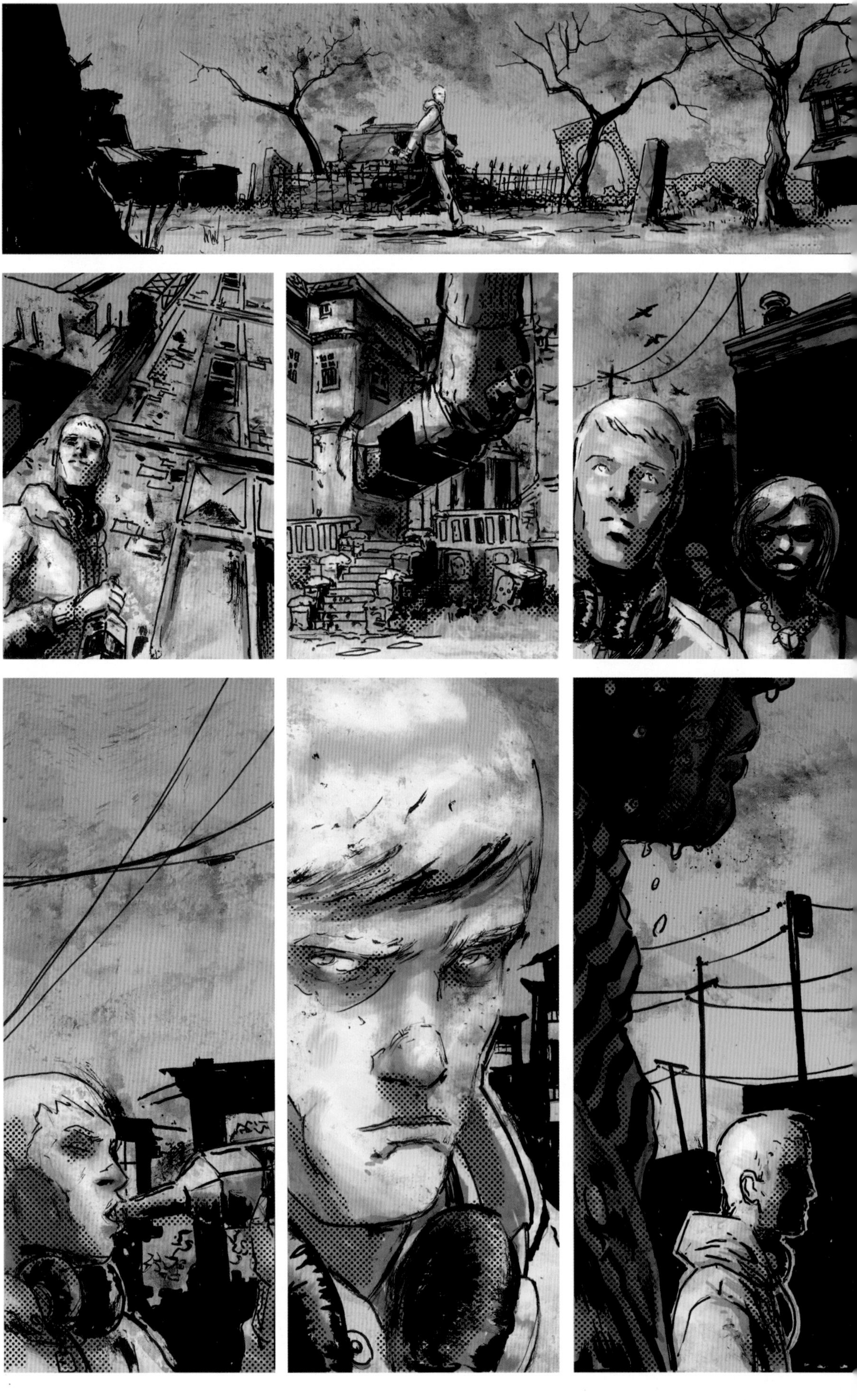

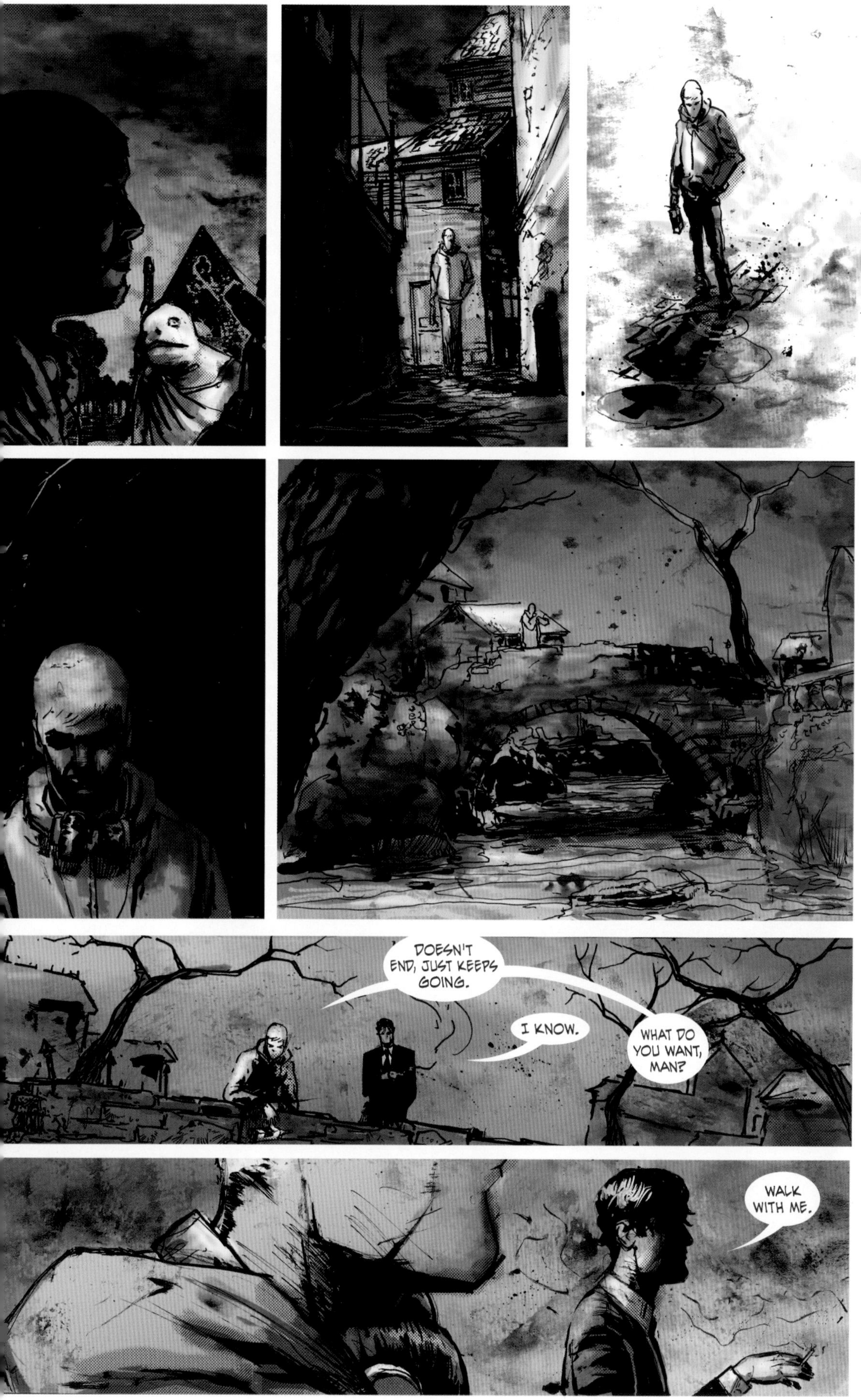
DOESN'T END, JUST KEEPS GOING.
I KNOW.
WHAT DO YOU WANT, MAN?
WALK WITH ME.

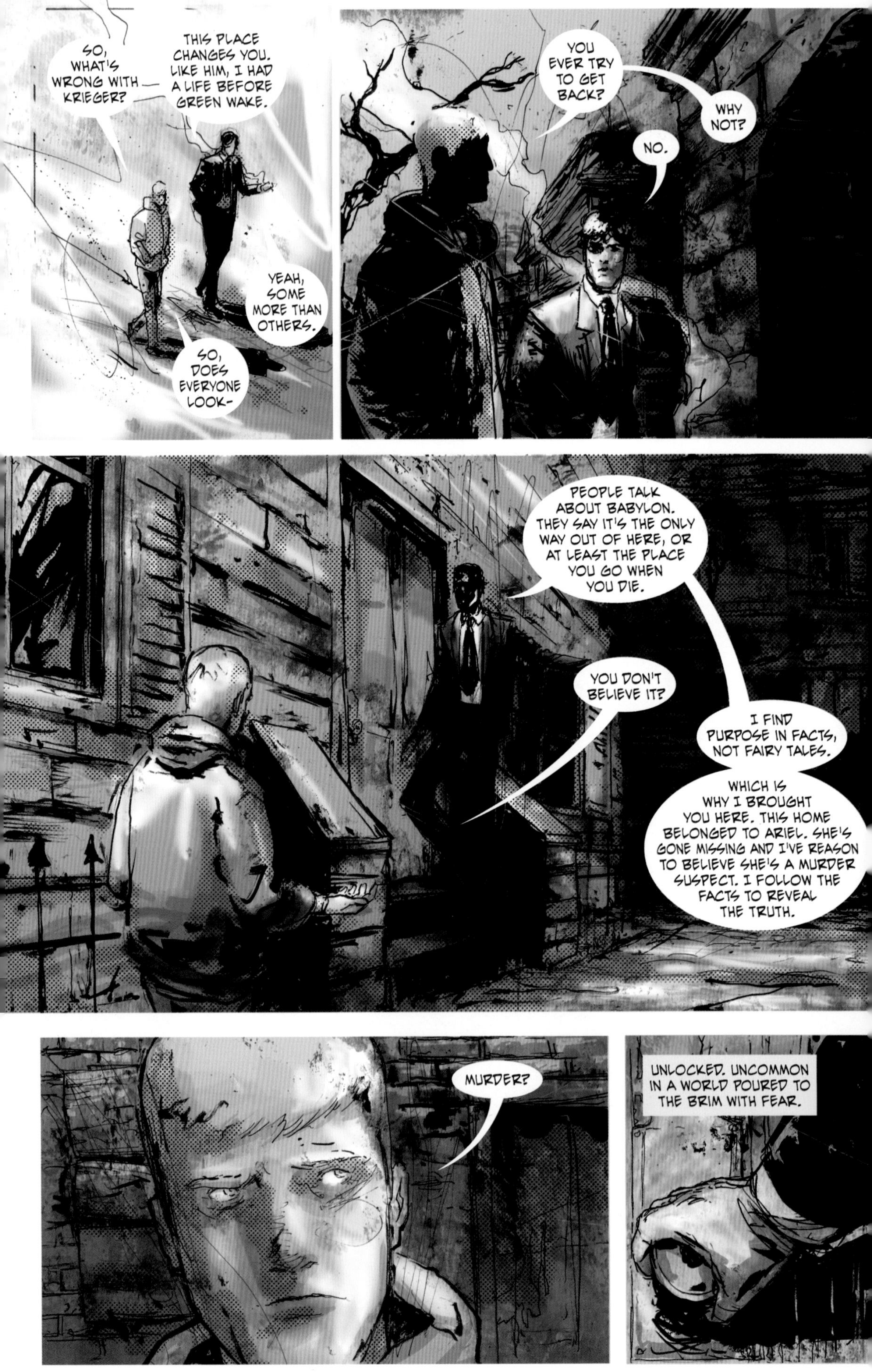

SO, WHAT'S WRONG WITH KRIEGER?
THIS PLACE CHANGES YOU. LIKE HIM, I HAD A LIFE BEFORE GREEN WAKE.
YEAH, SOME MORE THAN OTHERS.
SO, DOES EVERYONE LOOK-
YOU EVER TRY TO GET BACK?
NO.
WHY NOT?
PEOPLE TALK ABOUT BABYLON. THEY SAY IT'S THE ONLY WAY OUT OF HERE, OR AT LEAST THE PLACE YOU GO WHEN YOU DIE.
YOU DON'T BELIEVE IT?
I FIND PURPOSE IN FACTS, NOT FAIRY TALES.
WHICH IS WHY I BROUGHT YOU HERE. THIS HOME BELONGED TO ARIEL. SHE'S GONE MISSING AND I'VE REASON TO BELIEVE SHE'S A MURDER SUSPECT. I FOLLOW THE FACTS TO REVEAL THE TRUTH.
MURDER?
UNLOCKED. UNCOMMON IN A WORLD POURED TO THE BRIM WITH FEAR.

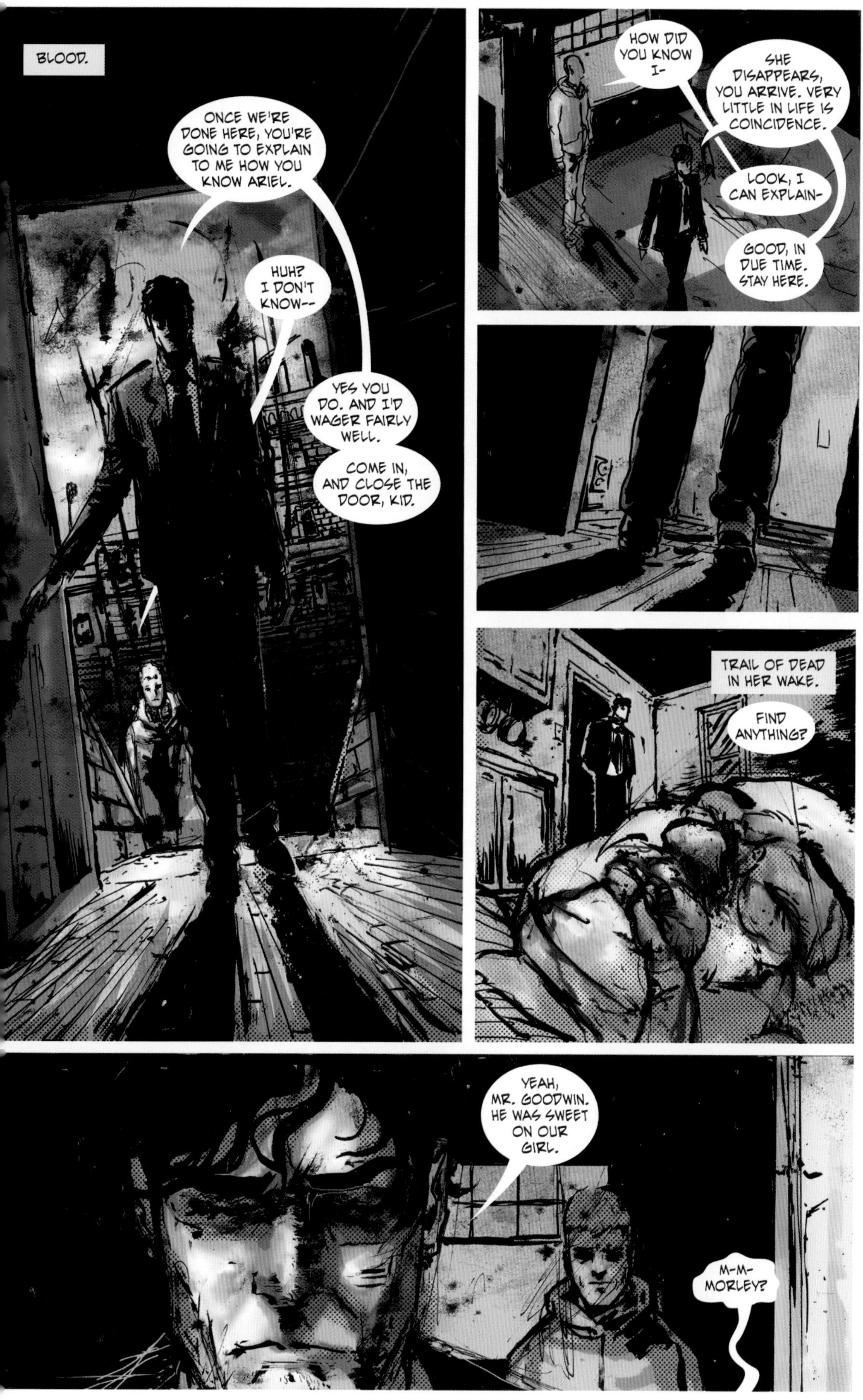
BLOOD.
ONCE WE'RE DONE HERE, YOU'RE GOING TO EXPLAIN TO ME HOW YOU KNOW ARIEL.
HUH? I DON'T KNOW--
YES YOU DO. AND I'D WAGER FAIRLY WELL.
COME IN, AND CLOSE THE DOOR, KID.
HOW DID YOU KNOW I-
SHE DISAPPEARS, YOU ARRIVE. VERY LITTLE IN LIFE IS COINCIDENCE.
LOOK, I CAN EXPLAIN-
GOOD, IN DUE TIME. STAY HERE.
TRAIL OF DEAD IN HER WAKE.
FIND ANYTHING?
YEAH, MR. GOODWIN. HE WAS SWEET ON OUR GIRL.
M-M-MORLEY?

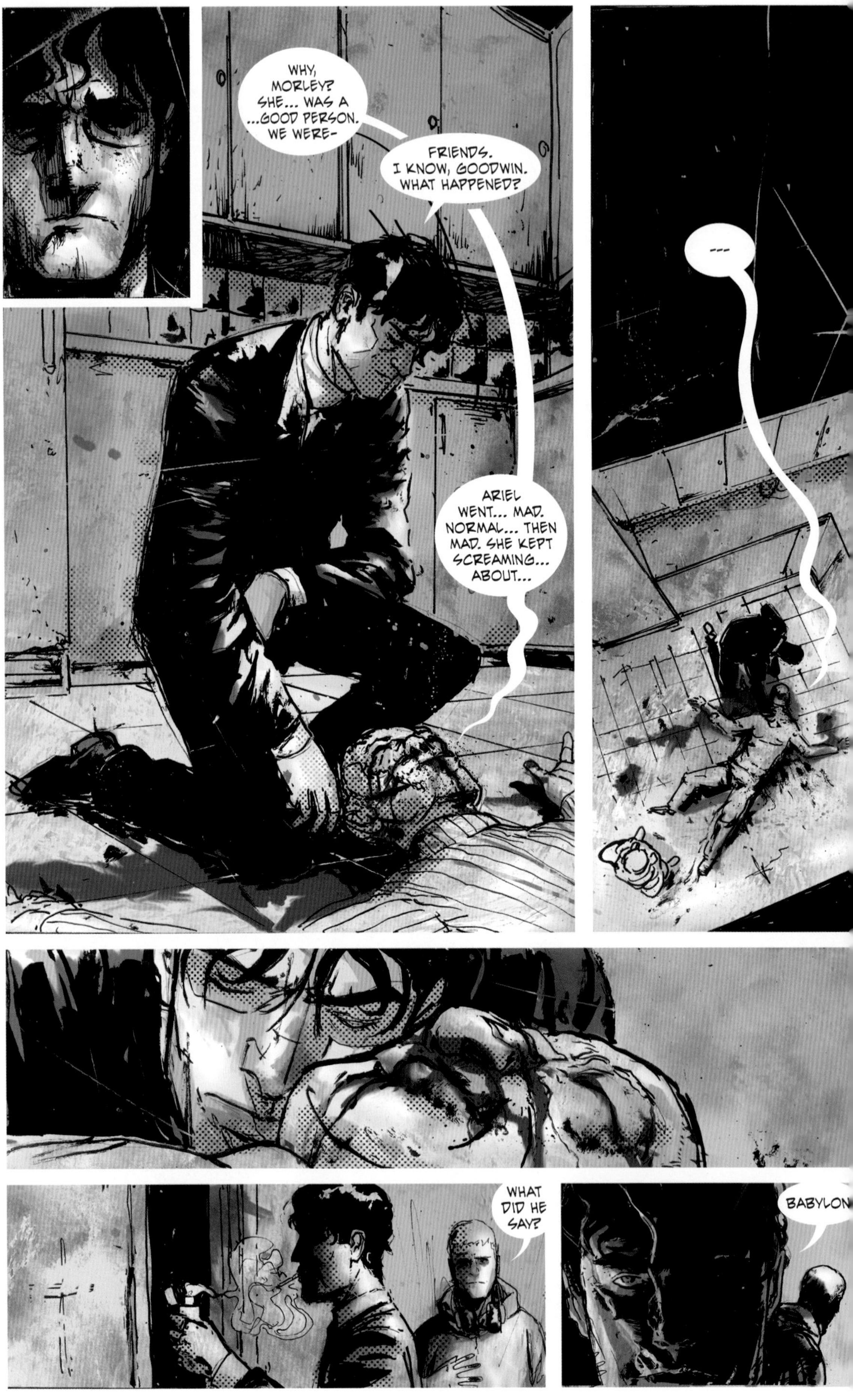
WHY, MORLEY? SHE... WAS A ...GOOD PERSON. WE WERE-
FRIENDS. I KNOW, GOODWIN. WHAT HAPPENED?
ARIEL WENT... MAD. NORMAL... THEN MAD. SHE KEPT SCREAMING... ABOUT...
...
WHAT DID HE SAY?
BABYLON

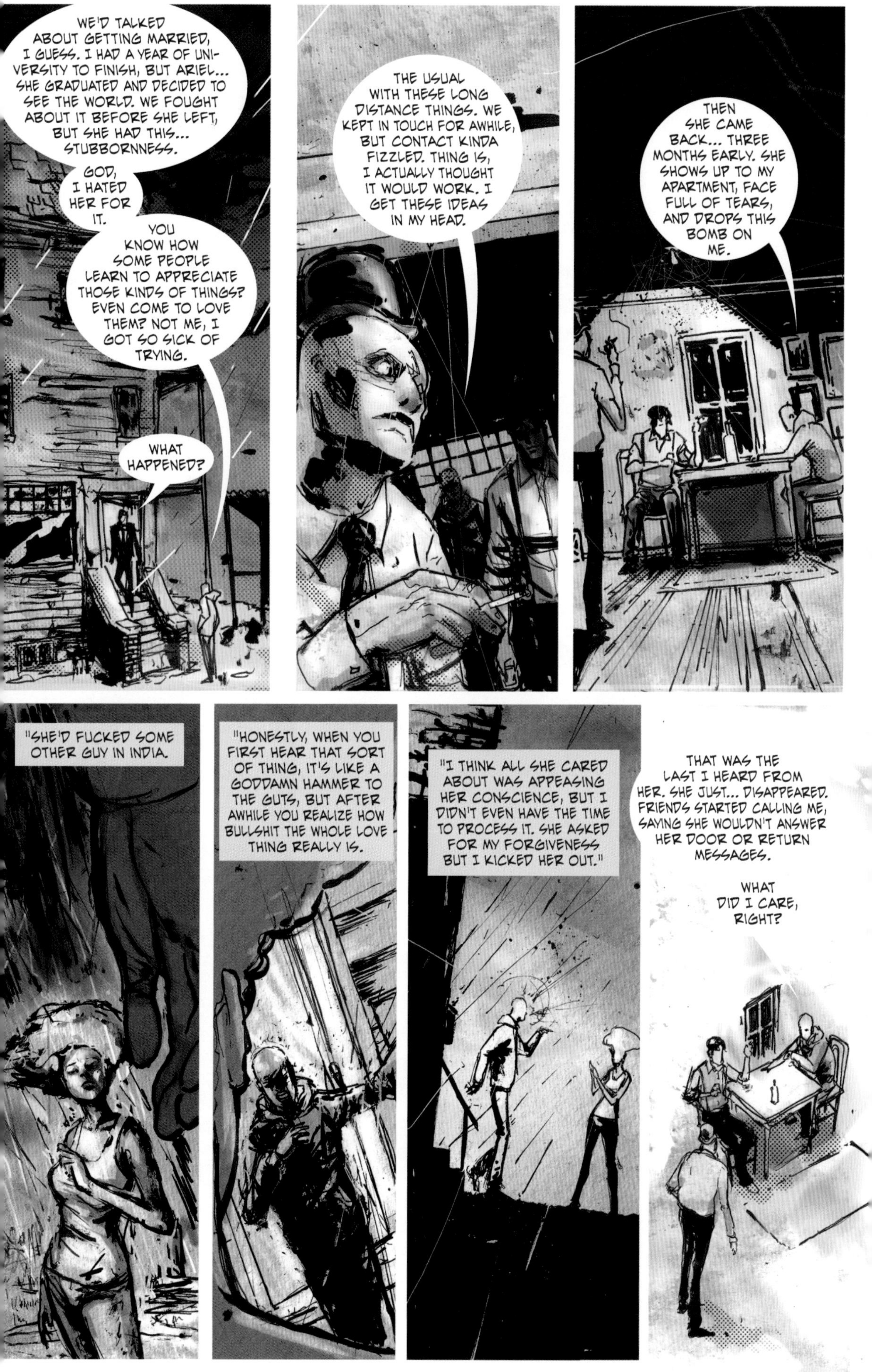
WE'D TALKED ABOUT GETTING MARRIED, I GUESS. I HAD A YEAR OF UNIVERSITY TO FINISH, BUT ARIEL... SHE GRADUATED AND DECIDED TO SEE THE WORLD. WE FOUGHT ABOUT IT BEFORE SHE LEFT, BUT SHE HAD THIS... STUBBORNNESS.
GOD, I HATED HER FOR IT.
YOU KNOW HOW SOME PEOPLE LEARN TO APPRECIATE THOSE KINDS OF THINGS? EVEN COME TO LOVE THEM? NOT ME, I GOT SO SICK OF TRYING.
WHAT HAPPENED?
THE USUAL WITH THESE LONG DISTANCE THINGS. WE KEPT IN TOUCH FOR AWHILE, BUT CONTACT KINDA FIZZLED. THING IS, I ACTUALLY THOUGHT IT WOULD WORK. I GET THESE IDEAS IN MY HEAD.
THEN SHE CAME BACK... THREE MONTHS EARLY. SHE SHOWS UP TO MY APARTMENT, FACE FULL OF TEARS, AND DROPS THIS BOMB ON ME.
"SHE'D FUCKED SOME OTHER GUY IN INDIA.
"HONESTLY, WHEN YOU FIRST HEAR THAT SORT OF THING, IT'S LIKE A GODDAMN HAMMER TO THE GUTS, BUT AFTER AWHILE YOU REALIZE HOW BULLSHIT THE WHOLE LOVE THING REALLY IS.
"I THINK ALL SHE CARED ABOUT WAS APPEASING HER CONSCIENCE, BUT I DIDN'T EVEN HAVE THE TIME TO PROCESS IT. SHE ASKED FOR MY FORGIVENESS BUT I KICKED HER OUT."
THAT WAS THE LAST I HEARD FROM HER. SHE JUST... DISAPPEARED. FRIENDS STARTED CALLING ME, SAYING SHE WOULDN'T ANSWER HER DOOR OR RETURN MESSAGES.
WHAT DID I CARE, RIGHT?

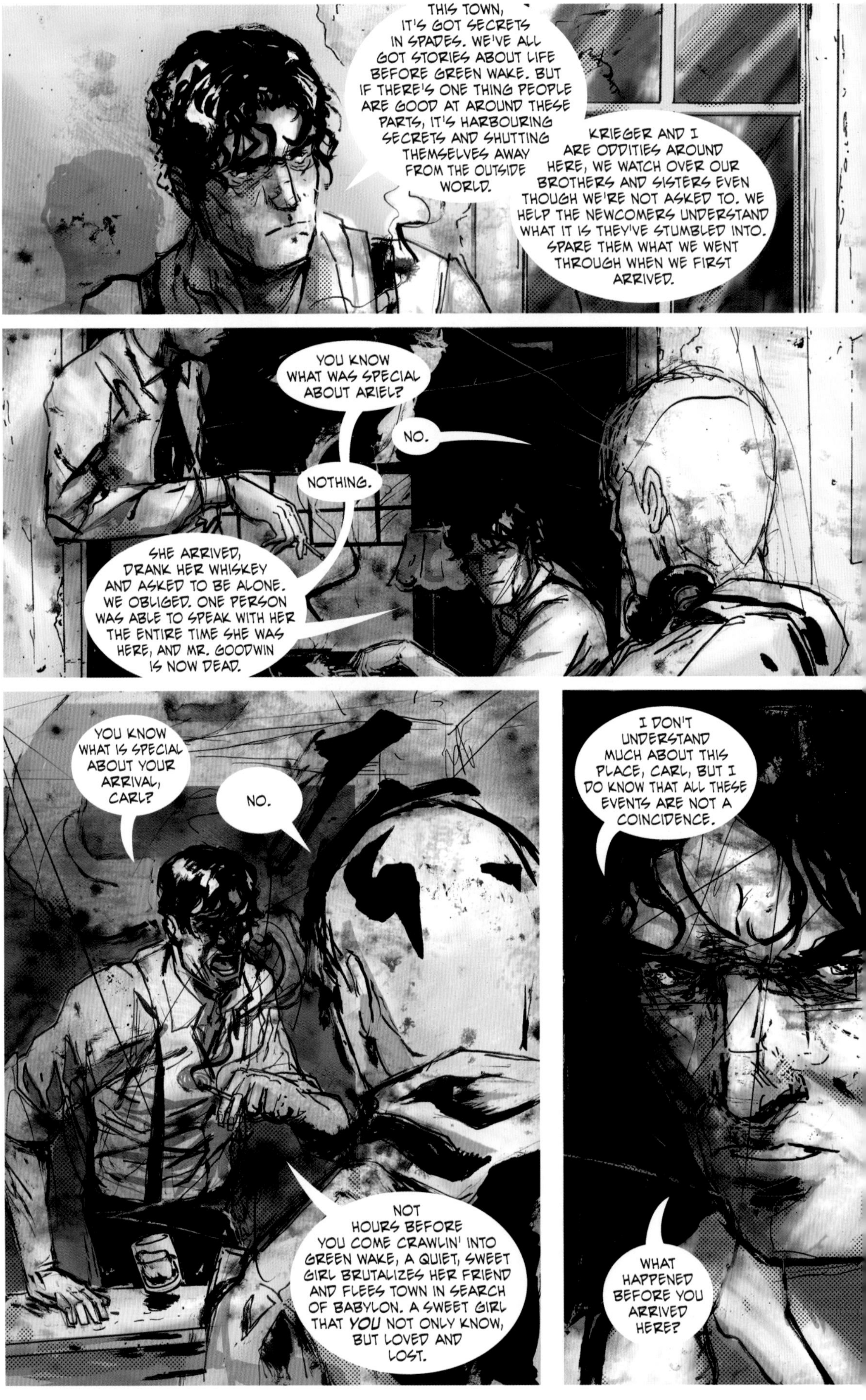
THIS TOWN, IT'S GOT SECRETS IN SPADES. WE'VE ALL GOT STORIES ABOUT LIFE BEFORE GREEN WAKE. BUT IF THERE'S ONE THING PEOPLE ARE GOOD AT AROUND THESE PARTS, IT'S HARBOURING SECRETS AND SHUTTING THEMSELVES AWAY FROM THE OUTSIDE WORLD.
KRIEGER AND I ARE ODDITIES AROUND HERE, WE WATCH OVER OUR BROTHERS AND SISTERS EVEN THOUGH WE'RE NOT ASKED TO. WE HELP THE NEWCOMERS UNDERSTAND WHAT IT IS THEY'VE STUMBLED INTO. SPARE THEM WHAT WE WENT THROUGH WHEN WE FIRST ARRIVED.
YOU KNOW WHAT WAS SPECIAL ABOUT ARIEL?
NO.
NOTHING.
SHE ARRIVED, DRANK HER WHISKEY AND ASKED TO BE ALONE. WE OBLIGED. ONE PERSON WAS ABLE TO SPEAK WITH HER THE ENTIRE TIME SHE WAS HERE, AND MR. GOODWIN IS NOW DEAD.
YOU KNOW WHAT IS SPECIAL ABOUT YOUR ARRIVAL, CARL?
NO.
NOT HOURS BEFORE YOU COME CRAWLIN' INTO GREEN WAKE, A QUIET, SWEET GIRL BRUTALIZES HER FRIEND AND FLEES TOWN IN SEARCH OF BABYLON. A SWEET GIRL THAT YOU NOT ONLY KNOW, BUT LOVED AND LOST.
I DON'T UNDERSTAND MUCH ABOUT THIS PLACE, CARL, BUT I DO KNOW THAT ALL THESE EVENTS ARE NOT A COINCIDENCE.
WHAT HAPPENED BEFORE YOU ARRIVED HERE?

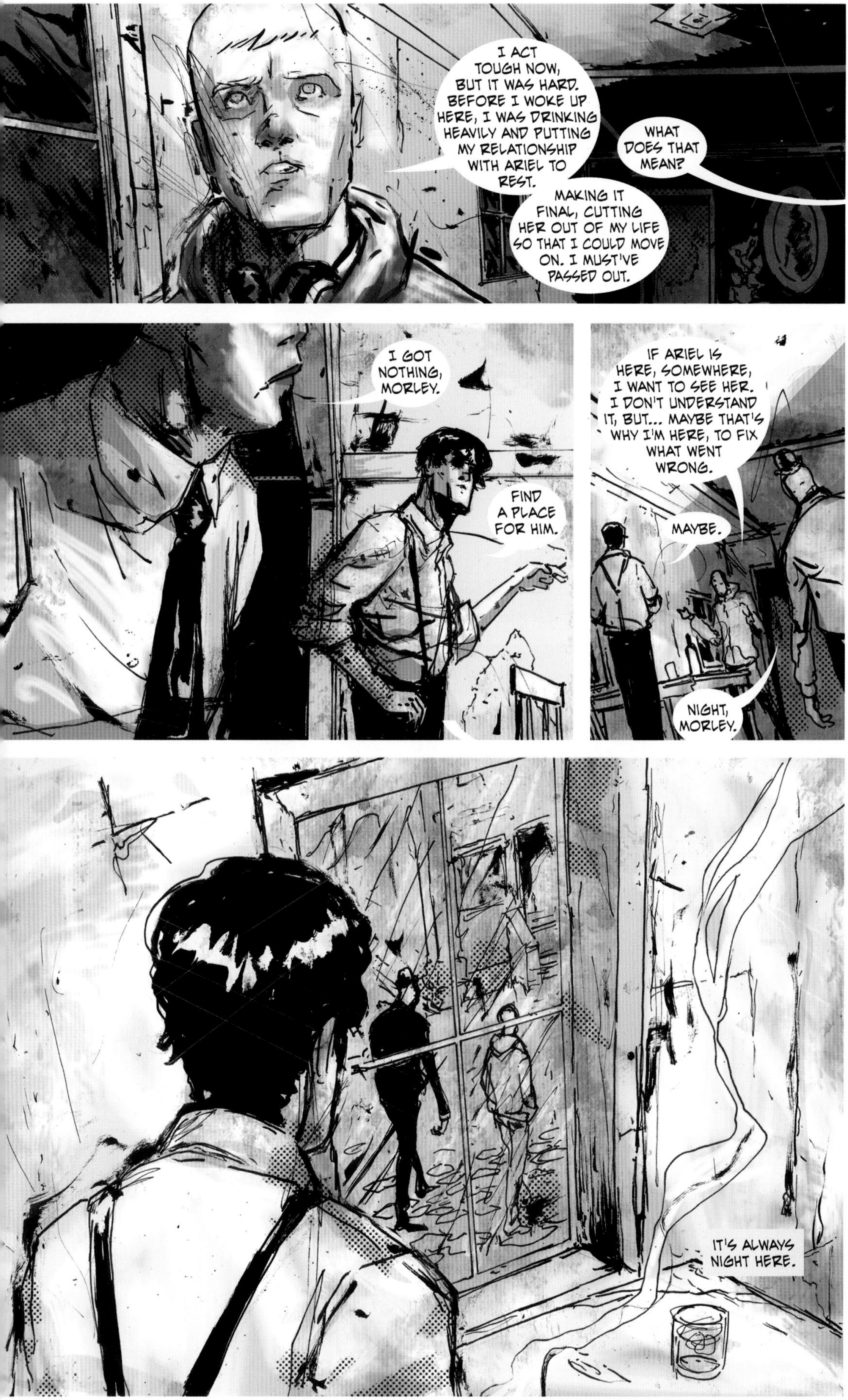
I ACT TOUGH NOW, BUT IT WAS HARD. BEFORE I WOKE UP HERE, I WAS DRINKING HEAVILY AND PUTTING MY RELATIONSHIP WITH ARIEL TO REST.
MAKING IT FINAL, CUTTING HER OUT OF MY LIFE SO THAT I COULD MOVE ON. I MUST'VE PASSED OUT.
WHAT DOES THAT MEAN?
I GOT NOTHING, MORLEY.
FIND A PLACE FOR HIM.
IF ARIEL IS HERE, SOMEWHERE, I WANT TO SEE HER. I DON'T UNDERSTAND IT, BUT... MAYBE THAT'S WHY I'M HERE, TO FIX WHAT WENT WRONG.
MAYBE.
NIGHT, MORLEY.
IT'S ALWAYS NIGHT HERE.

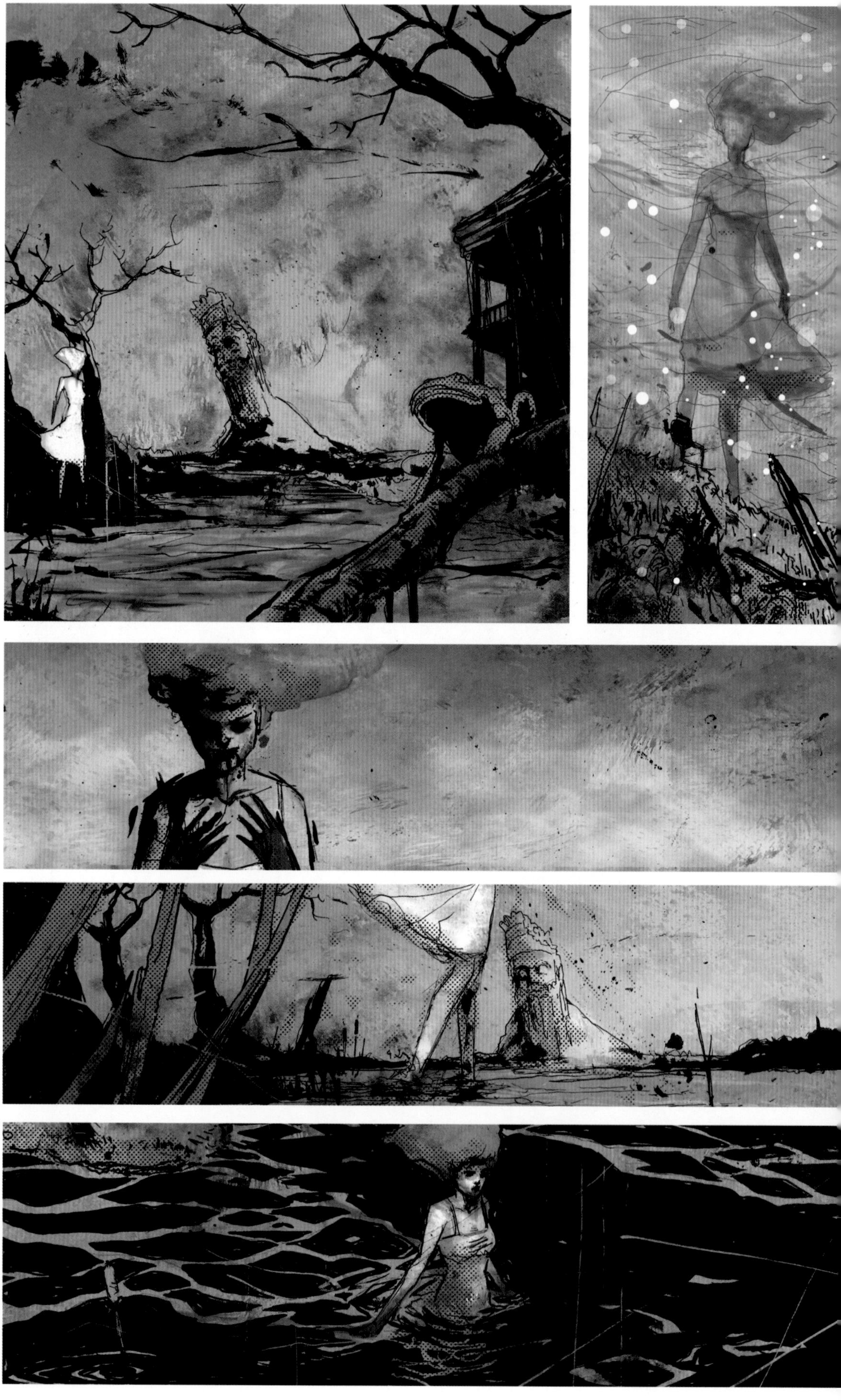

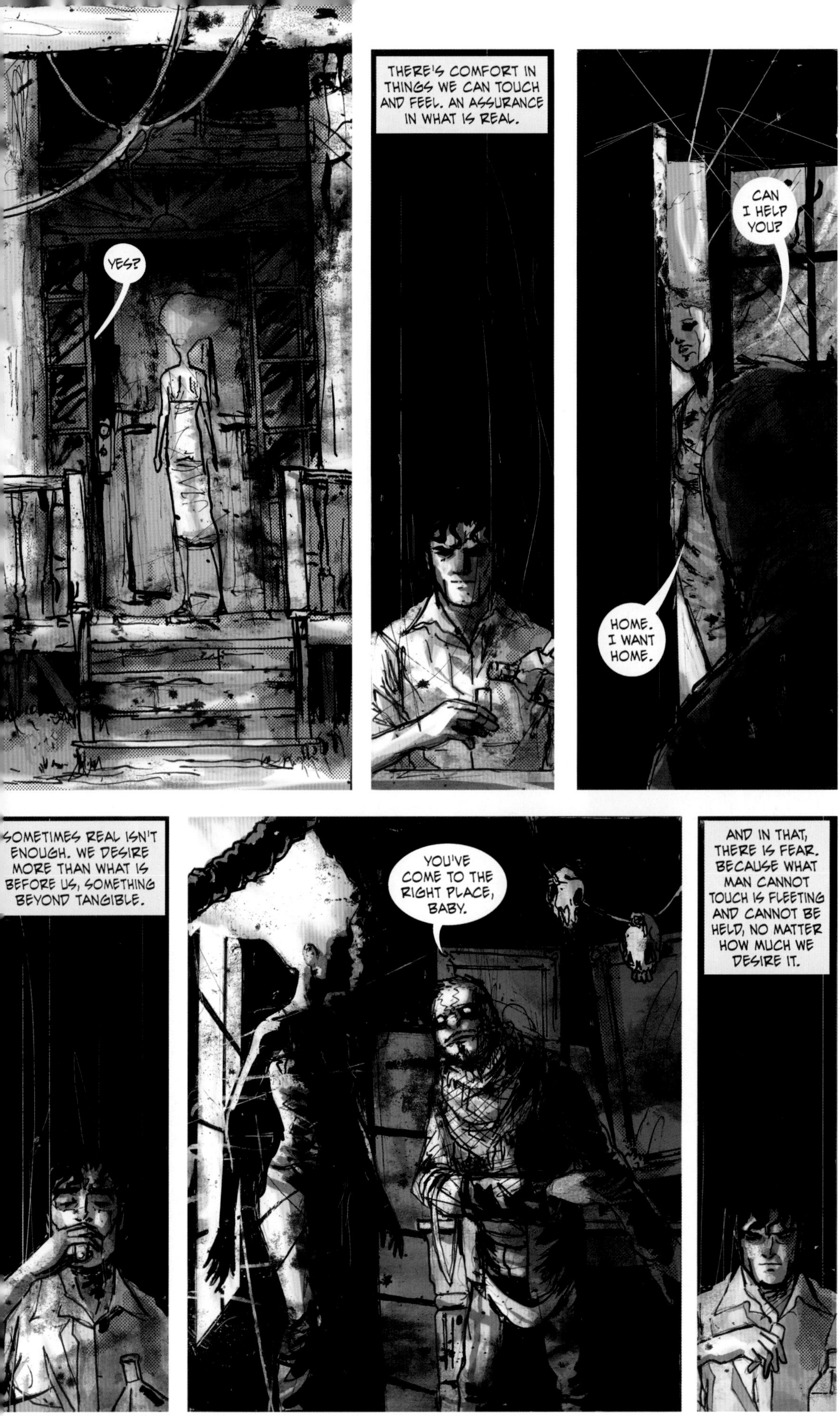
YES?
THERE'S COMFORT IN THINGS WE CAN TOUCH AND FEEL. AN ASSURANCE IN WHAT IS REAL.
CAN I HELP YOU?
HOME. I WANT HOME.
SOMETIMES REAL ISN'T ENOUGH. WE DESIRE MORE THAN WHAT IS BEFORE US, SOMETHING BEYOND TANGIBLE.
YOU'VE COME TO THE RIGHT PLACE, BABY.
AND IN THAT, THERE IS FEAR. BECAUSE WHAT MAN CANNOT TOUCH IS FLEETING AND CANNOT BE HELD, NO MATTER HOW MUCH WE DESIRE IT.

WE FIND THE
NEXT BEST THING.

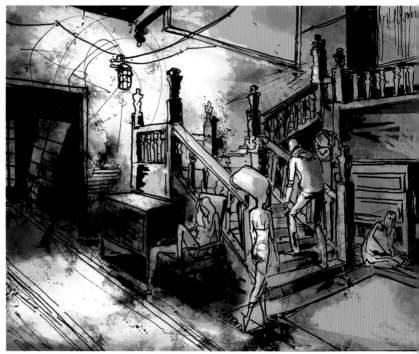

WELCOME TO
BABYLON, LOVE.

.BUT IT'S NEVER
ENOUGH. WE
ALWAYS WANT
WHAT SLIPPED
THROUGH OUR
FINGERS.

WHAT'S BEEN
TAKEN FROM
US.

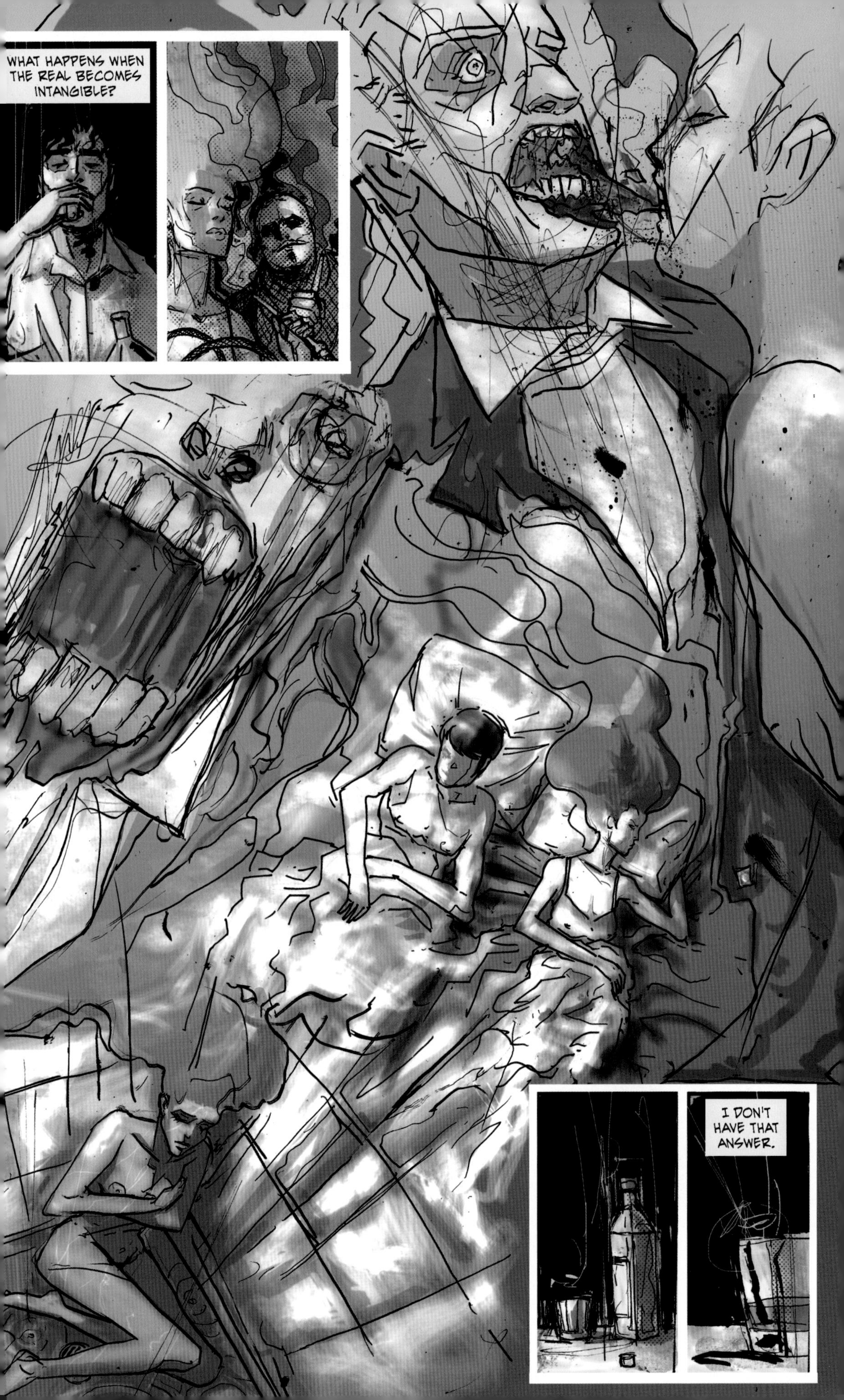
WHAT HAPPENS WHEN THE REAL BECOMES INTANGIBLE?
I DON'T HAVE THAT ANSWER.

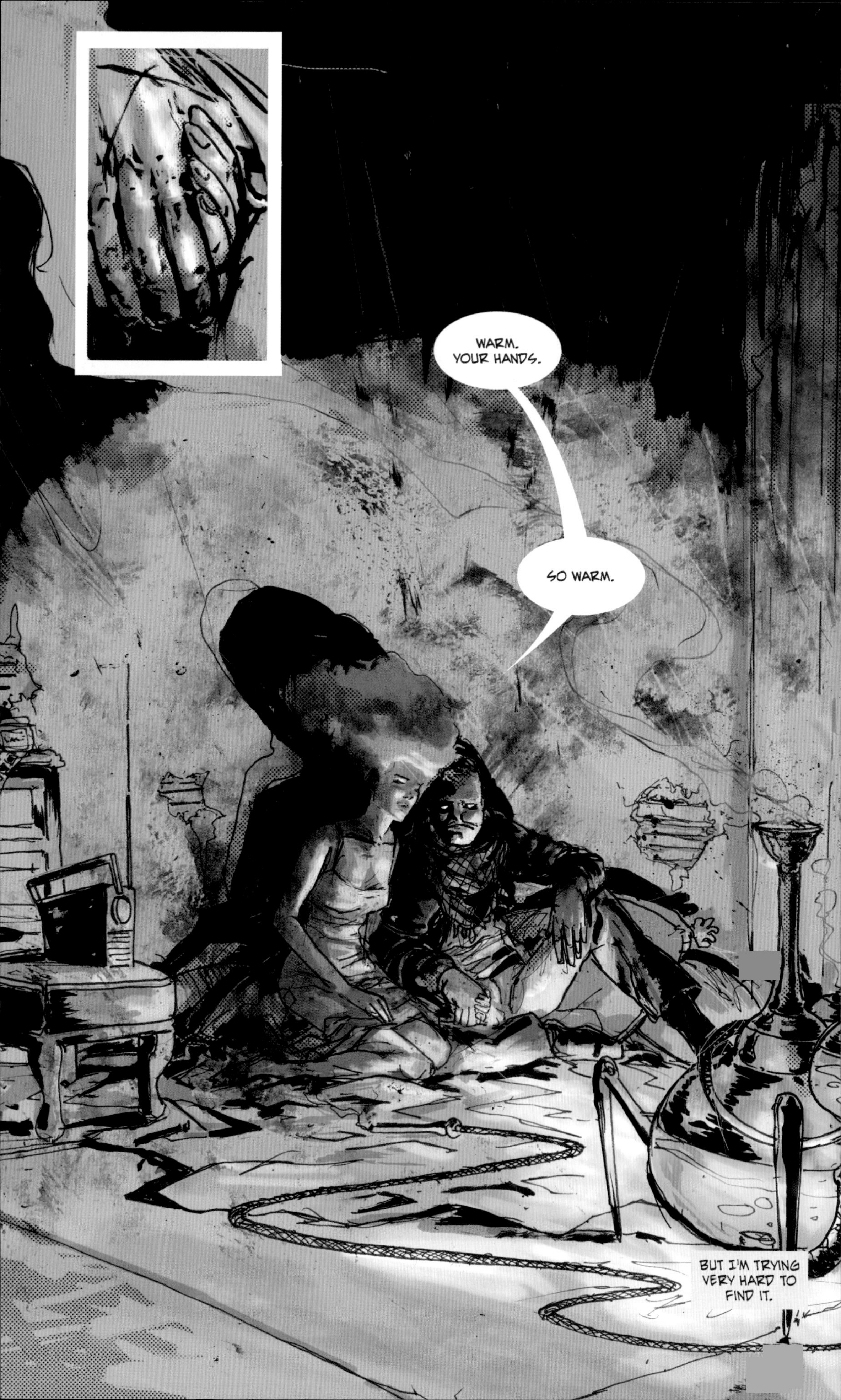
WARM. YOUR HANDS.
SO WARM.
BUT I'M TRYING VERY HARD TO FIND IT.

Green Wake #2 cover

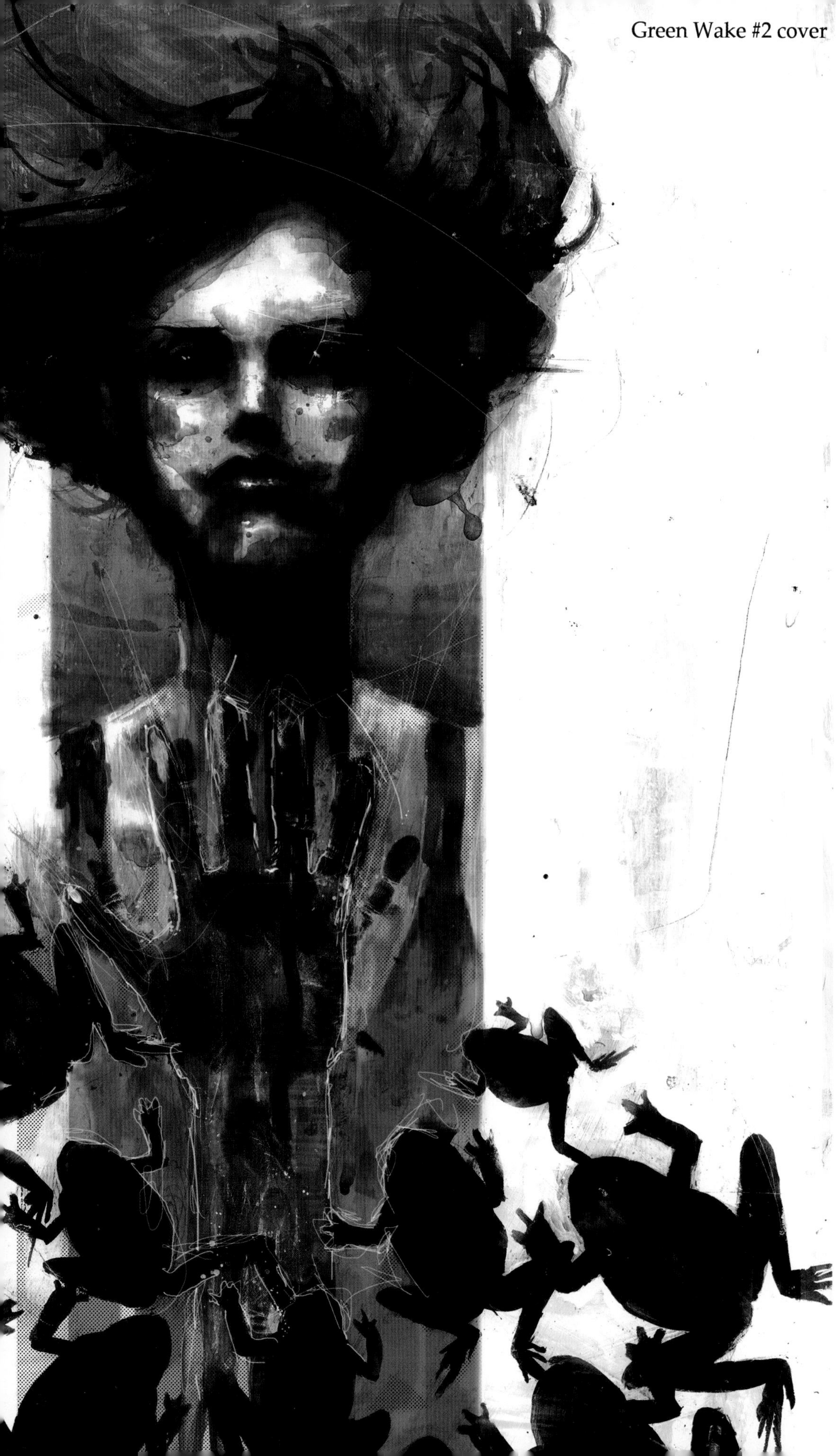

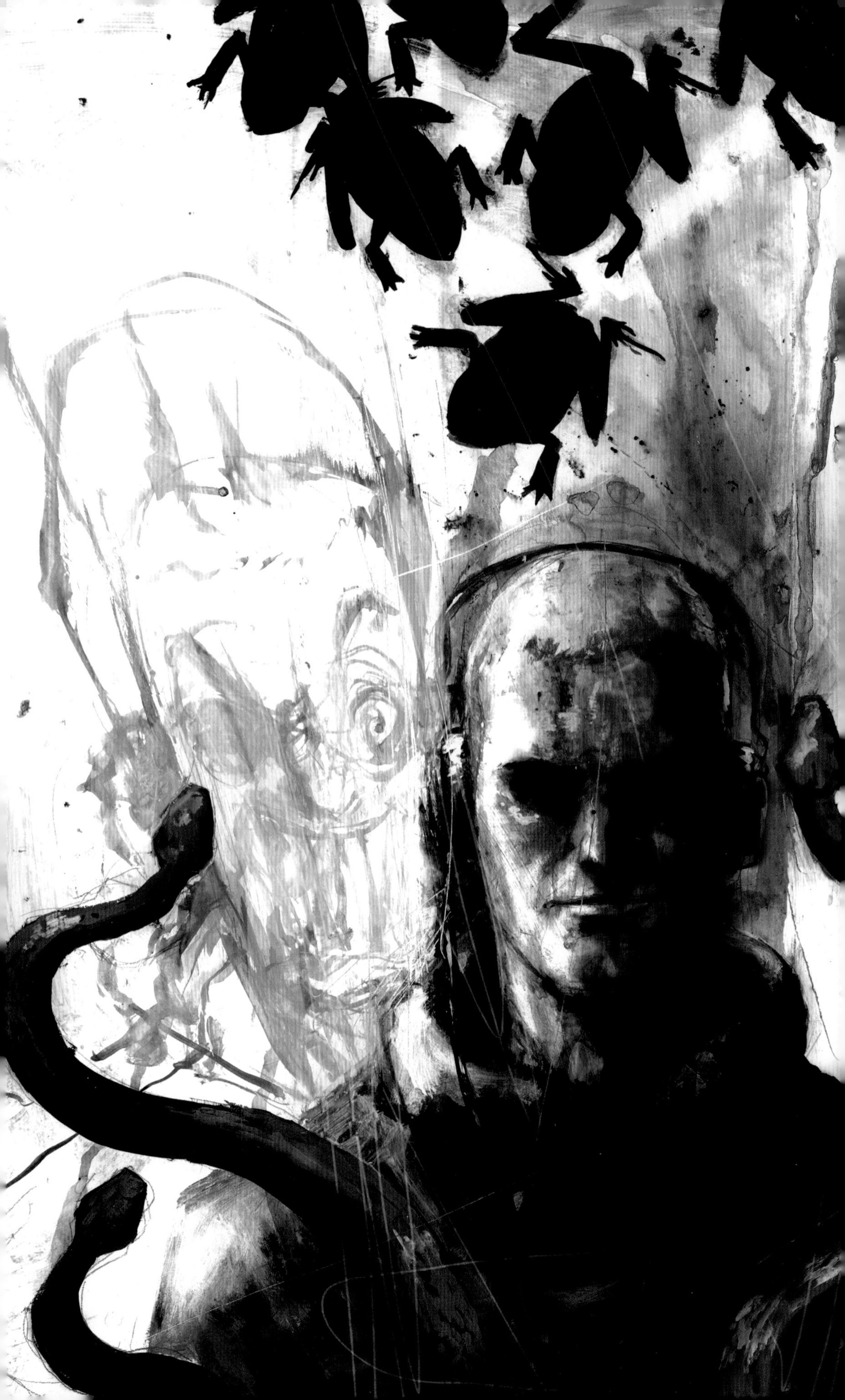

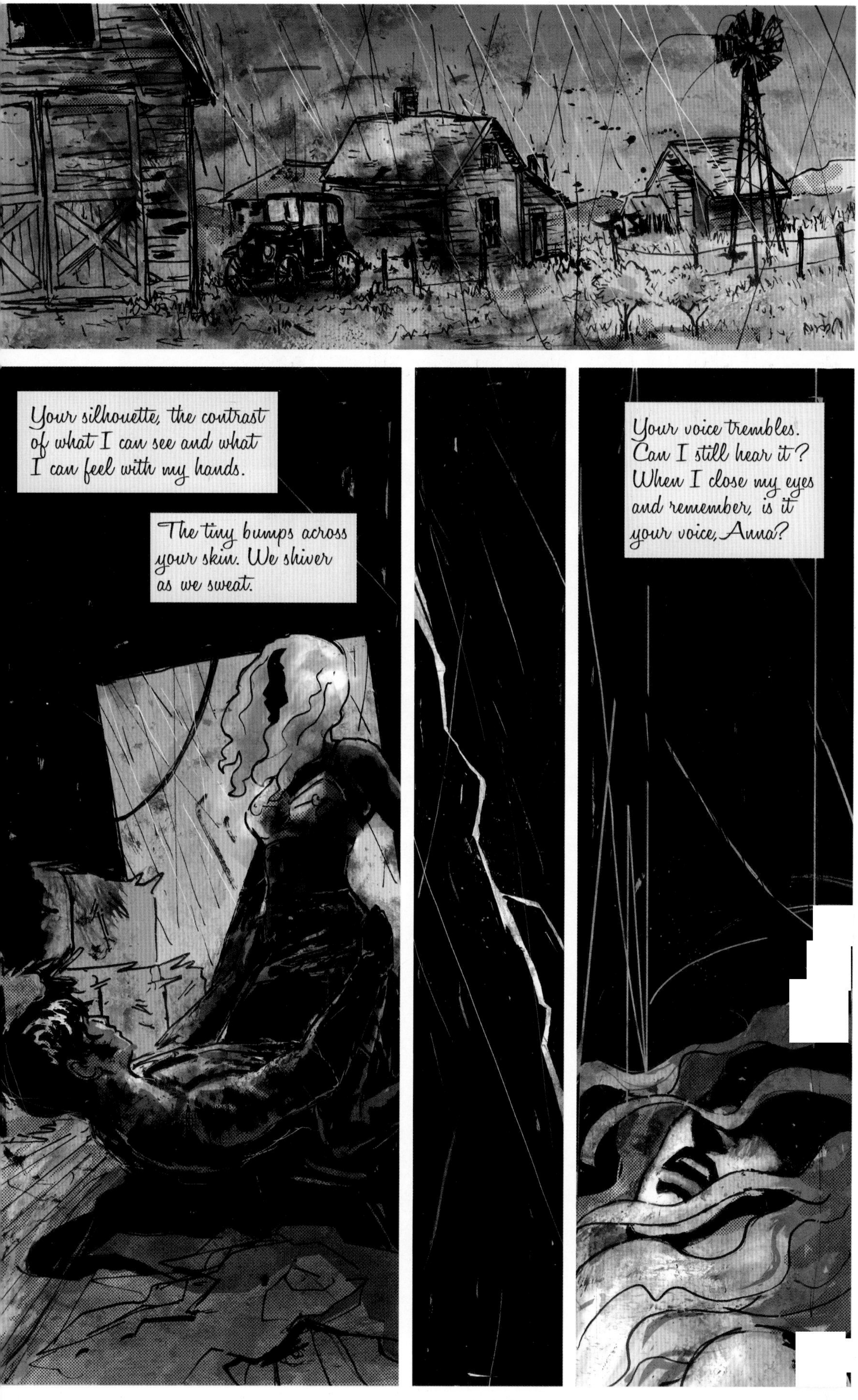
Your silhouette, the contrast of what I can see and what I can feel with my hands.
The tiny bumps across your skin. We shiver as we sweat.
Your voice trembles. Can I still hear it? When I close my eyes and remember, is it your voice, Anna?

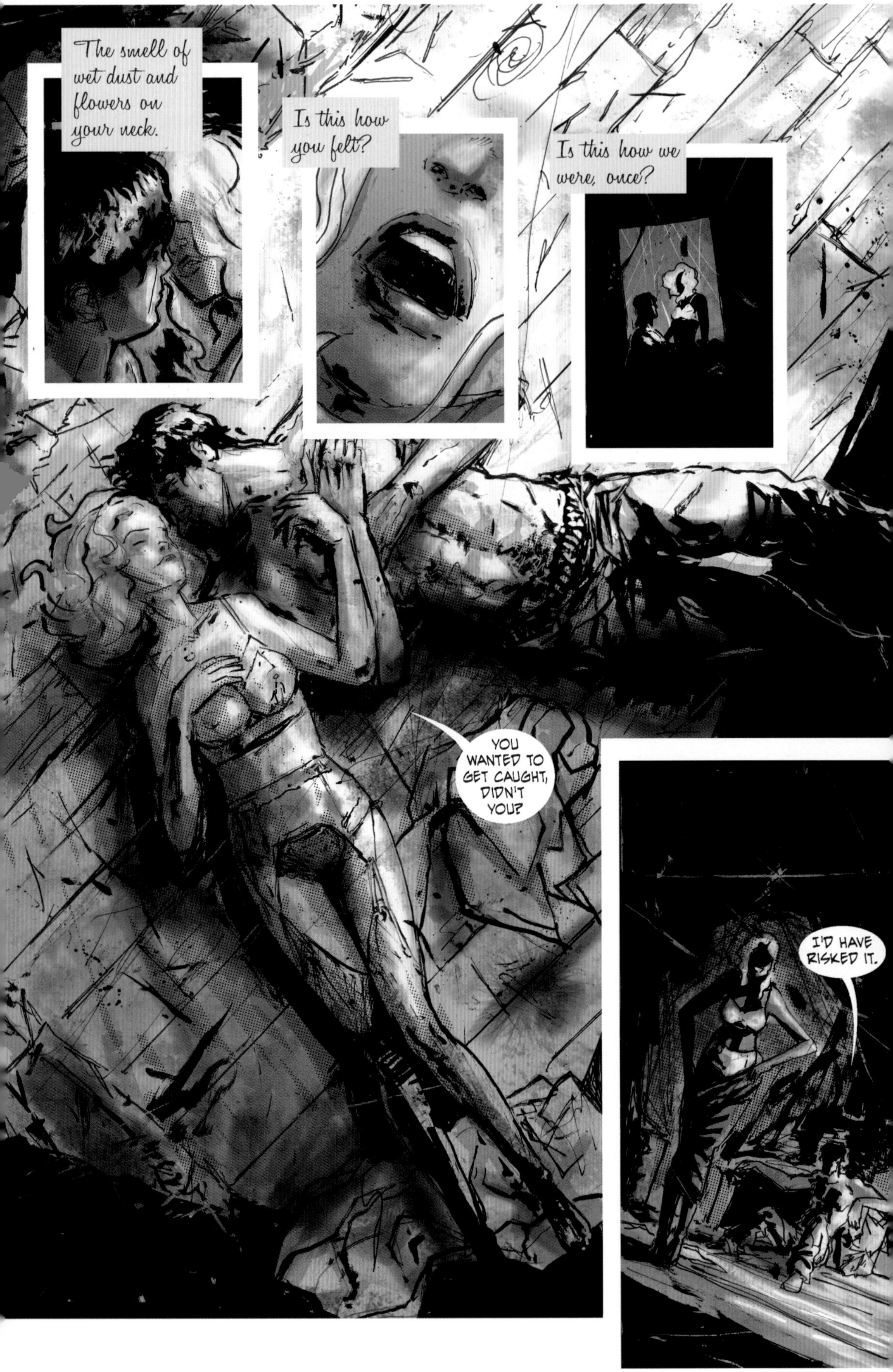
The smell of wet dust and flowers on your neck.
Is this how you felt?
Is this how we were, once?
YOU WANTED TO GET CAUGHT, DIDN'T YOU?
I'D HAVE RISKED IT.

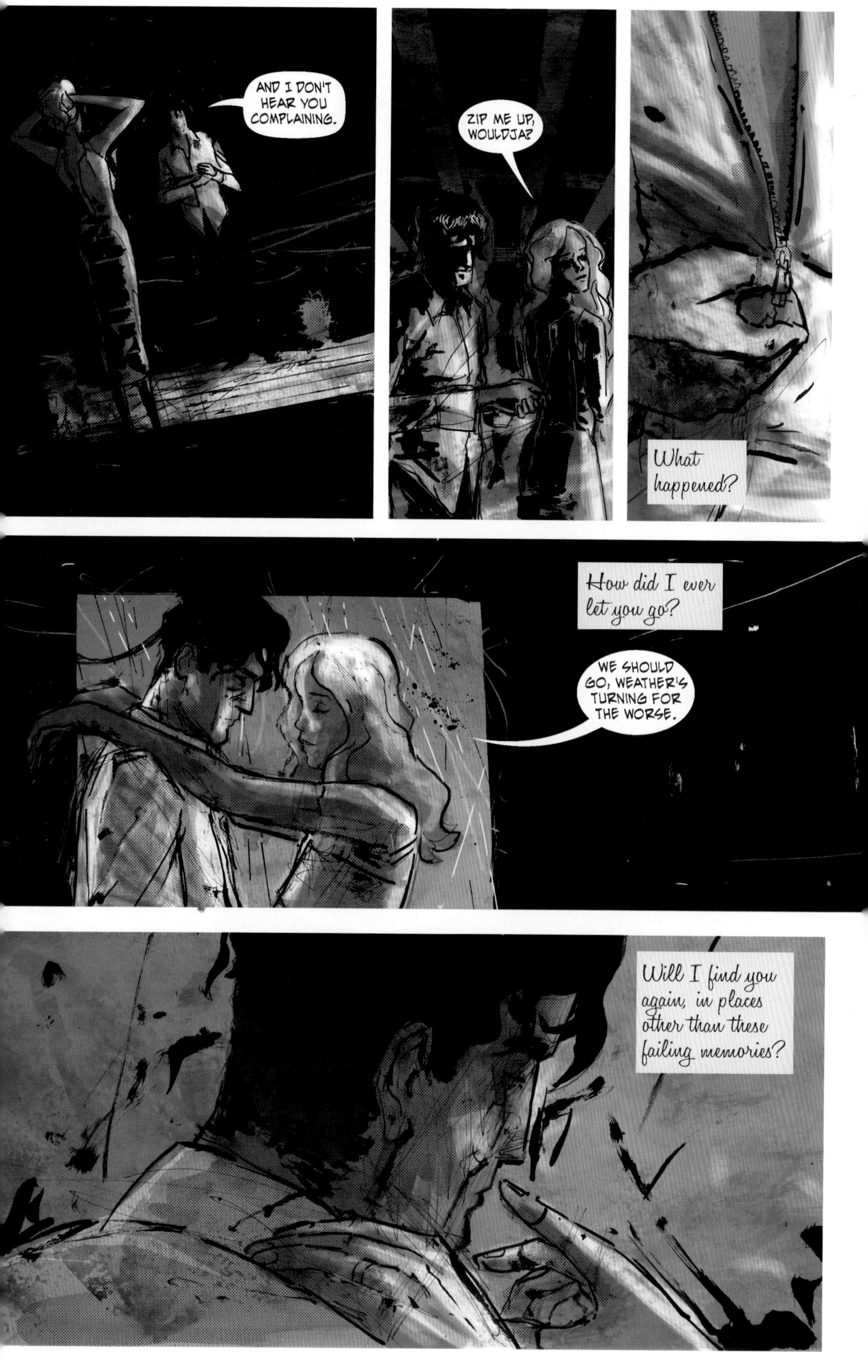
AND I DON'T HEAR YOU COMPLAINING.
ZIP ME UP, WOULDJA?
What happened?
How did I ever let you go?
WE SHOULD GO, WEATHER'S TURNING FOR THE WORSE.
Will I find you again, in places other than these failing memories?

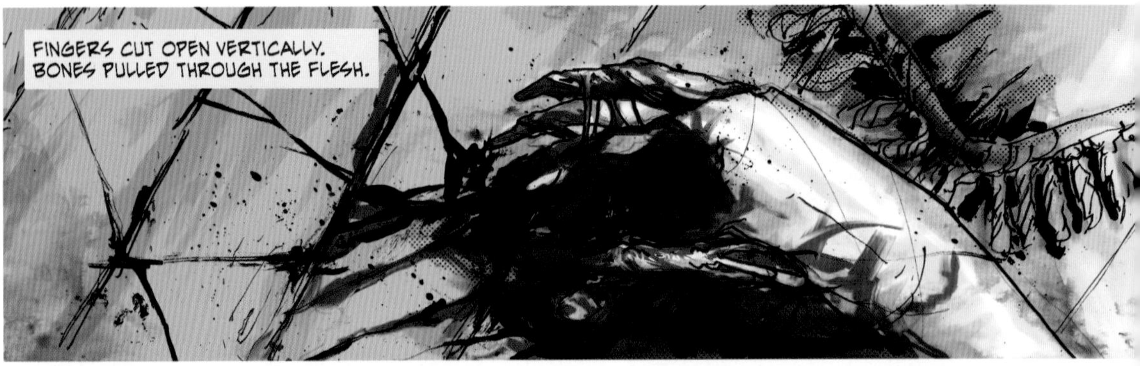

FINGERS CUT OPEN VERTICALLY.
BONES PULLED THROUGH THE FLESH.

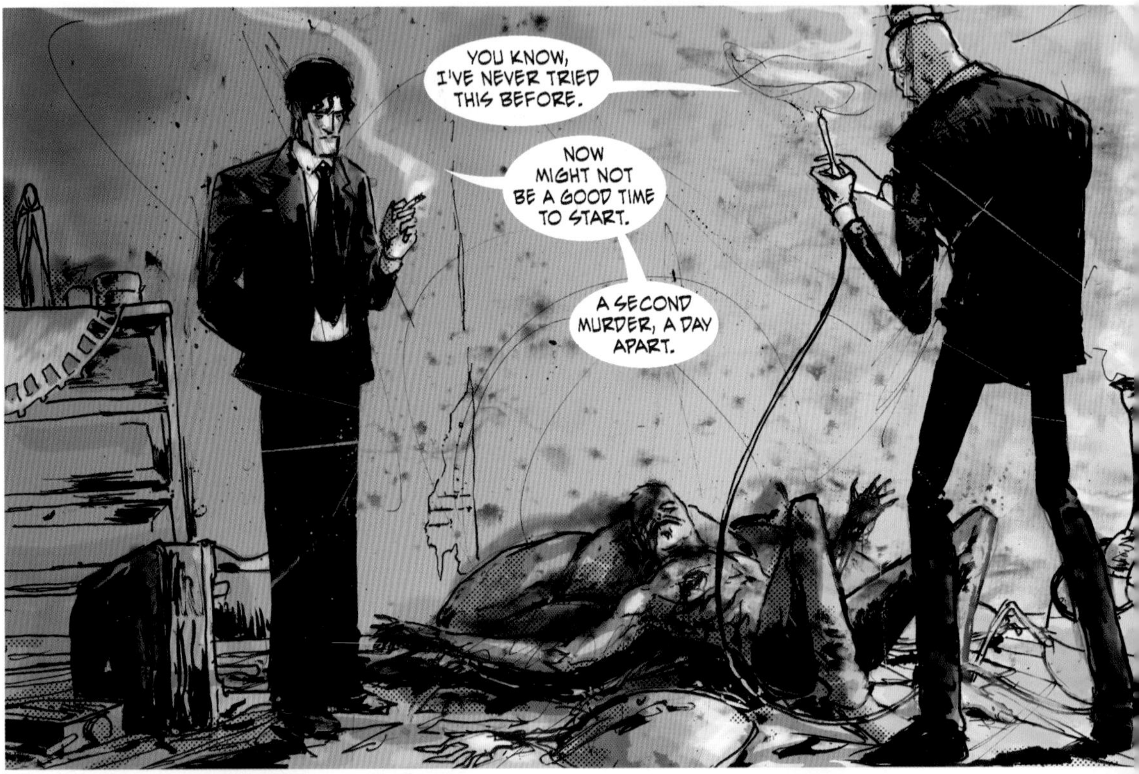

YOU KNOW, I'VE NEVER TRIED THIS BEFORE.
NOW MIGHT NOT BE A GOOD TIME TO START.
A SECOND MURDER, A DAY APART.

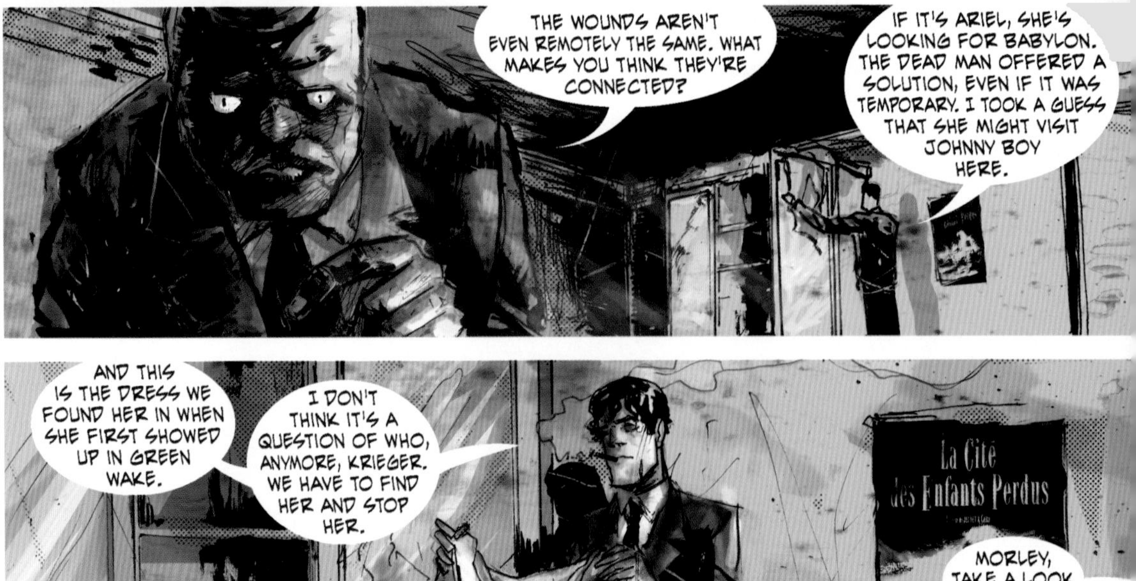

THE WOUNDS AREN'T EVEN REMOTELY THE SAME. WHAT MAKES YOU THINK THEY'RE CONNECTED?
IF IT'S ARIEL, SHE'S LOOKING FOR BABYLON. THE DEAD MAN OFFERED A SOLUTION, EVEN IF IT WAS TEMPORARY. I TOOK A GUESS THAT SHE MIGHT VISIT JOHNNY BOY HERE.

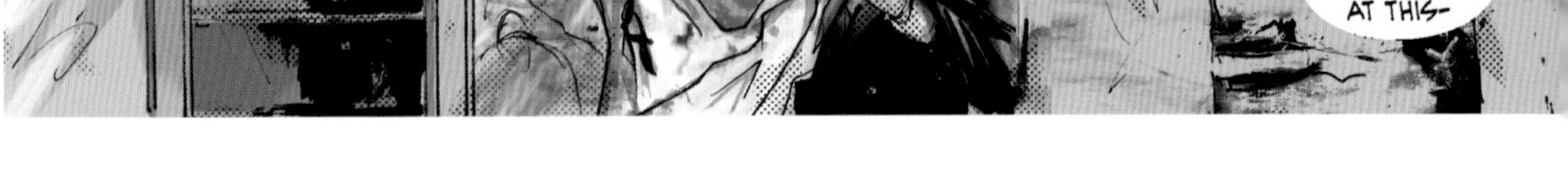

AND THIS IS THE DRESS WE FOUND HER IN WHEN SHE FIRST SHOWED UP IN GREEN WAKE.
I DON'T THINK IT'S A QUESTION OF WHO, ANYMORE, KRIEGER. WE HAVE TO FIND HER AND STOP HER.
La Cité des Enfants Perdus
MORLEY, TAKE A LOOK AT THIS-

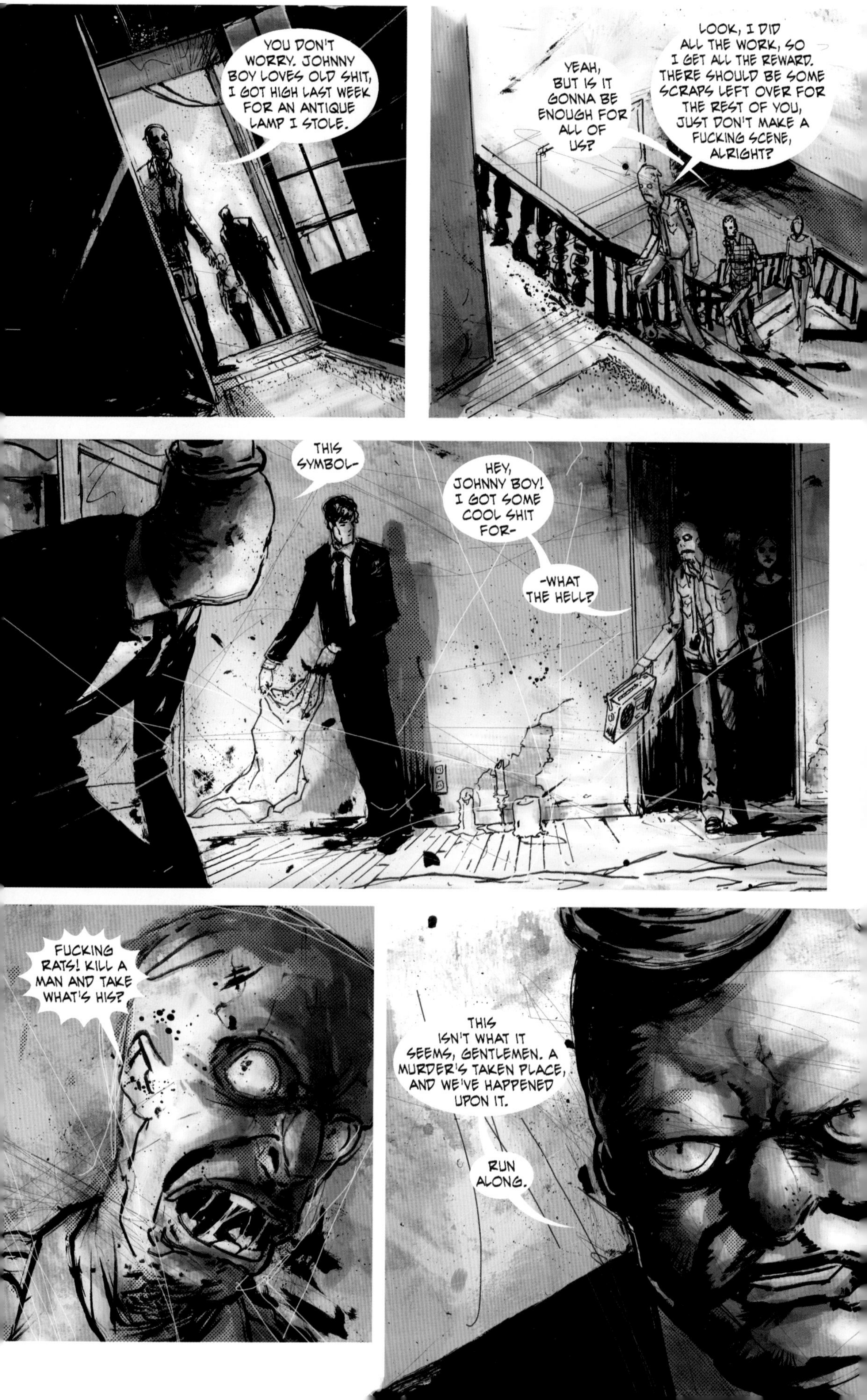
YOU DON'T WORRY. JOHNNY BOY LOVES OLD SHIT, I GOT HIGH LAST WEEK FOR AN ANTIQUE LAMP I STOLE.
YEAH, BUT IS IT GONNA BE ENOUGH FOR ALL OF US?
LOOK, I DID ALL THE WORK, SO I GET ALL THE REWARD. THERE SHOULD BE SOME SCRAPS LEFT OVER FOR THE REST OF YOU, JUST DON'T MAKE A FUCKING SCENE, ALRIGHT?
THIS SYMBOL-
HEY, JOHNNY BOY! I GOT SOME COOL SHIT FOR-
-WHAT THE HELL?
FUCKING RATS! KILL A MAN AND TAKE WHAT'S HIS?
THIS ISN'T WHAT IT SEEMS, GENTLEMEN. A MURDER'S TAKEN PLACE, AND WE'VE HAPPENED UPON IT.
RUN ALONG.

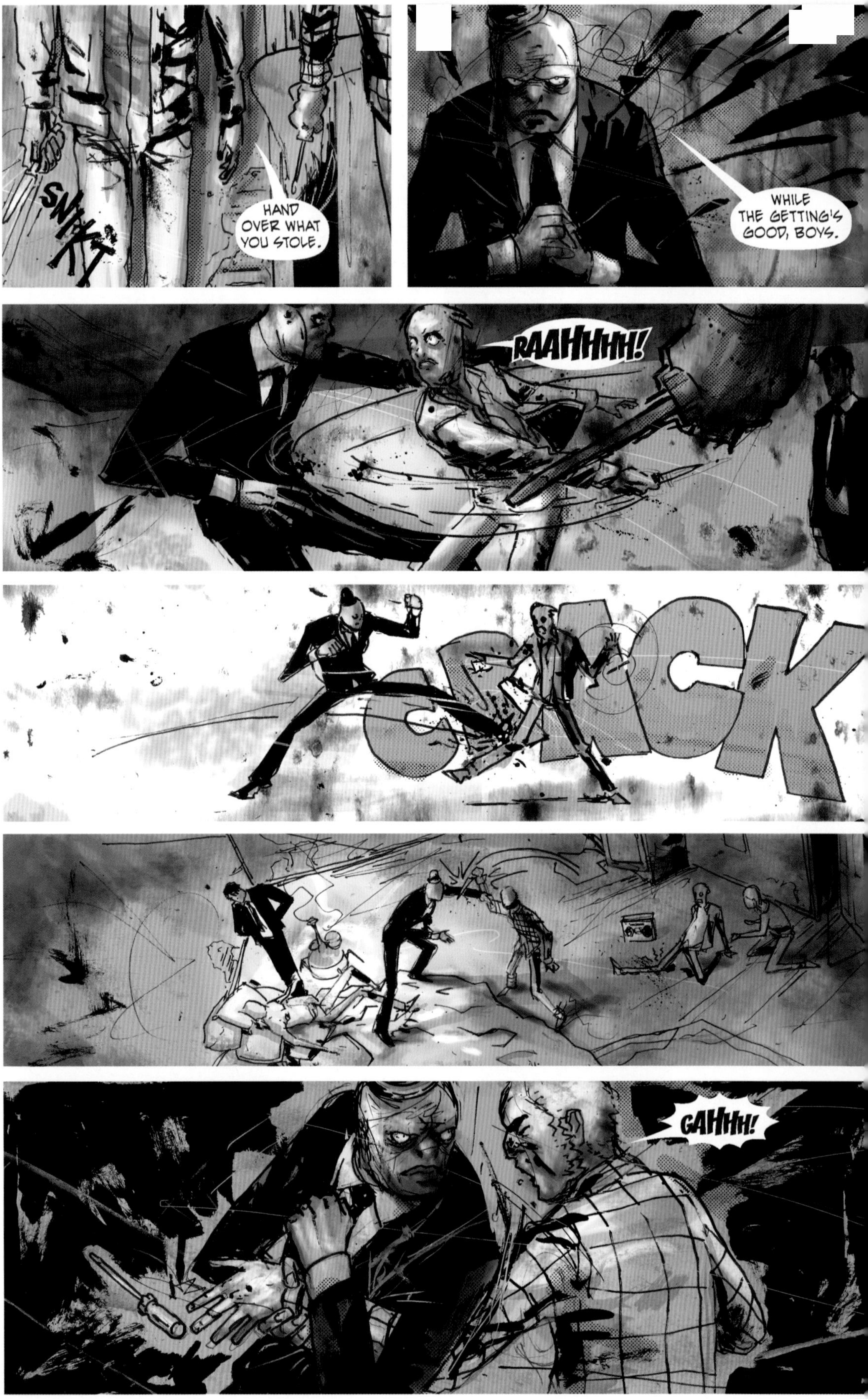
SNIKT
HAND OVER WHAT YOU STOLE.
WHILE THE GETTING'S GOOD, BOYS.
RAAHHHH!
SMACK
GAHHH!

THIS IS EATING INVESTIGATIVE TIME. RECONSIDER YOUR CHANCE FOR SUCCESS.

JESUS.

UH, YOU WERE SAYING SOMETHING ABOUT THE SYMBOL?

WHAT?

ON THE BODY.

I WONDER IF HAWTHORNE HAS A SIMILAR MARKING. IT'S WORTH CHECKING.

SOME JUNKIES GOT WHAT WAS COMING TO THEM.

WHAT JUST HAPPENED?

CHRIST.

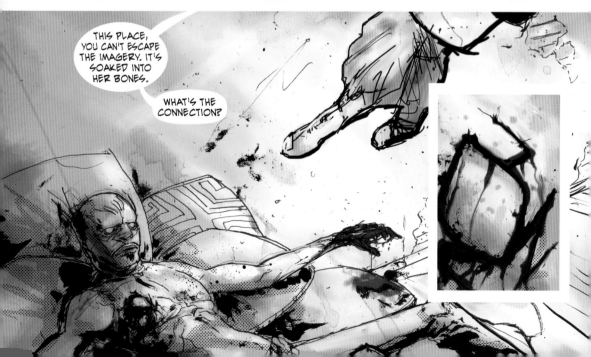

THIS PLACE, YOU CAN'T ESCAPE THE IMAGERY. IT'S SOAKED INTO HER BONES.

WHAT'S THE CONNECTION?

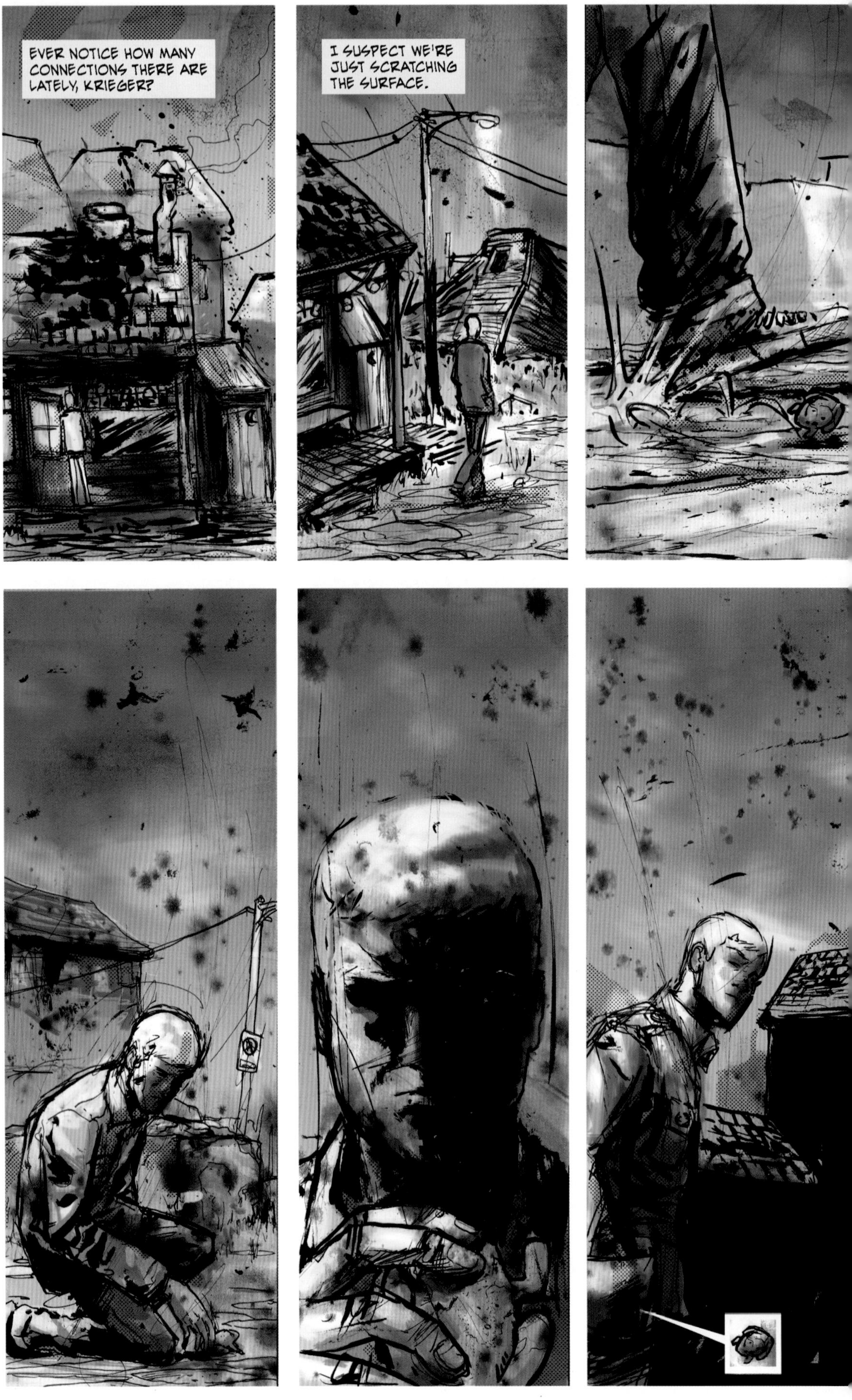
EVER NOTICE HOW MANY CONNECTIONS THERE ARE LATELY, KRIEGER?
I SUSPECT WE'RE JUST SCRATCHING THE SURFACE.

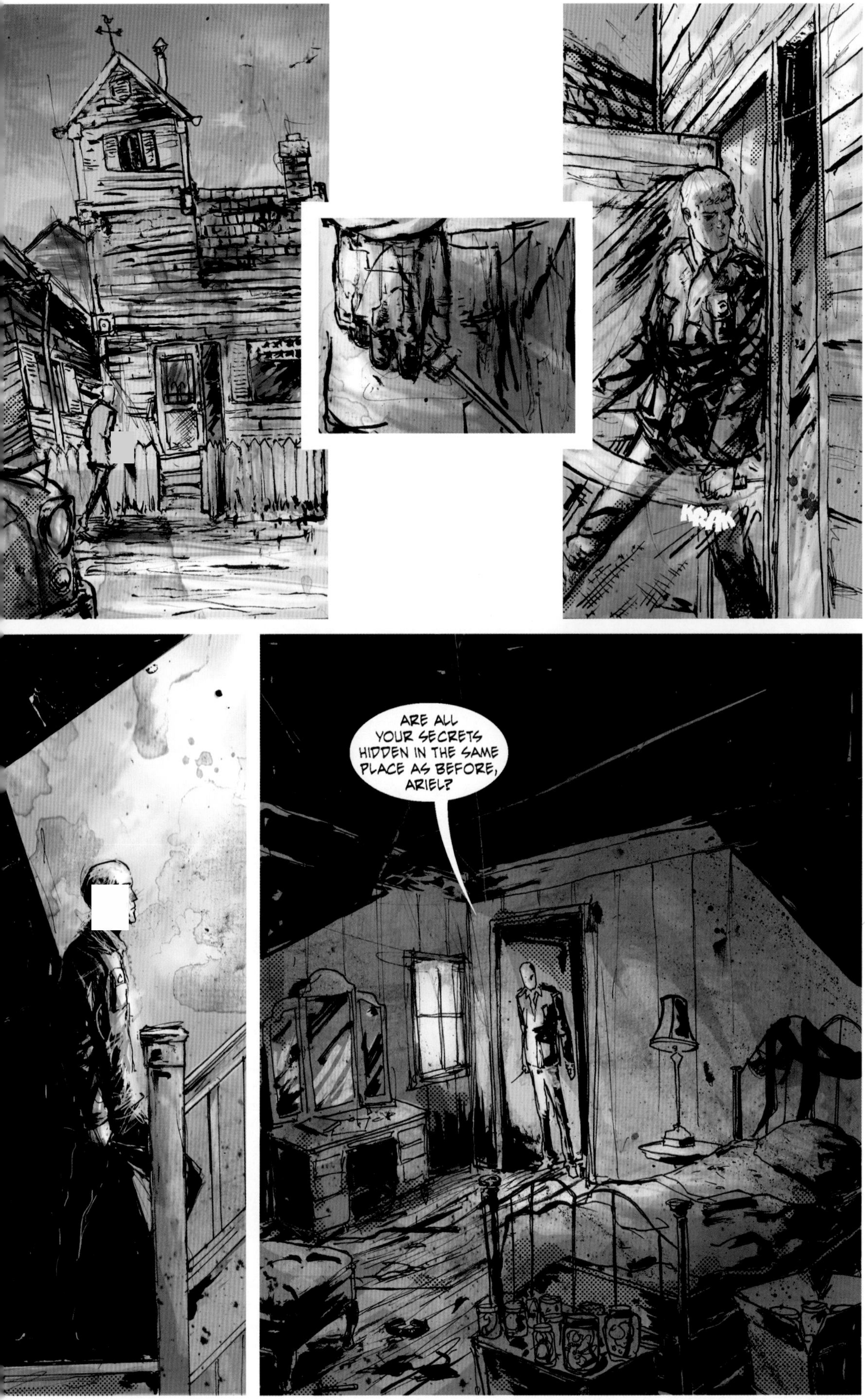
KRAK
ARE ALL YOUR SECRETS HIDDEN IN THE SAME PLACE AS BEFORE, ARIEL?

AND, LIKE I SAID, THERE WAS NOTHING IN HER ROOM. CHECKED THE DRAWERS, THE CABINETS.

WELL, WHAT WERE YOU HOPING TO FIND? WE ALL CAME TO GREEN WAKE WITH THE CLOTHES ON OUR BACKS AND, REALLY, THAT'S ALL.

MAYBE A FULL CONFESSION, CLEARLY EXPLAINING WHY SHE HAS DECIDED TO GO ON A MUTILATION MURDER SPREE.

FUNNY GUY.

CARL, YOU THERE?

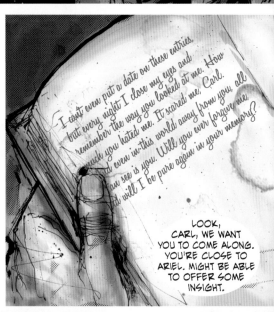

I can't even put a date on these entries, but every night I close my eyes and remember the way you looked at me. How much you hated me. It scared me, Carl. And even in this world away from you, all I can see is you. Will you ever forgive me, and will I be pure again in your memory?

LOOK, CARL, WE WANT YOU TO COME ALONG. YOU'RE CLOSE TO ARIEL. MIGHT BE ABLE TO OFFER SOME INSIGHT.

BE RIGHT WITH YOU.

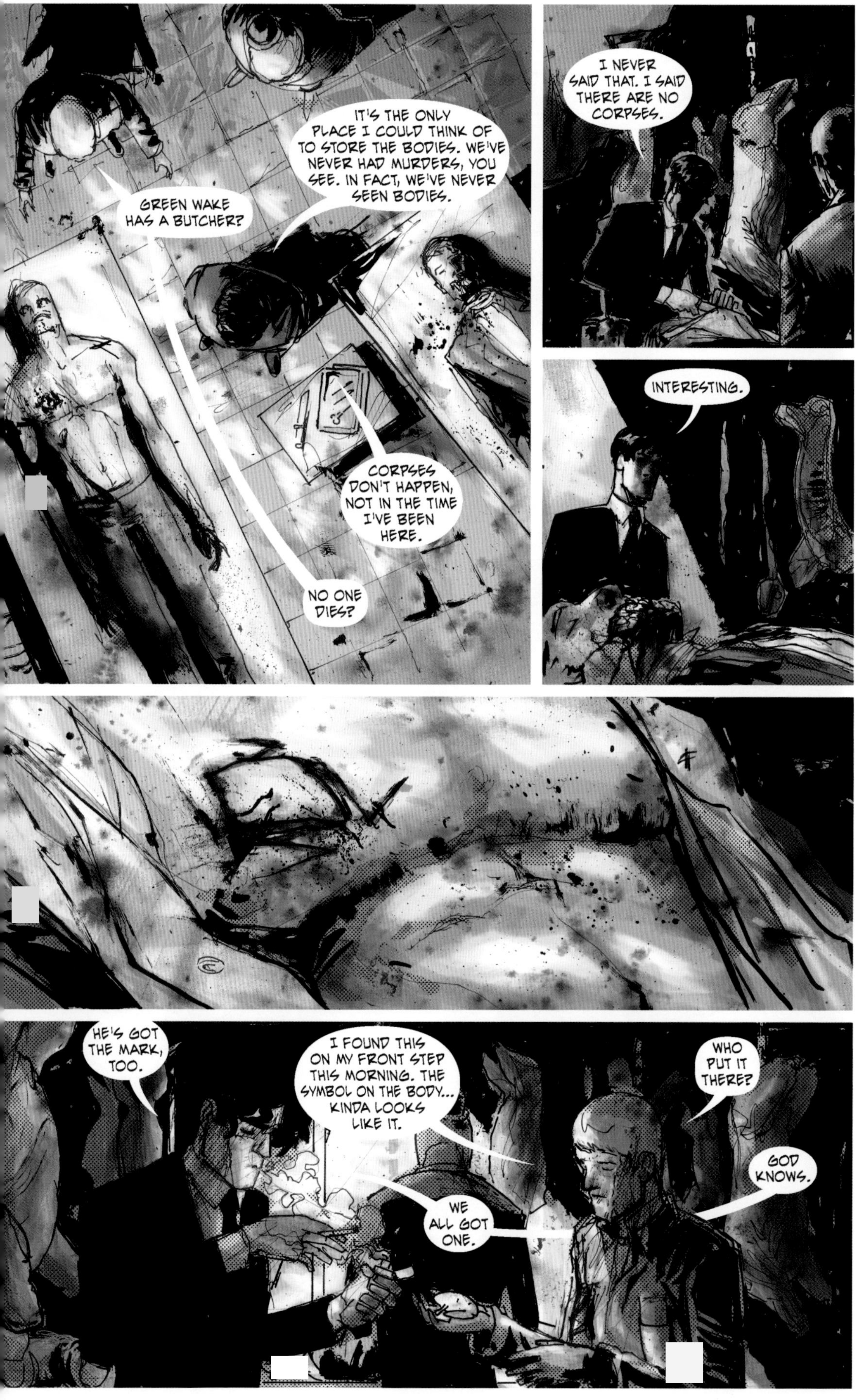
GREEN WAKE HAS A BUTCHER?
IT'S THE ONLY PLACE I COULD THINK OF TO STORE THE BODIES. WE'VE NEVER HAD MURDERS, YOU SEE. IN FACT, WE'VE NEVER SEEN BODIES.
NO ONE DIES?
CORPSES DON'T HAPPEN, NOT IN THE TIME I'VE BEEN HERE.
I NEVER SAID THAT. I SAID THERE ARE NO CORPSES.
INTERESTING.
HE'S GOT THE MARK, TOO.
I FOUND THIS ON MY FRONT STEP THIS MORNING. THE SYMBOL ON THE BODY... KINDA LOOKS LIKE IT.
WHO PUT IT THERE?
GOD KNOWS.
WE ALL GOT ONE.

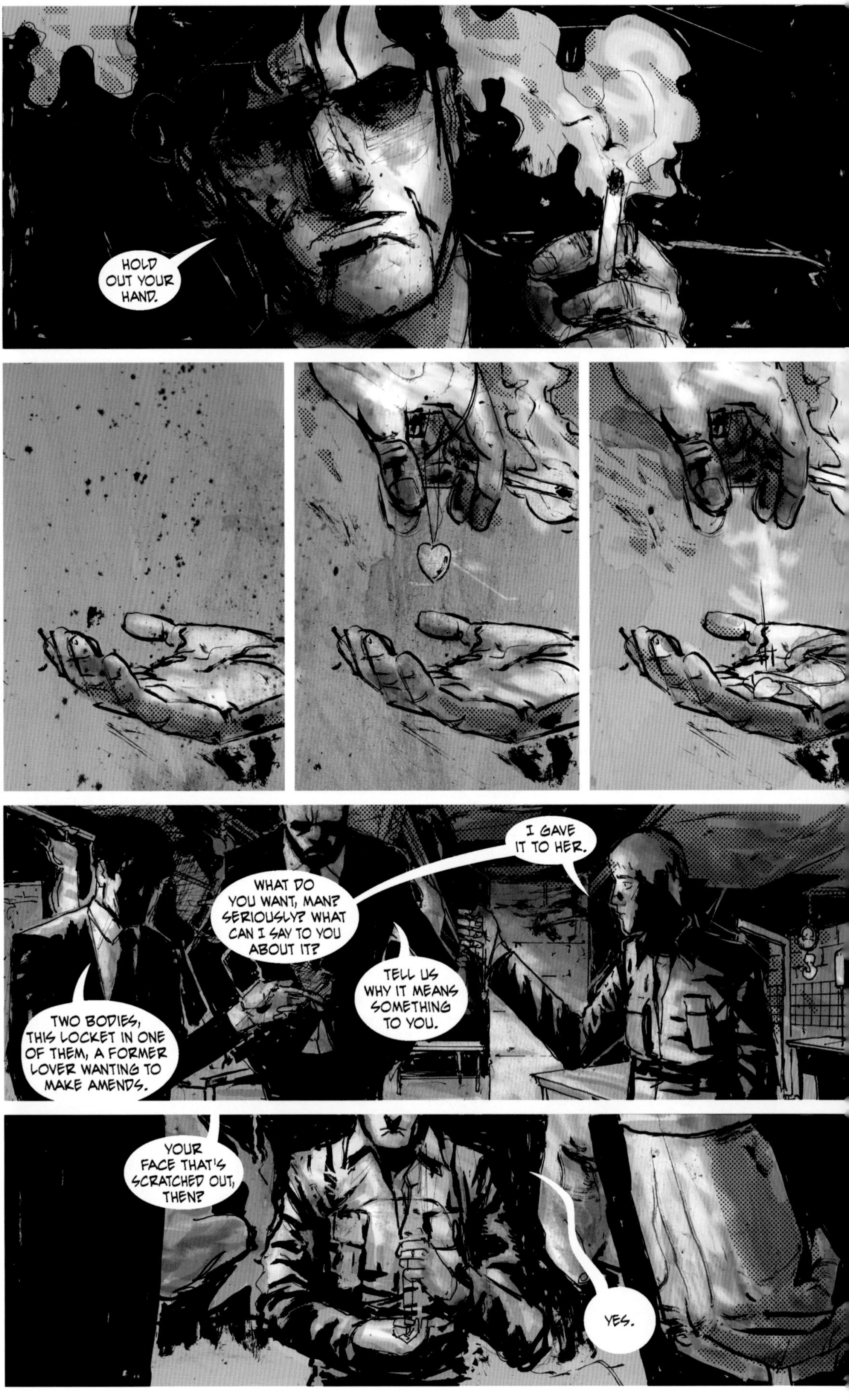
HOLD OUT YOUR HAND.
I GAVE IT TO HER.
WHAT DO YOU WANT, MAN? SERIOUSLY? WHAT CAN I SAY TO YOU ABOUT IT?
TELL US WHY IT MEANS SOMETHING TO YOU.
TWO BODIES, THIS LOCKET IN ONE OF THEM, A FORMER LOVER WANTING TO MAKE AMENDS.
YOUR FACE THAT'S SCRATCHED OUT, THEN?
YES.

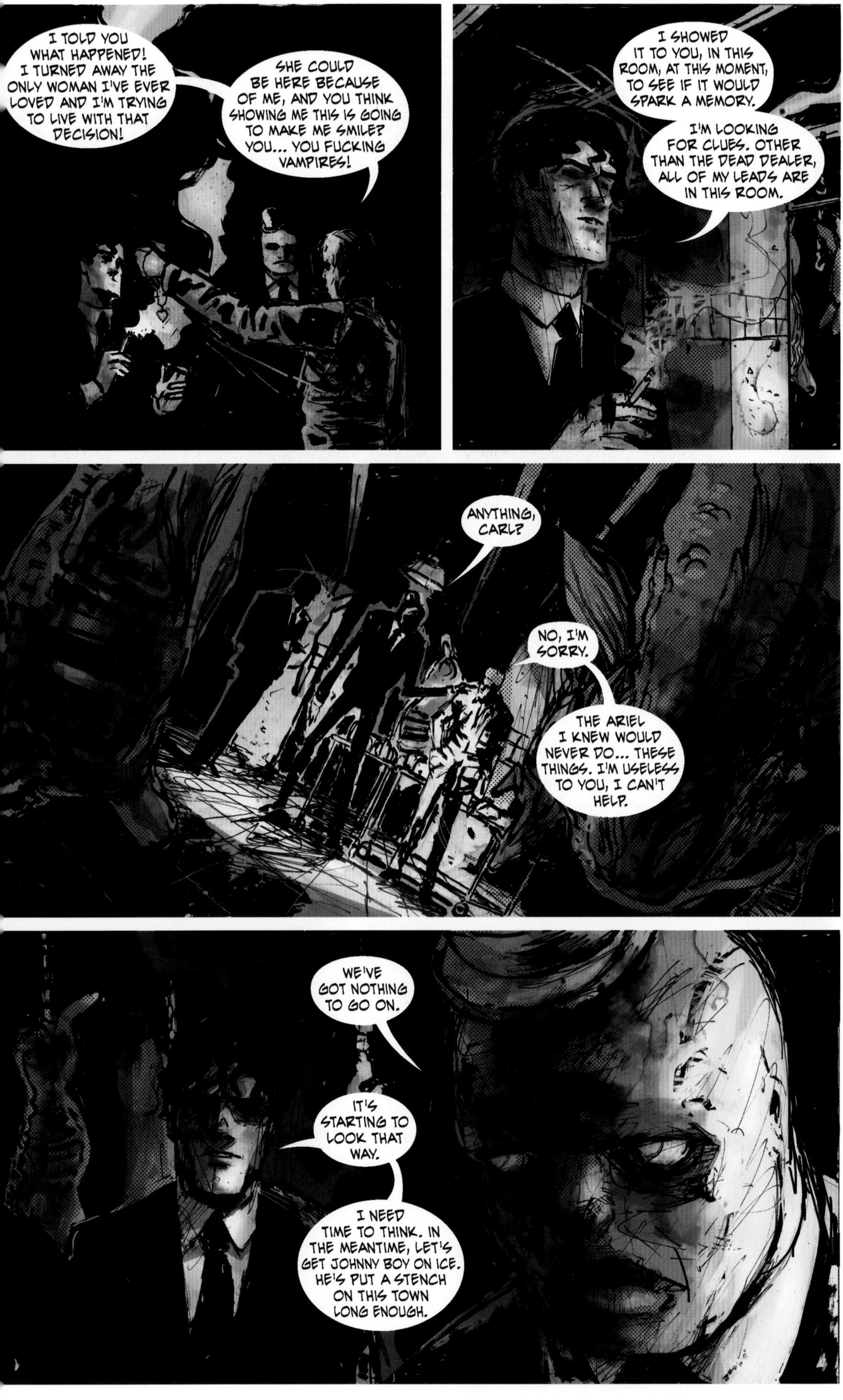
I TOLD YOU WHAT HAPPENED! I TURNED AWAY THE ONLY WOMAN I'VE EVER LOVED AND I'M TRYING TO LIVE WITH THAT DECISION!
SHE COULD BE HERE BECAUSE OF ME, AND YOU THINK SHOWING ME THIS IS GOING TO MAKE ME SMILE? YOU... YOU FUCKING VAMPIRES!
I SHOWED IT TO YOU, IN THIS ROOM, AT THIS MOMENT, TO SEE IF IT WOULD SPARK A MEMORY.
I'M LOOKING FOR CLUES. OTHER THAN THE DEAD DEALER, ALL OF MY LEADS ARE IN THIS ROOM.
ANYTHING, CARL?
NO, I'M SORRY.
THE ARIEL I KNEW WOULD NEVER DO... THESE THINGS. I'M USELESS TO YOU, I CAN'T HELP.
WE'VE GOT NOTHING TO GO ON.
IT'S STARTING TO LOOK THAT WAY.
I NEED TIME TO THINK. IN THE MEANTIME, LET'S GET JOHNNY BOY ON ICE. HE'S PUT A STENCH ON THIS TOWN LONG ENOUGH.

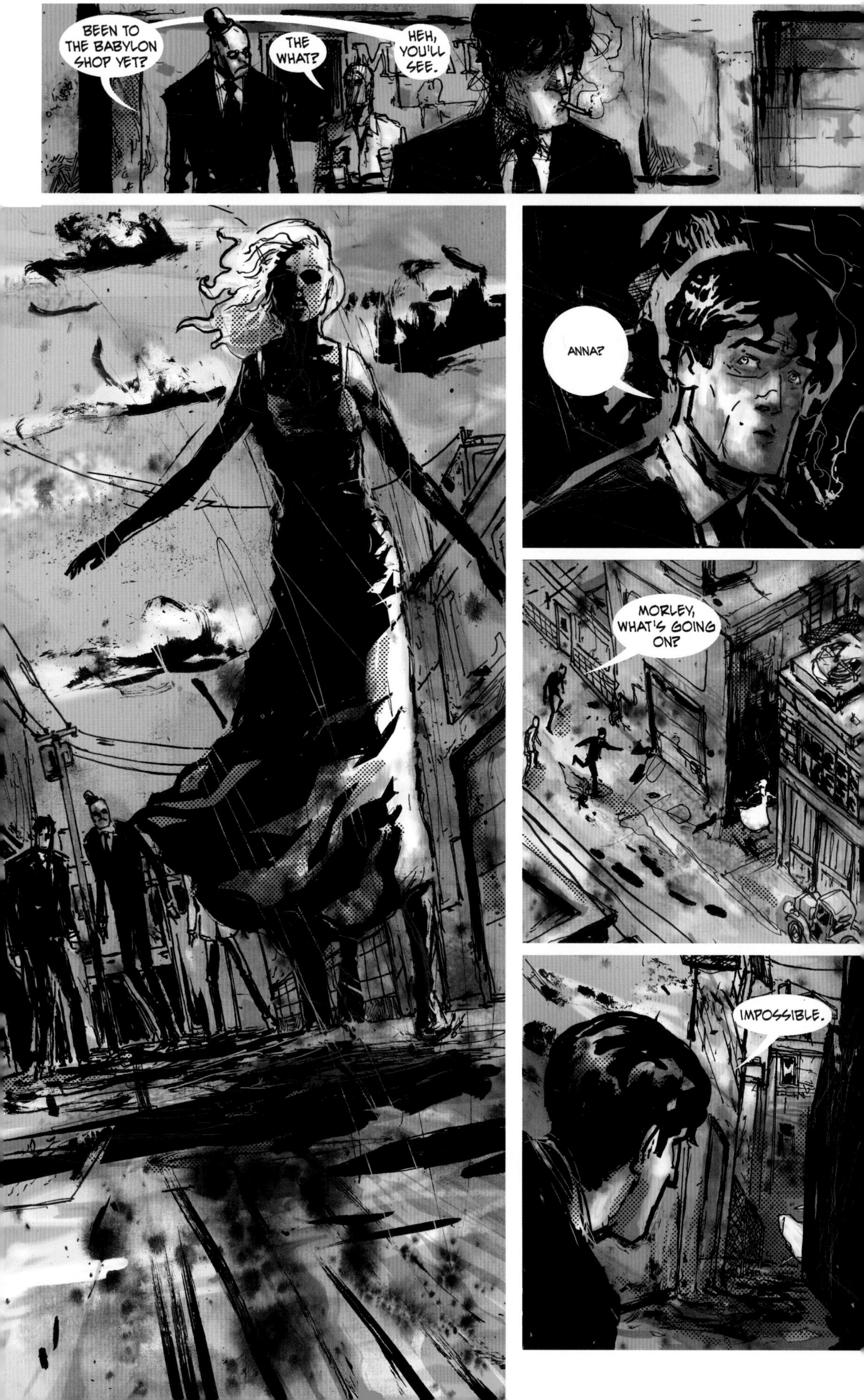
BEEN TO THE BABYLON SHOP YET?
THE WHAT?
HEH, YOU'LL SEE.
ANNA?
MORLEY, WHAT'S GOING ON?
IMPOSSIBLE.

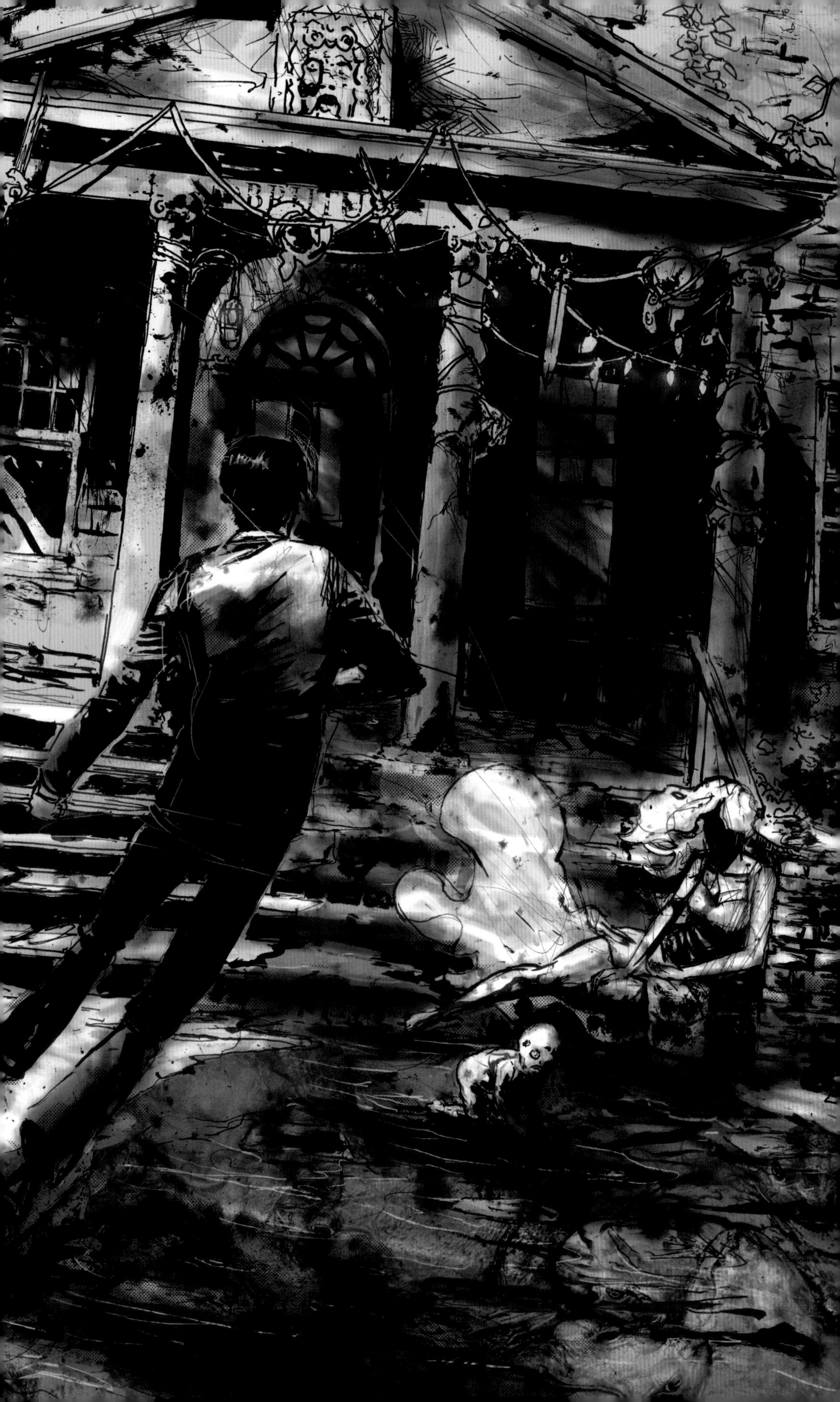

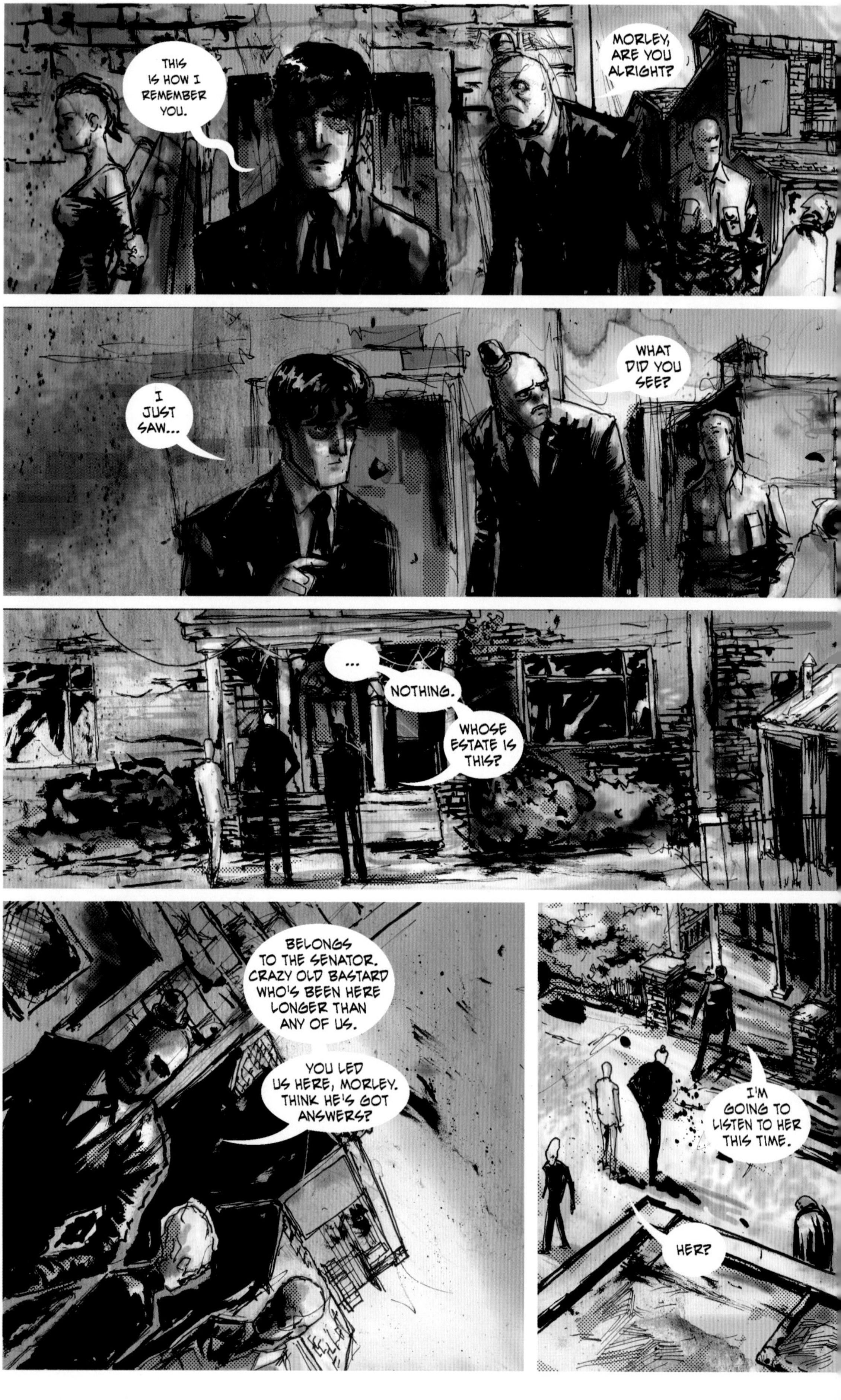
THIS IS HOW I REMEMBER YOU.
MORLEY, ARE YOU ALRIGHT?
I JUST SAW...
WHAT DID YOU SEE?
...
NOTHING.
WHOSE ESTATE IS THIS?
BELONGS TO THE SENATOR. CRAZY OLD BASTARD WHO'S BEEN HERE LONGER THAN ANY OF US.
YOU LED US HERE, MORLEY. THINK HE'S GOT ANSWERS?
I'M GOING TO LISTEN TO HER THIS TIME.
HER?

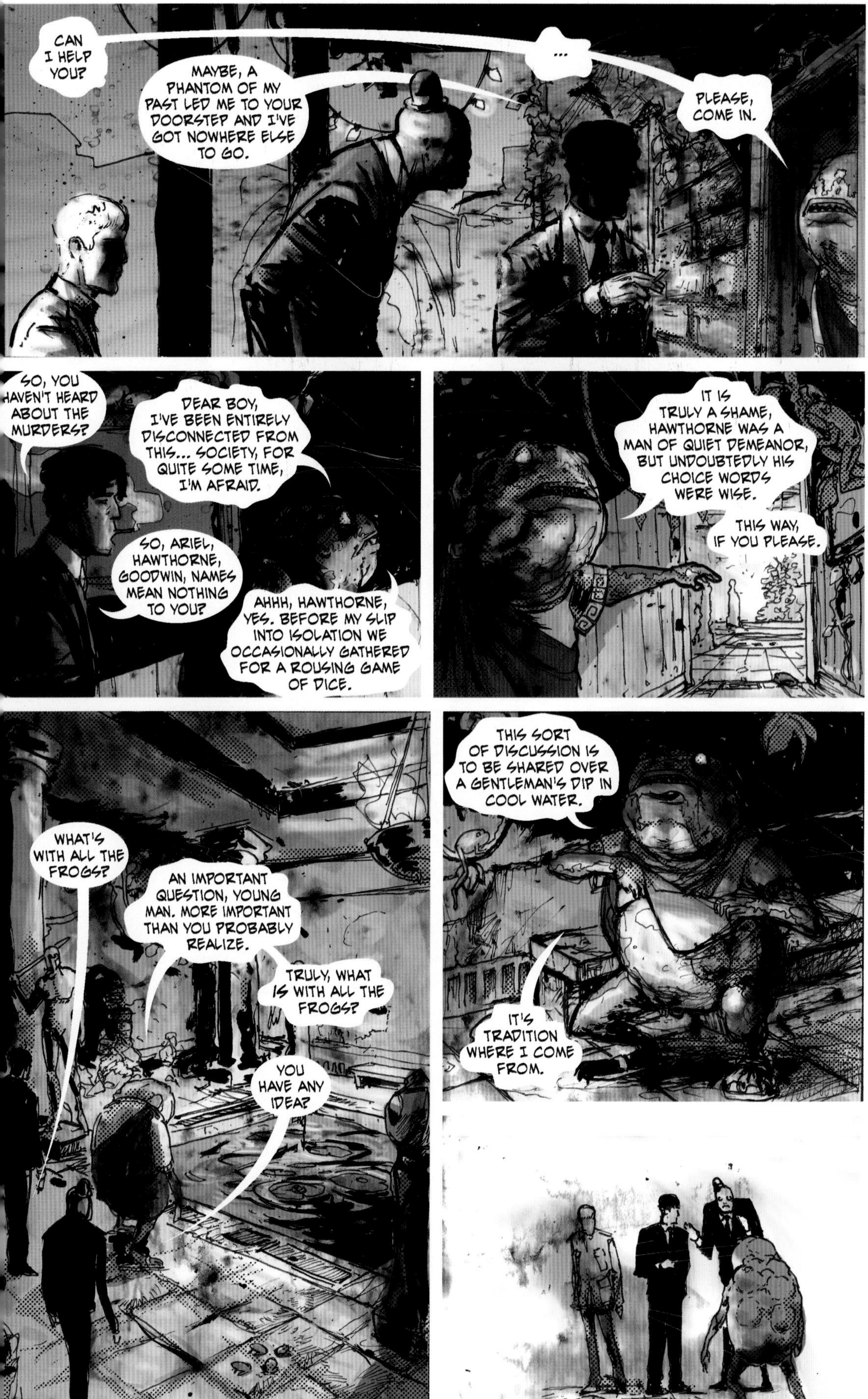
CAN I HELP YOU?
MAYBE, A PHANTOM OF MY PAST LED ME TO YOUR DOORSTEP AND I'VE GOT NOWHERE ELSE TO GO.
...
PLEASE, COME IN.
SO, YOU HAVEN'T HEARD ABOUT THE MURDERS?
DEAR BOY, I'VE BEEN ENTIRELY DISCONNECTED FROM THIS... SOCIETY, FOR QUITE SOME TIME, I'M AFRAID.
SO, ARIEL, HAWTHORNE, GOODWIN, NAMES MEAN NOTHING TO YOU?
AHHH, HAWTHORNE, YES. BEFORE MY SLIP INTO ISOLATION WE OCCASIONALLY GATHERED FOR A ROUSING GAME OF DICE.
IT IS TRULY A SHAME, HAWTHORNE WAS A MAN OF QUIET DEMEANOR, BUT UNDOUBTEDLY HIS CHOICE WORDS WERE WISE.
THIS WAY, IF YOU PLEASE.
WHAT'S WITH ALL THE FROGS?
AN IMPORTANT QUESTION, YOUNG MAN. MORE IMPORTANT THAN YOU PROBABLY REALIZE.
TRULY, WHAT IS WITH ALL THE FROGS?
YOU HAVE ANY IDEA?
THIS SORT OF DISCUSSION IS TO BE SHARED OVER A GENTLEMAN'S DIP IN COOL WATER.
IT'S TRADITION WHERE I COME FROM.

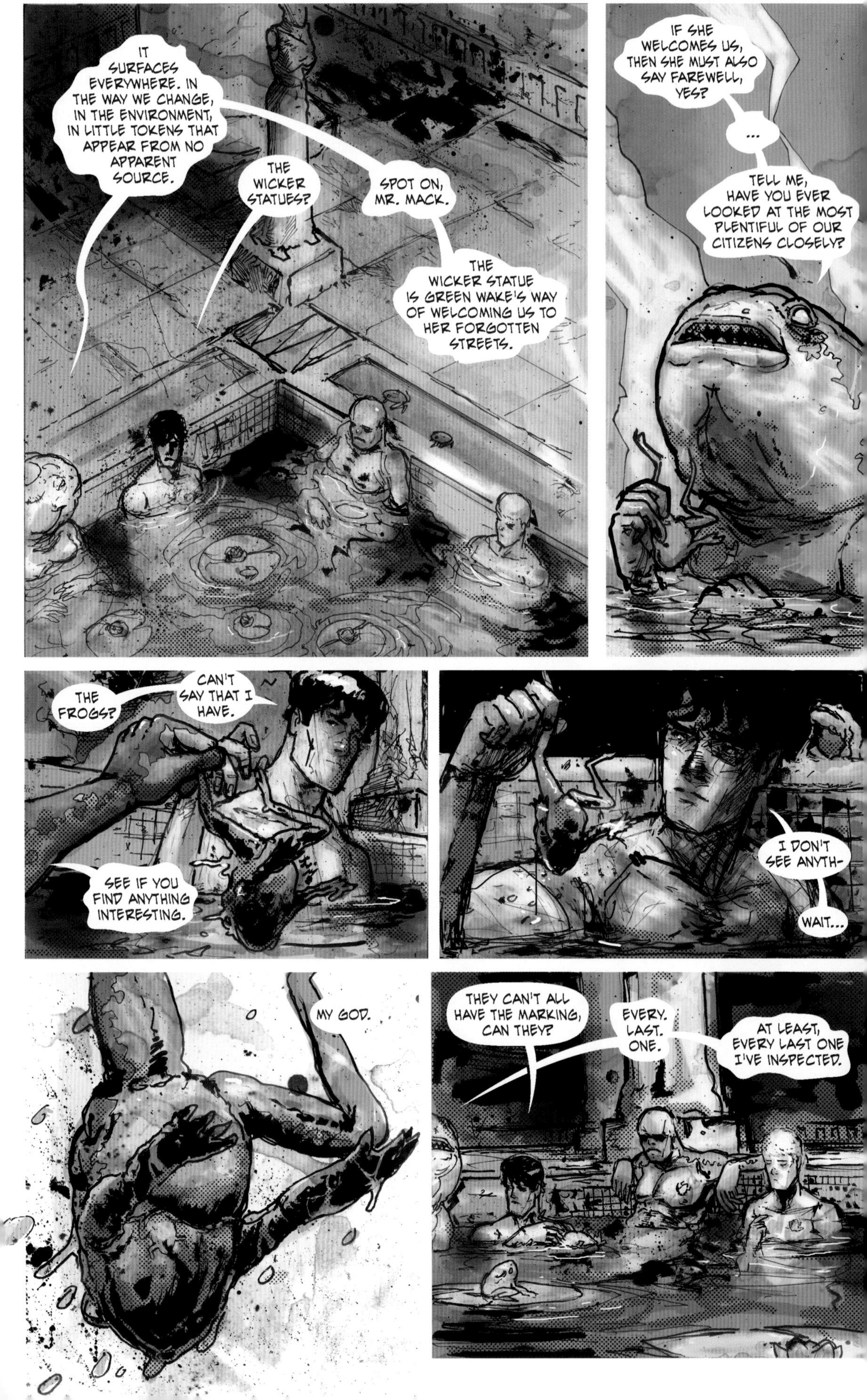
IT SURFACES EVERYWHERE. IN THE WAY WE CHANGE, IN THE ENVIRONMENT, IN LITTLE TOKENS THAT APPEAR FROM NO APPARENT SOURCE.
THE WICKER STATUES?
SPOT ON, MR. MACK.
THE WICKER STATUE IS GREEN WAKE'S WAY OF WELCOMING US TO HER FORGOTTEN STREETS.
IF SHE WELCOMES US, THEN SHE MUST ALSO SAY FAREWELL, YES?
...
TELL ME, HAVE YOU EVER LOOKED AT THE MOST PLENTIFUL OF OUR CITIZENS CLOSELY?
THE FROGS?
CAN'T SAY THAT I HAVE.
SEE IF YOU FIND ANYTHING INTERESTING.
I DON'T SEE ANYTH-
WAIT...
MY GOD.
THEY CAN'T ALL HAVE THE MARKING, CAN THEY?
EVERY. LAST. ONE.
AT LEAST, EVERY LAST ONE I'VE INSPECTED.

NO BODIES IN GREEN WAKE.

EVER HEARD OF A RESIDENT ACTING IN THE WAY THAT ARIEL HAS?

YES. IT HAS HAPPENED BEFORE.

A SERIES OF MURDERS, HORRIFIC AND VIOLENT. IT LASTS A VERY SHORT TIME AND THEN...

THE VILLAIN SIMPLY DISAPPEARS.

ALMOST LIKE GREEN WAKE IS PROTECTING HERSELF.

FROM WHAT?

ANOTHER EXCELLENT QUESTION, MY BOY.

BUT, I TIRE OF COMPANY. SHOW YOURSELVES OUT.

IF YOU KNOW ANYTHING--

GOOD DAY, MR. MACK.

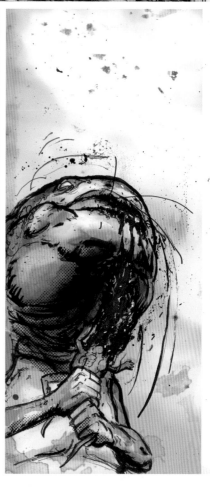

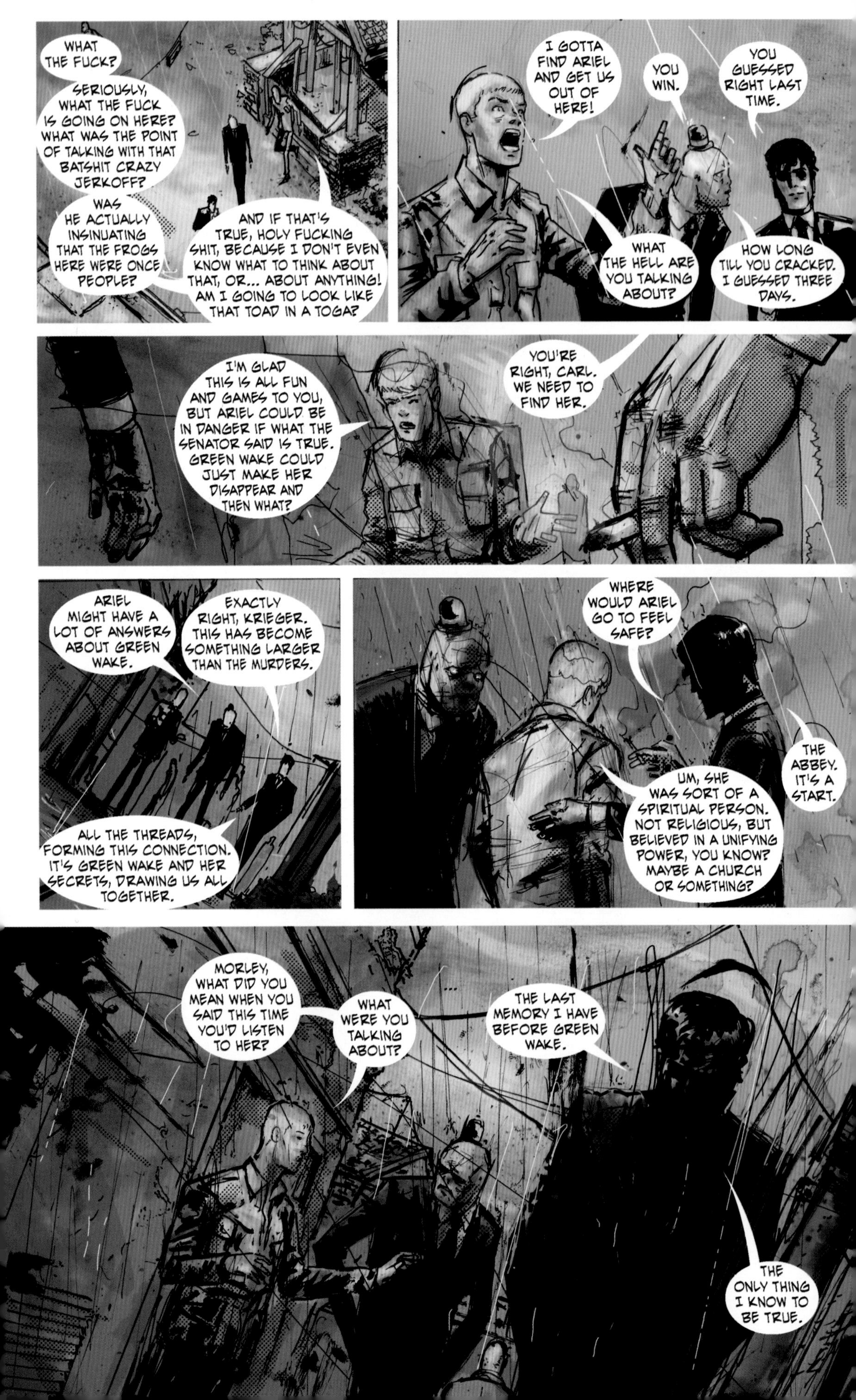

WHAT THE FUCK?
SERIOUSLY, WHAT THE FUCK IS GOING ON HERE? WHAT WAS THE POINT OF TALKING WITH THAT BATSHIT CRAZY JERKOFF?
WAS HE ACTUALLY INSINUATING THAT THE FROGS HERE WERE ONCE PEOPLE?
AND IF THAT'S TRUE, HOLY FUCKING SHIT, BECAUSE I DON'T EVEN KNOW WHAT TO THINK ABOUT THAT, OR... ABOUT ANYTHING! AM I GOING TO LOOK LIKE THAT TOAD IN A TOGA?
I GOTTA FIND ARIEL AND GET US OUT OF HERE!
YOU WIN.
YOU GUESSED RIGHT LAST TIME.
WHAT THE HELL ARE YOU TALKING ABOUT?
HOW LONG TILL YOU CRACKED. I GUESSED THREE DAYS.
I'M GLAD THIS IS ALL FUN AND GAMES TO YOU, BUT ARIEL COULD BE IN DANGER IF WHAT THE SENATOR SAID IS TRUE. GREEN WAKE COULD JUST MAKE HER DISAPPEAR AND THEN WHAT?
YOU'RE RIGHT, CARL. WE NEED TO FIND HER.
ARIEL MIGHT HAVE A LOT OF ANSWERS ABOUT GREEN WAKE.
EXACTLY RIGHT, KRIEGER. THIS HAS BECOME SOMETHING LARGER THAN THE MURDERS.
ALL THE THREADS, FORMING THIS CONNECTION. IT'S GREEN WAKE AND HER SECRETS, DRAWING US ALL TOGETHER.
WHERE WOULD ARIEL GO TO FEEL SAFE?
UM, SHE WAS SORT OF A SPIRITUAL PERSON. NOT RELIGIOUS, BUT BELIEVED IN A UNIFYING POWER, YOU KNOW? MAYBE A CHURCH OR SOMETHING?
THE ABBEY. IT'S A START.
MORLEY, WHAT DID YOU MEAN WHEN YOU SAID THIS TIME YOU'D LISTEN TO HER?
WHAT WERE YOU TALKING ABOUT?
THE LAST MEMORY I HAVE BEFORE GREEN WAKE.
THE ONLY THING I KNOW TO BE TRUE.

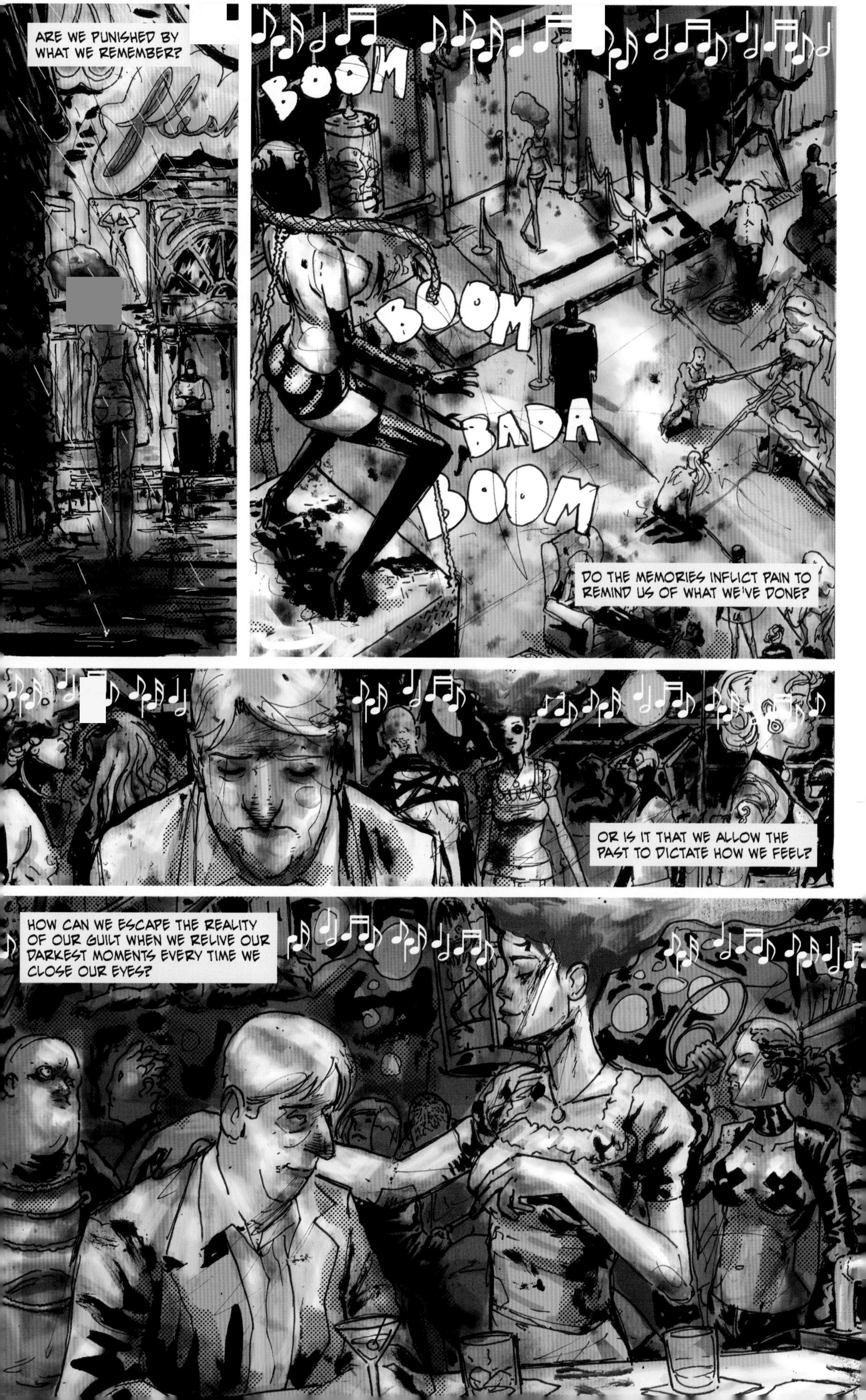

ARE WE PUNISHED BY WHAT WE REMEMBER?
BOOM
BOOM
BADA
BOOM
DO THE MEMORIES INFLICT PAIN TO REMIND US OF WHAT WE'VE DONE?
OR IS IT THAT WE ALLOW THE PAST TO DICTATE HOW WE FEEL?
HOW CAN WE ESCAPE THE REALITY OF OUR GUILT WHEN WE RELIVE OUR DARKEST MOMENTS EVERY TIME WE CLOSE OUR EYES?

WE FIND OURSELVES DRIVEN FORWARD BY THE VERY THING THAT STAGNATES US, MAKES US LESS THAN WHAT WE ARE.

DRIVEN BY WHAT HOLDS US BACK.

I WANT TO FEEL THIS. MAKE ME FEEL YOU.

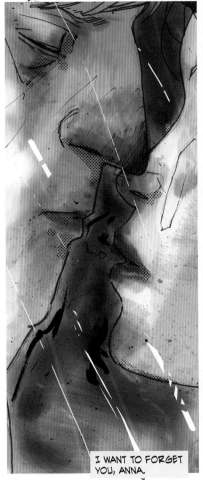

I WANT TO FORGET YOU, ANNA.

I WANT YOU TO BE FICTION. A WOMAN I CREATED.

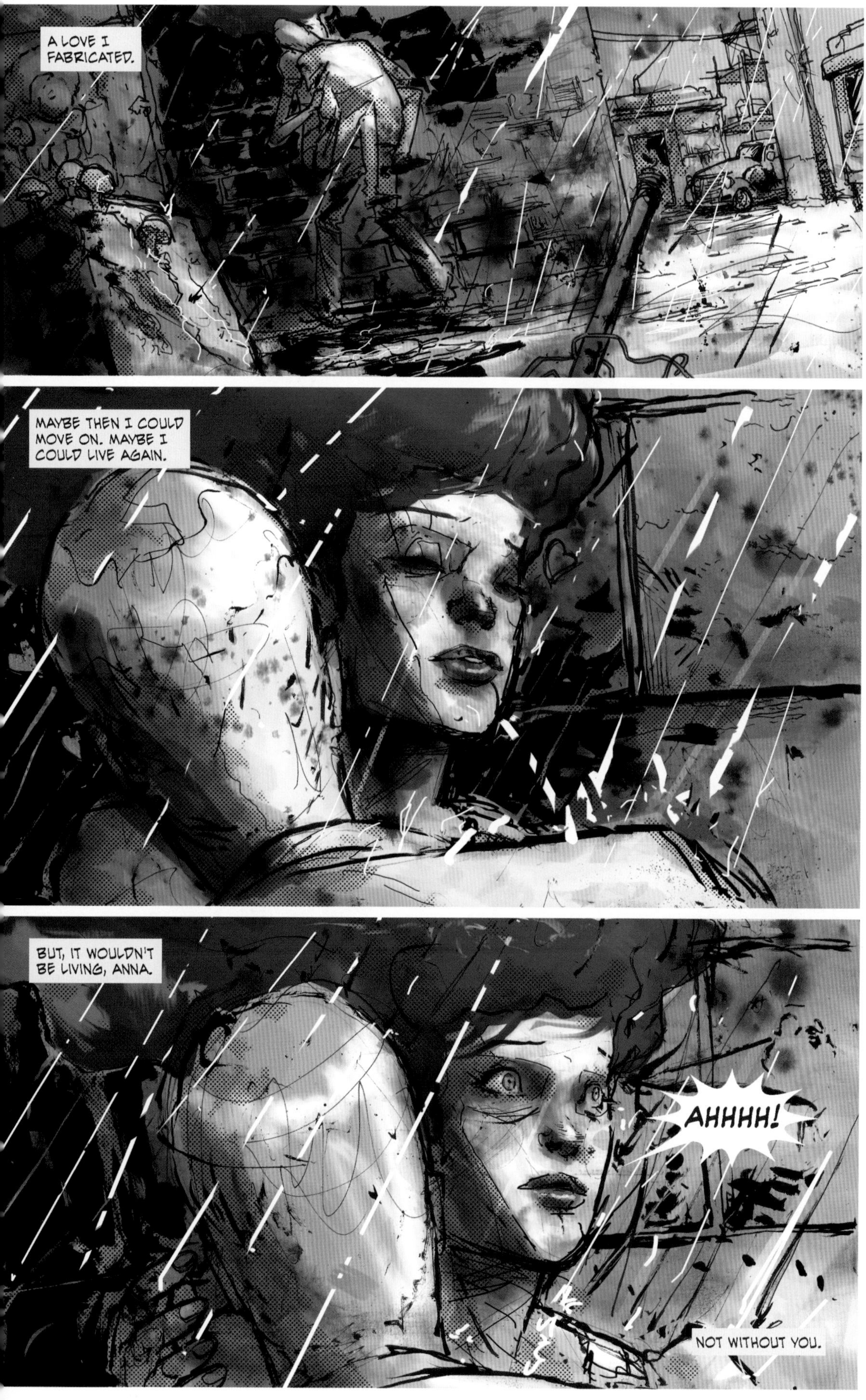
A LOVE I FABRICATED.
MAYBE THEN I COULD MOVE ON. MAYBE I COULD LIVE AGAIN.
BUT, IT WOULDN'T BE LIVING, ANNA.
AHHHH!
NOT WITHOUT YOU.

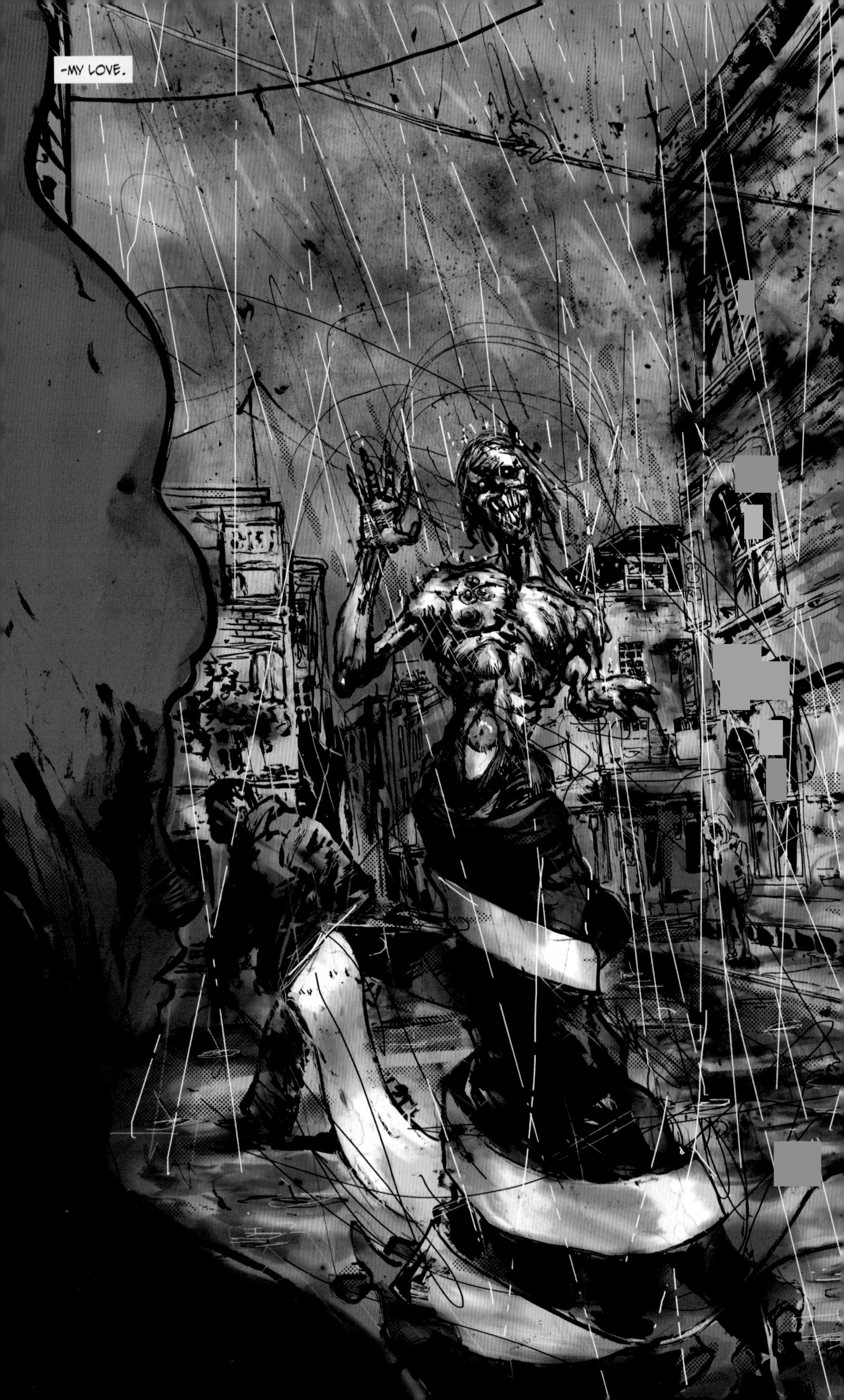
-MY LOVE.

Green Wake #3 cover

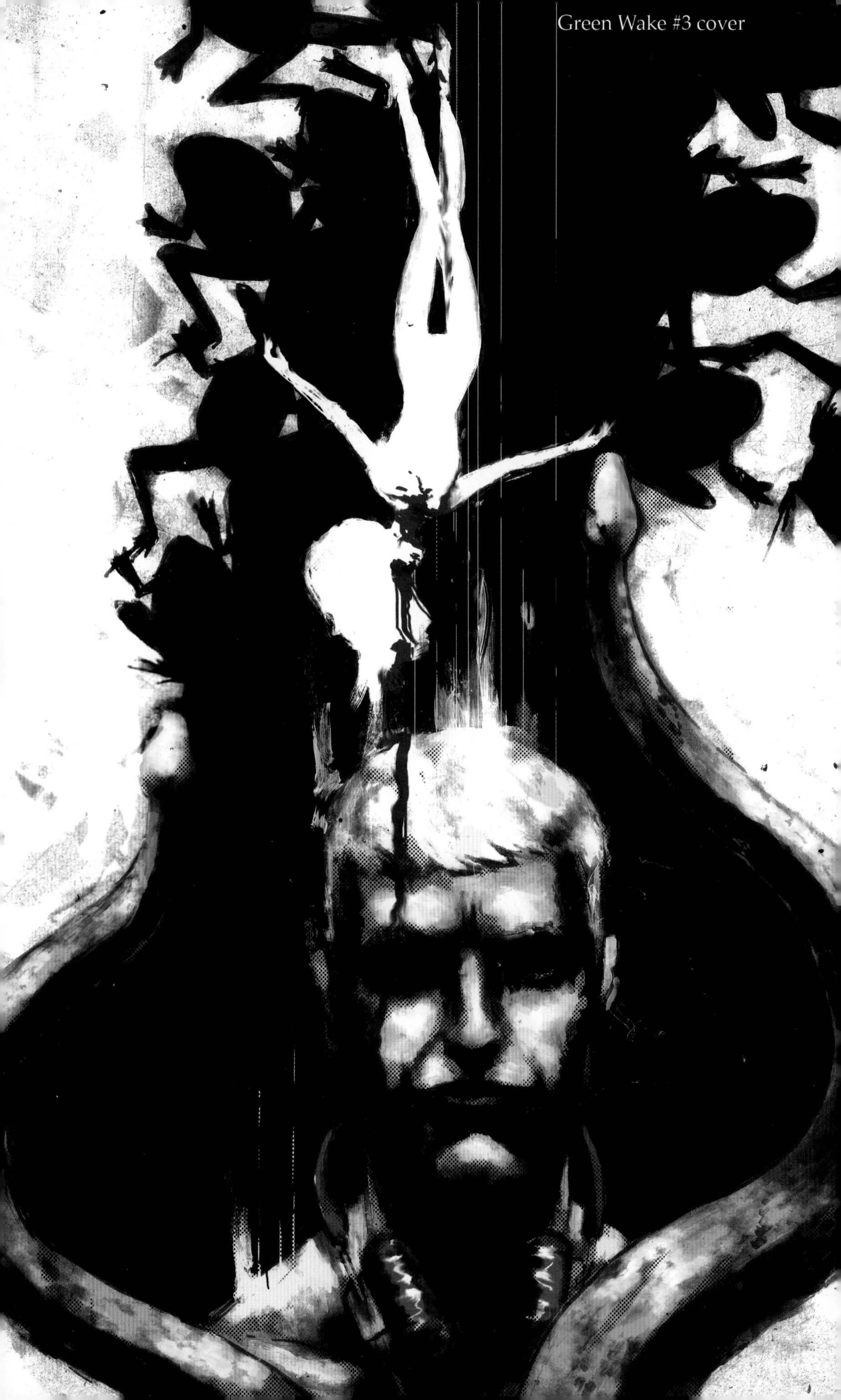

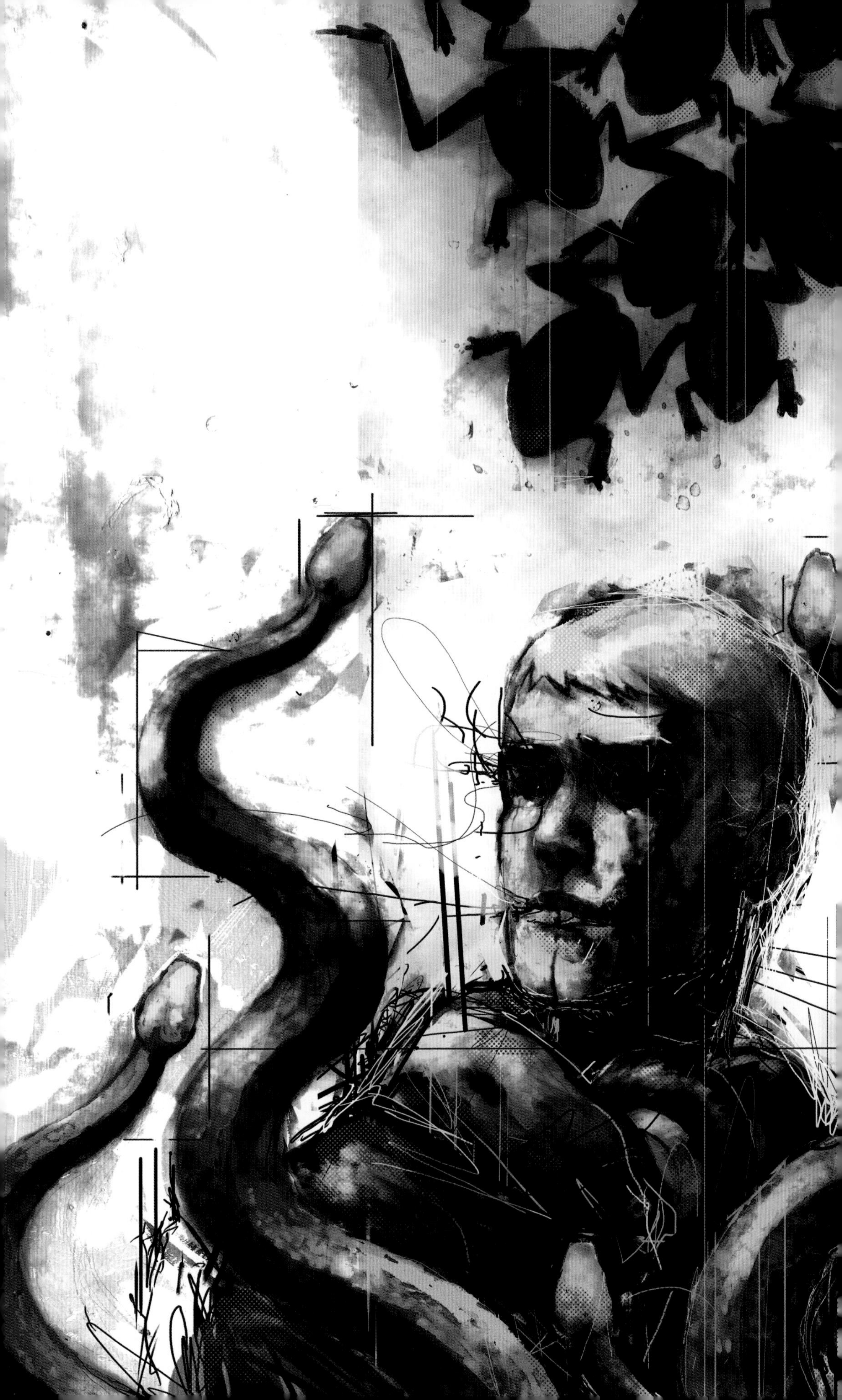

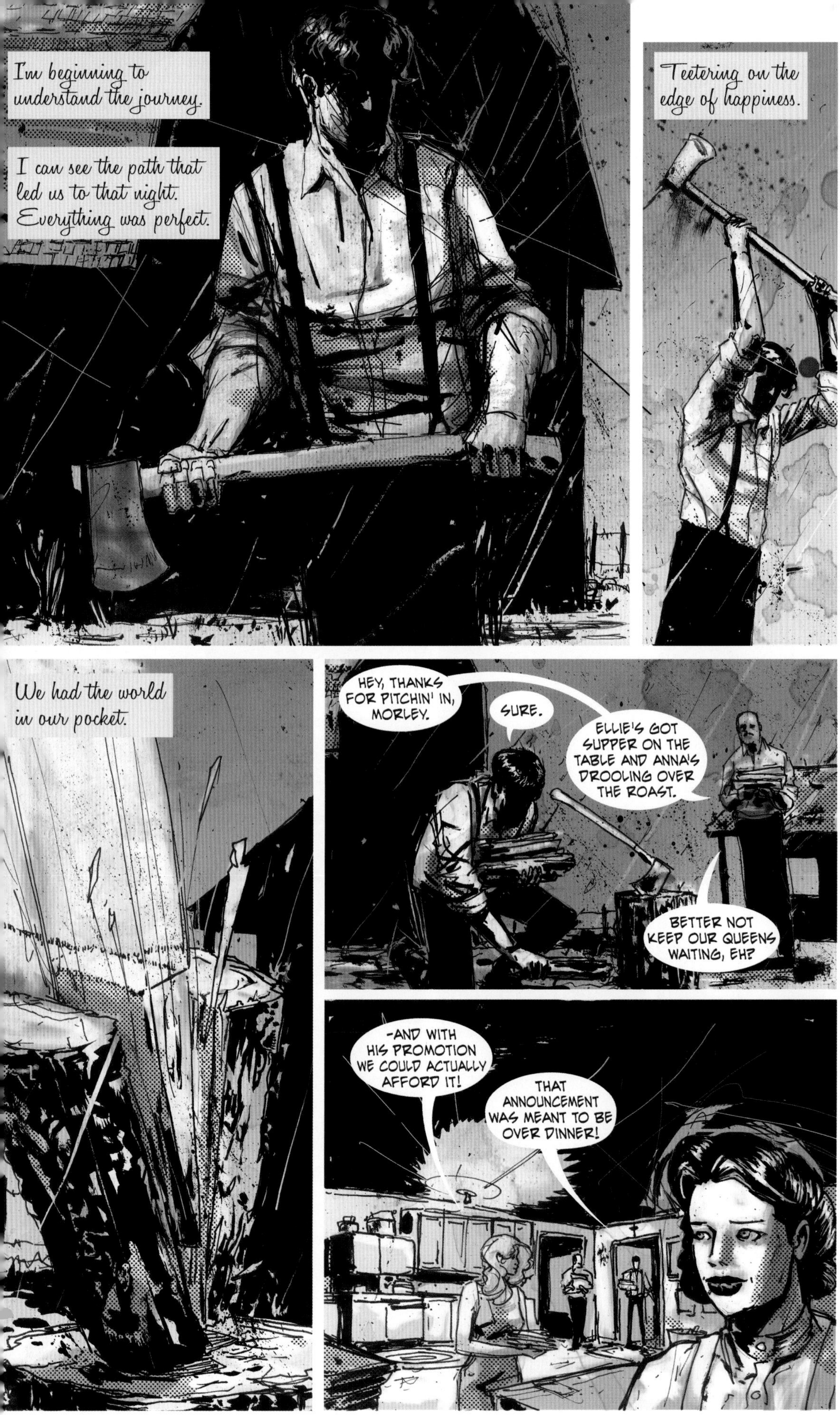
I'm beginning to understand the journey.
I can see the path that led us to that night. Everything was perfect.
Teetering on the edge of happiness.
We had the world in our pocket.
HEY, THANKS FOR PITCHIN' IN, MORLEY.
SURE.
ELLIE'S GOT SUPPER ON THE TABLE AND ANNA'S DROOLING OVER THE ROAST.
BETTER NOT KEEP OUR QUEENS WAITING, EH?
-AND WITH HIS PROMOTION WE COULD ACTUALLY AFFORD IT!
THAT ANNOUNCEMENT WAS MEANT TO BE OVER DINNER!

SORRY, SWEETHEART. I WAS TELLING ELLIE ABOUT THE HOUSE IN TOWN, AND... ONE THING LED TO ANOTHER.

MAYBE I'LL JUST TELL DOUG THE OTHER NEWS?

YOU WOULDN'T DARE!

OTHER NEWS?

THIS DAY IS FULL OF SURPRISES!

WELL, THEN, LET'S EAT SOME GRUB!

THANKS SO MUCH FOR HAVING US, IT'S BEEN TOO LONG!

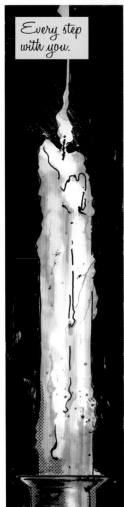

Every step with you.

Every waking hour.

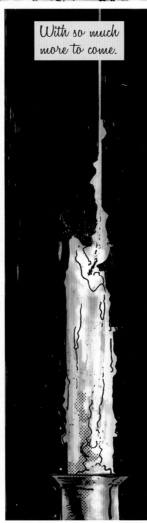

With so much more to come.

On the edge of happiness.

ALRIGHT, ENOUGH SMALL TALK, YOU GUYS, WHAT'S BIGGER NEWS THAN A PROMOTION?

C'MON, LET'S HEAR IT ALREADY!

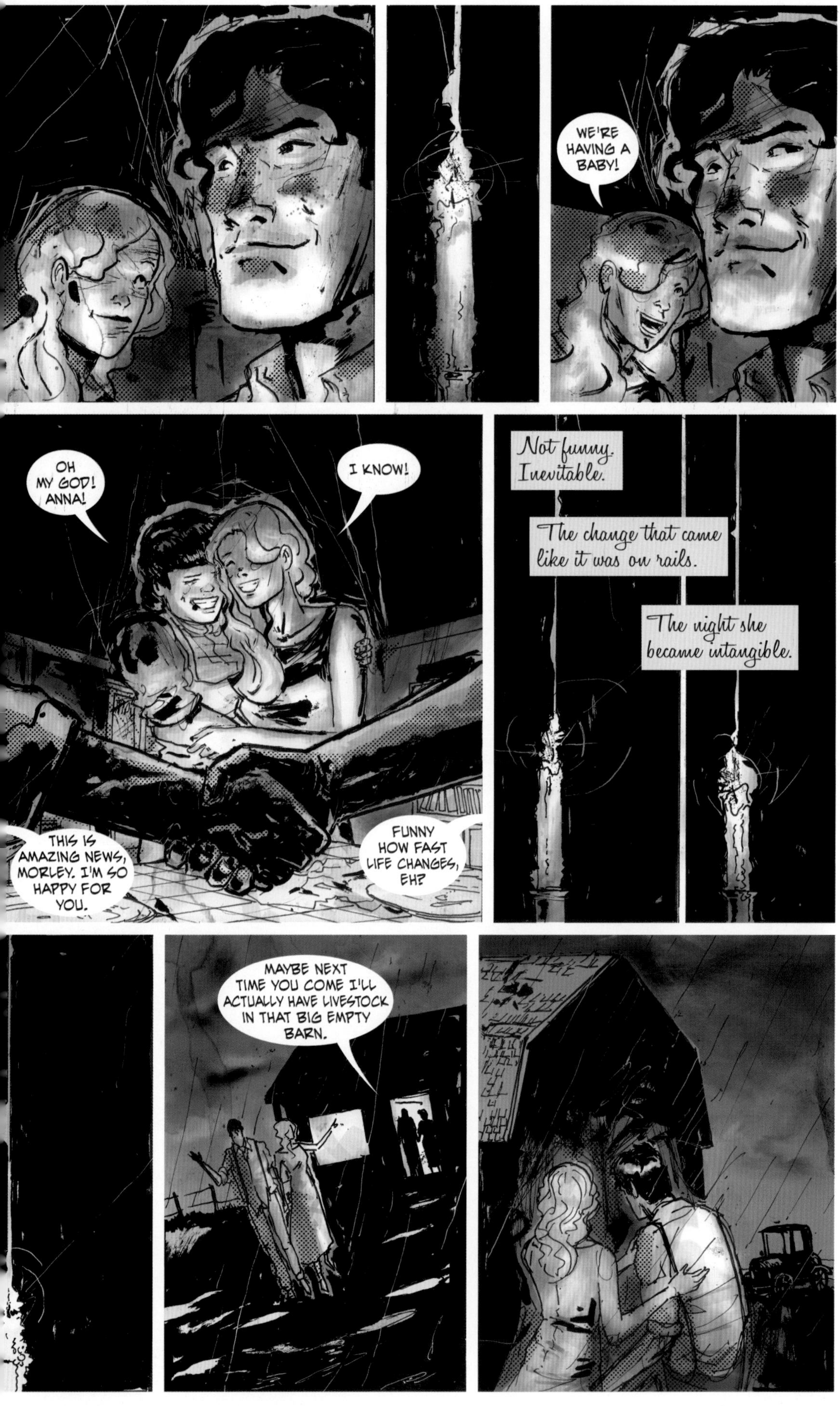
WE'RE HAVING A BABY!
OH MY GOD! ANNA!
I KNOW!
THIS IS AMAZING NEWS, MORLEY. I'M SO HAPPY FOR YOU.
FUNNY HOW FAST LIFE CHANGES, EH?
Not funny. Inevitable.
The change that came like it was on rails.
The night she became intangible.
MAYBE NEXT TIME YOU COME I'LL ACTUALLY HAVE LIVESTOCK IN THAT BIG EMPTY BARN.

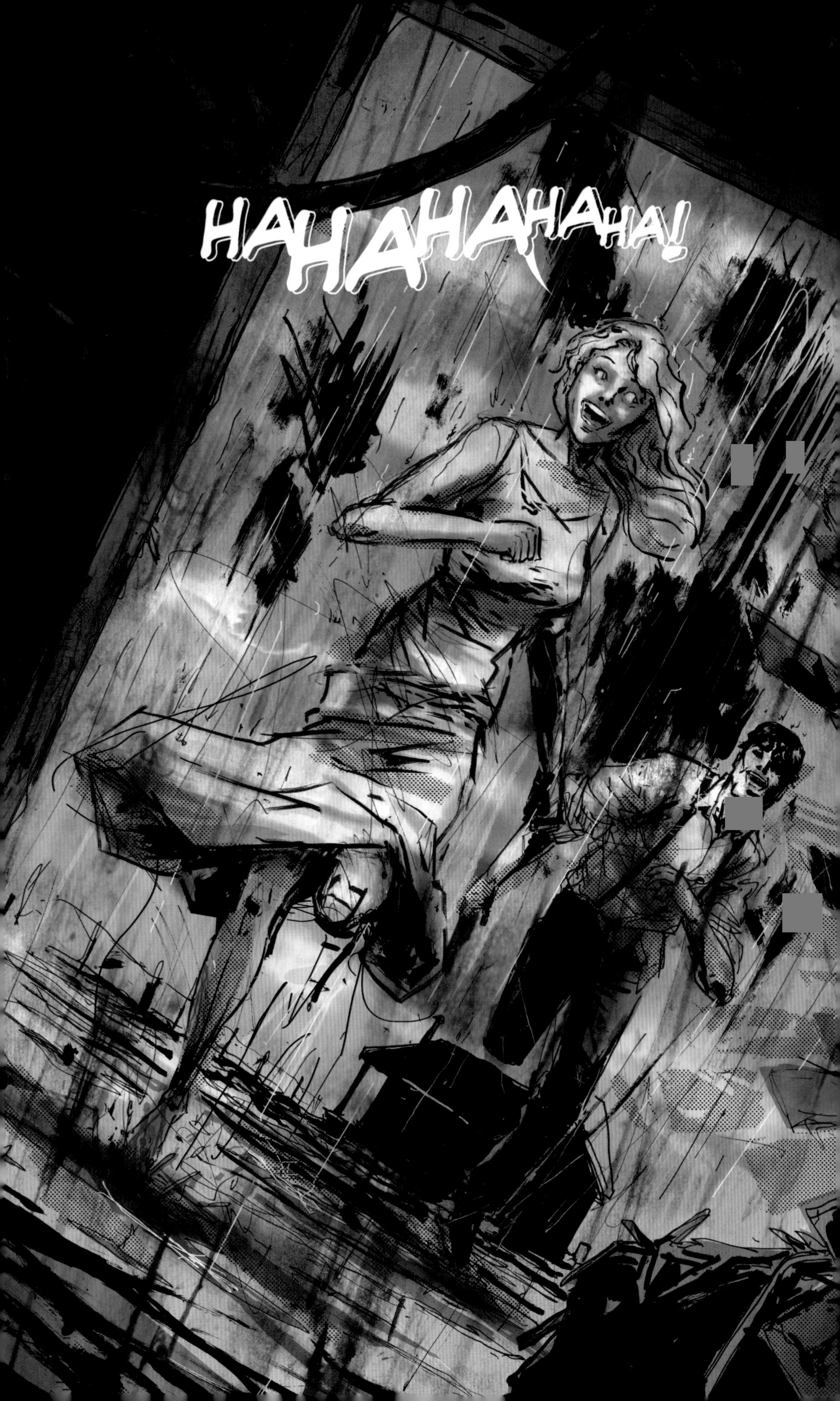
HAHAHAHAHAHA!

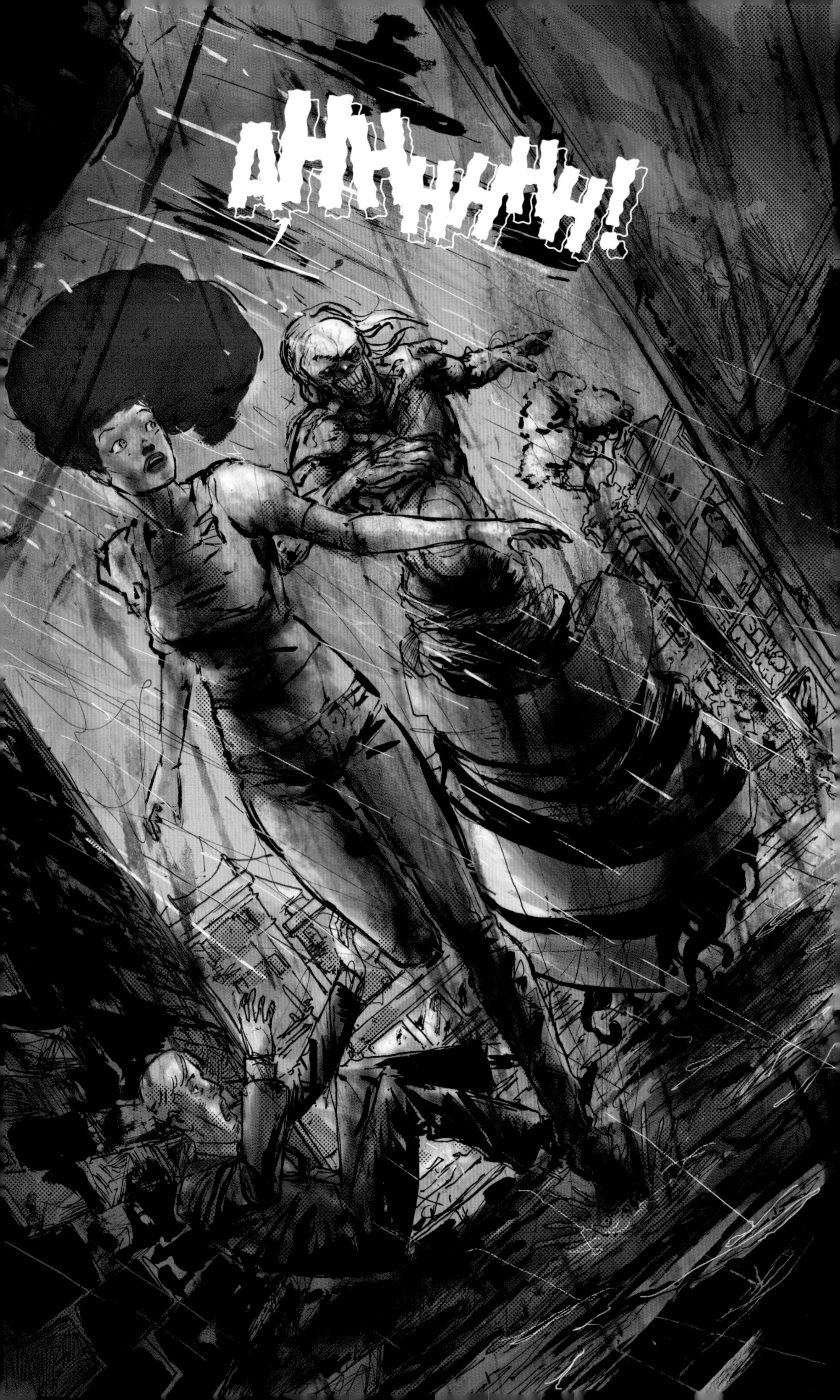
AHHHHHH!

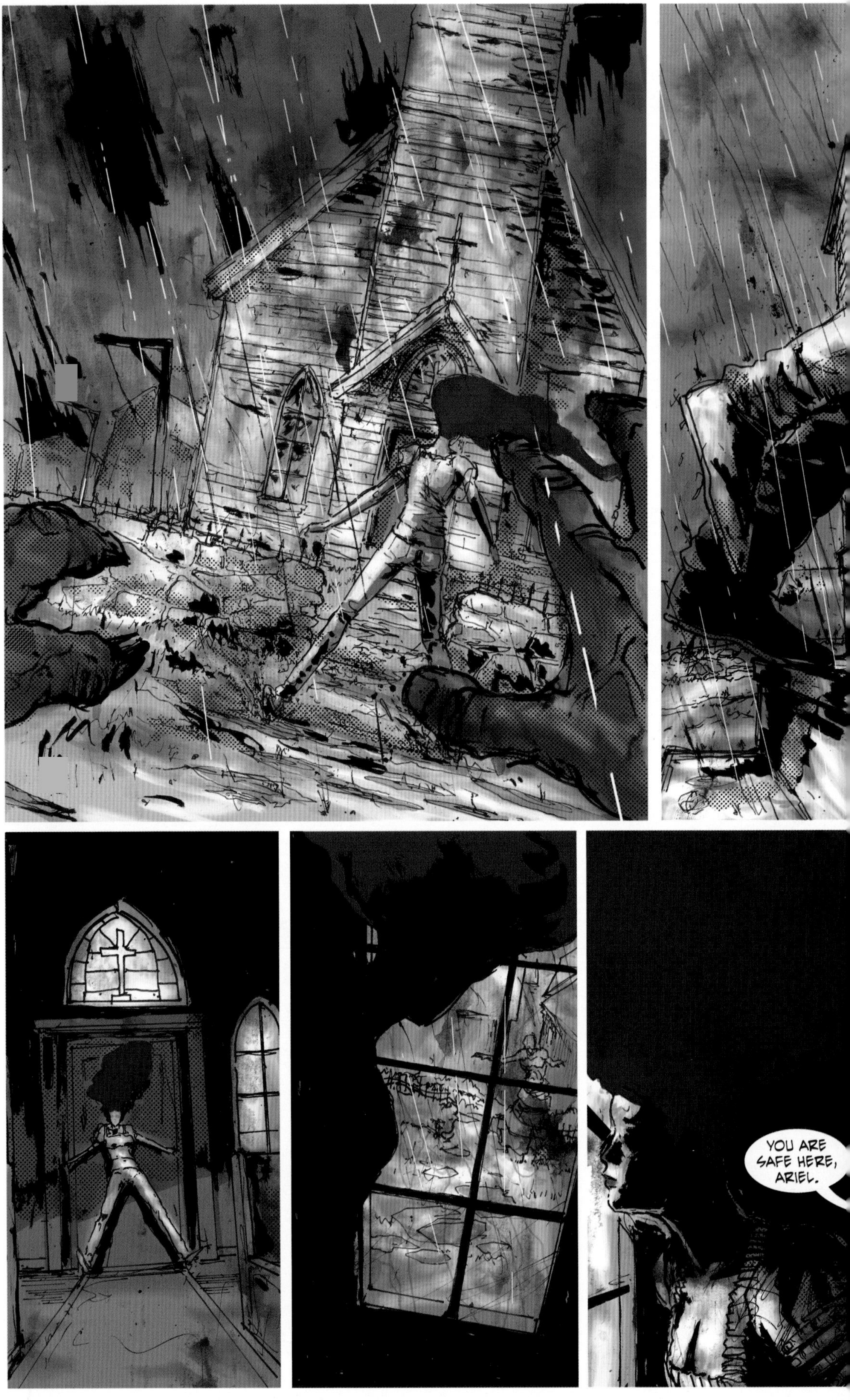
YOU ARE SAFE HERE, ARIEL.

I AM FATHER ISHUM. WELCOME TO THE ABBEY.

THE WARMTH OF THE CANDLES. I CAN'T REMEMBER WHAT WARM FEELS LIKE.

THE EMOTION DURING A SERVICE, THE CONNECTION AS WE ALL SANG.

THE SONGS ARE SO FAR AWAY.

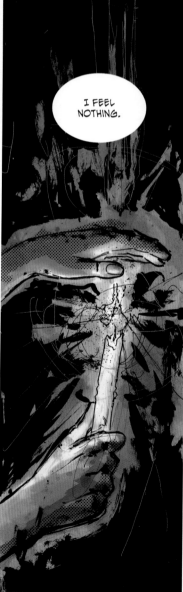

I FEEL NOTHING.

YOU'VE LOST YOUR TETHER, ARIEL. YOU'RE ADRIFT WITHOUT A COMPASS. THERE IS LITTLE I CAN DO, BUT YOU HAVE YET TO FULFILL YOUR PURPOSE HERE.

I WANT TO SHOW YOU HOW YOU CAN BE AT PEACE, HOW YOUR SOUL CAN FIND REST.

LET'S TALK ABOUT CARL.

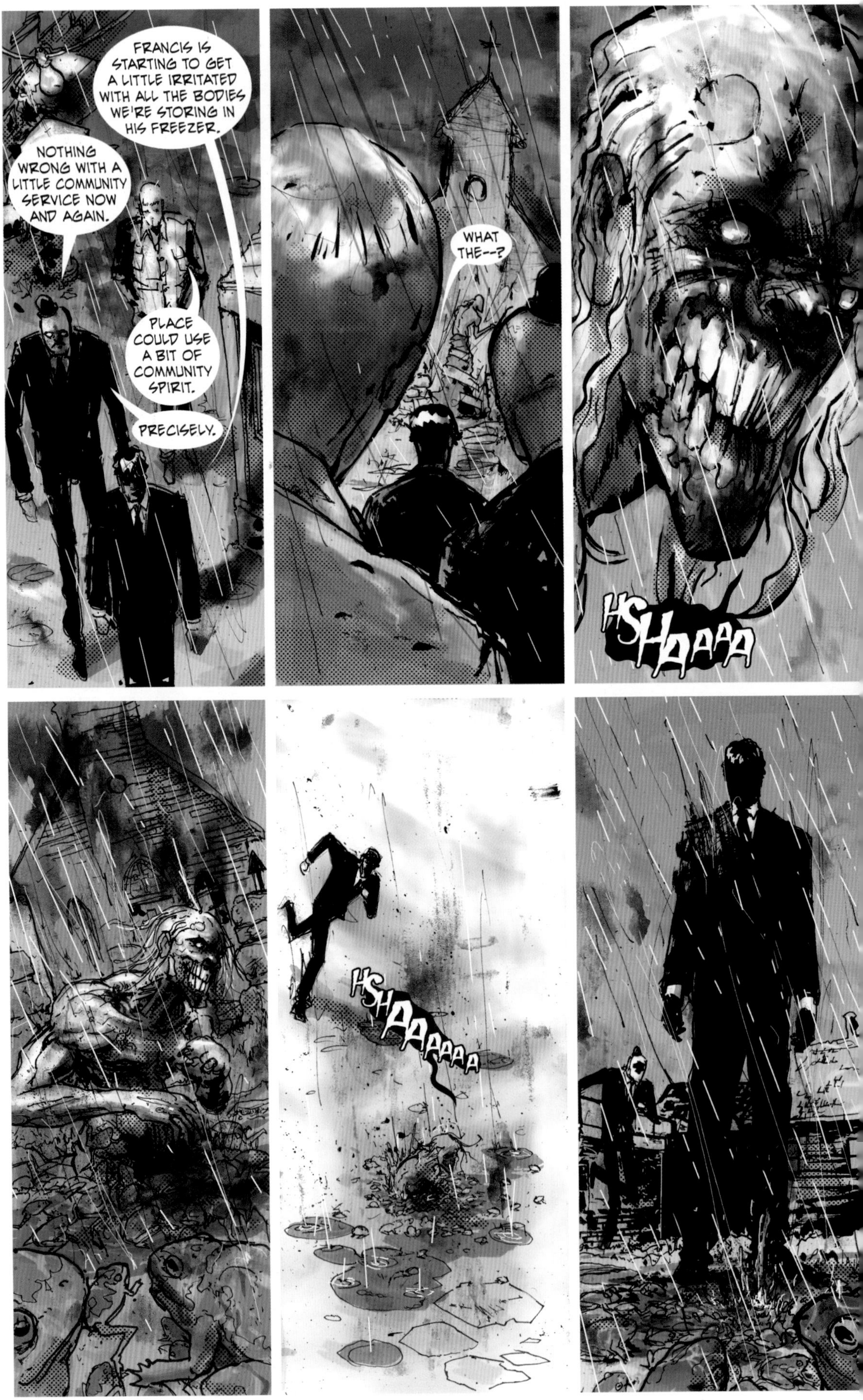
FRANCIS IS STARTING TO GET A LITTLE IRRITATED WITH ALL THE BODIES WE'RE STORING IN HIS FREEZER.
NOTHING WRONG WITH A LITTLE COMMUNITY SERVICE NOW AND AGAIN.
PLACE COULD USE A BIT OF COMMUNITY SPIRIT.
PRECISELY.
WHAT THE--?
HSHAAAA
HSHAAAAAA

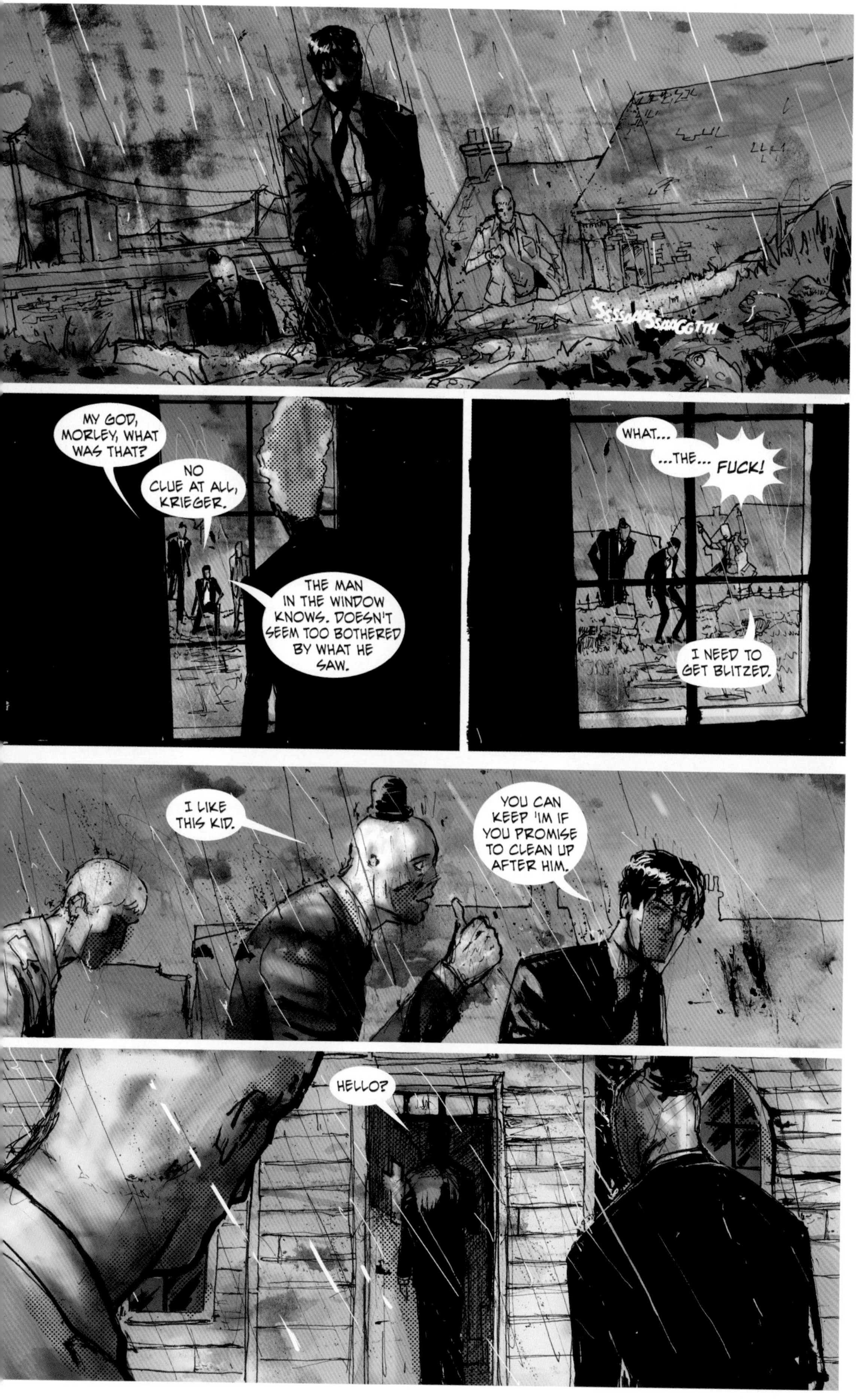

MY GOD, MORLEY, WHAT WAS THAT?
NO CLUE AT ALL, KRIEGER.
THE MAN IN THE WINDOW KNOWS. DOESN'T SEEM TOO BOTHERED BY WHAT HE SAW.
WHAT...
...THE... FUCK!
I NEED TO GET BLITZED.
I LIKE THIS KID.
YOU CAN KEEP 'IM IF YOU PROMISE TO CLEAN UP AFTER HIM.
HELLO?

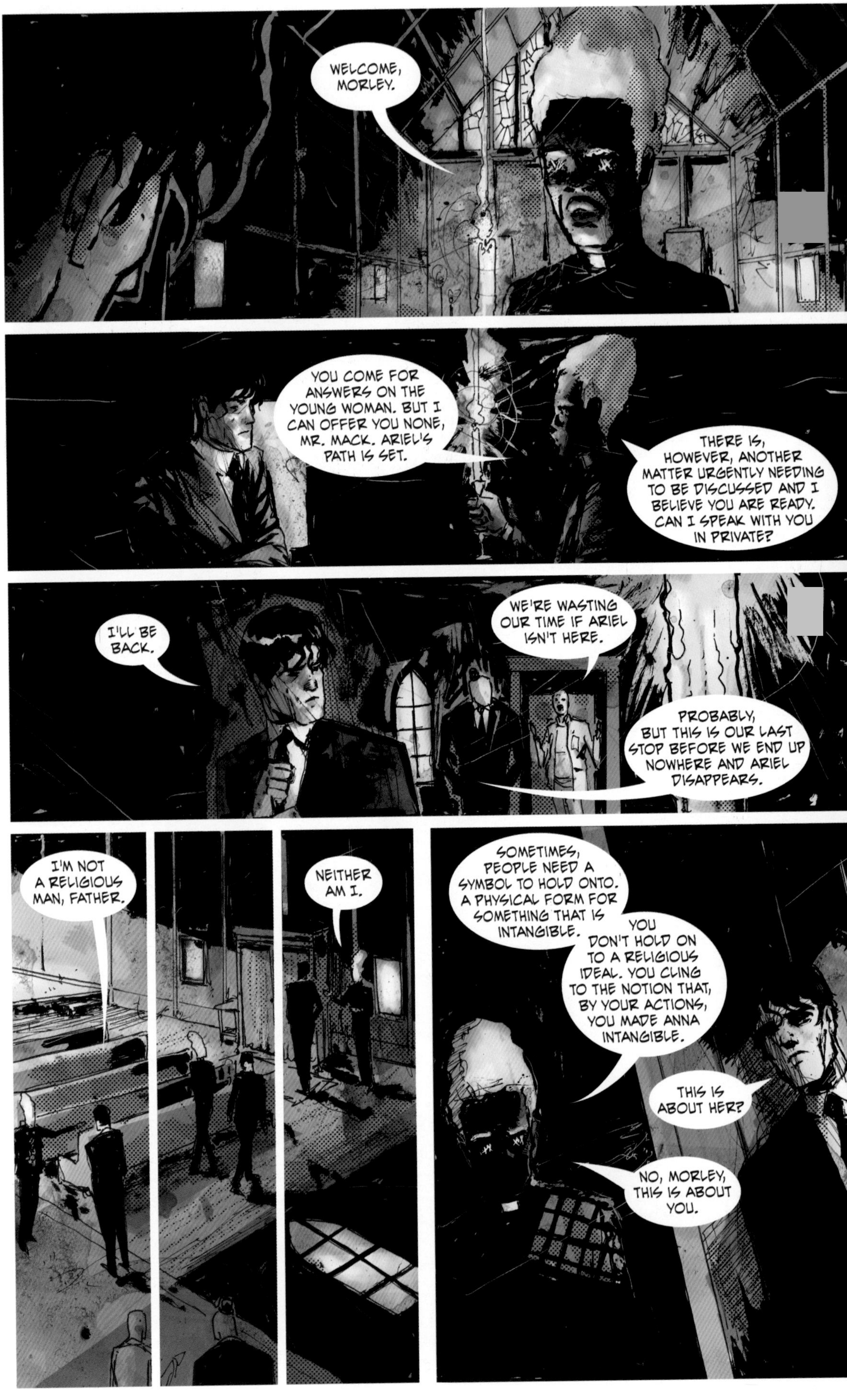
WELCOME, MORLEY.
YOU COME FOR ANSWERS ON THE YOUNG WOMAN. BUT I CAN OFFER YOU NONE, MR. MACK. ARIEL'S PATH IS SET.
THERE IS, HOWEVER, ANOTHER MATTER URGENTLY NEEDING TO BE DISCUSSED AND I BELIEVE YOU ARE READY. CAN I SPEAK WITH YOU IN PRIVATE?
I'LL BE BACK.
WE'RE WASTING OUR TIME IF ARIEL ISN'T HERE.
PROBABLY, BUT THIS IS OUR LAST STOP BEFORE WE END UP NOWHERE AND ARIEL DISAPPEARS.
I'M NOT A RELIGIOUS MAN, FATHER.
NEITHER AM I.
SOMETIMES, PEOPLE NEED A SYMBOL TO HOLD ONTO. A PHYSICAL FORM FOR SOMETHING THAT IS INTANGIBLE.
YOU DON'T HOLD ON TO A RELIGIOUS IDEAL. YOU CLING TO THE NOTION THAT, BY YOUR ACTIONS, YOU MADE ANNA INTANGIBLE.
THIS IS ABOUT HER?
NO, MORLEY, THIS IS ABOUT YOU.

I'LL PUT THIS ASIDE, AS IT BEARS NO SIGNIFICANCE TO THE NATURE OF OUR CONVERSATION.

NOR DOES IT HAVE ANY MEANING IN THIS PLACE.

TELL ME, MORLEY MACK, WHAT DO YOU BELIEVE GREEN WAKE TO BE?

...

HELL.

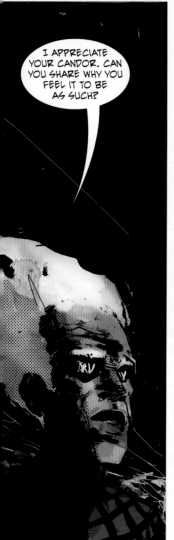

I APPRECIATE YOUR CANDOR. CAN YOU SHARE WHY YOU FEEL IT TO BE AS SUCH?

BECAUSE EVERYWHERE I GO, I'M REMINDED OF HER.

I DREAM OF THOSE LAST MOMENTS WITH ANNA EVERY NIGHT, WITH SUCH CLARITY THAT I'M STARTING TO DOUBT THE REALITY OF HER EVER EXISTING. HOW CAN THE MEMORY BE SO CLEAR WHEN SO MUCH TIME HAS PASSED?

I JUST WANT TO FORGET, BUT THIS PLACE WON'T LET ME.

GREEN WAKE IS MY HELL.

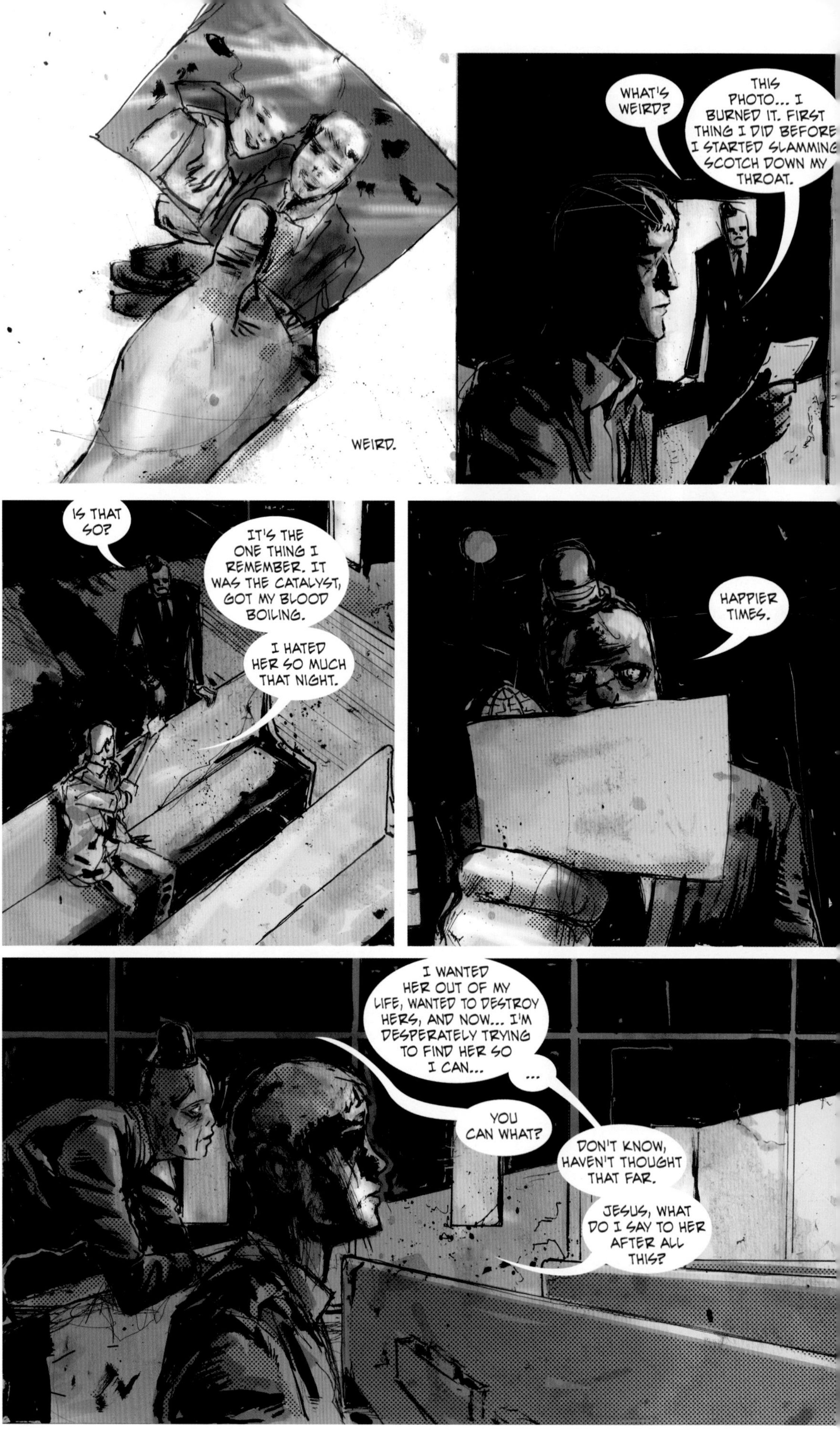
WEIRD.
WHAT'S WEIRD?
THIS PHOTO... I BURNED IT. FIRST THING I DID BEFORE I STARTED SLAMMING SCOTCH DOWN MY THROAT.
IS THAT SO?
IT'S THE ONE THING I REMEMBER. IT WAS THE CATALYST, GOT MY BLOOD BOILING.
I HATED HER SO MUCH THAT NIGHT.
HAPPIER TIMES.
I WANTED HER OUT OF MY LIFE, WANTED TO DESTROY HERS, AND NOW... I'M DESPERATELY TRYING TO FIND HER SO I CAN...
...
YOU CAN WHAT?
DON'T KNOW, HAVEN'T THOUGHT THAT FAR.
JESUS, WHAT DO I SAY TO HER AFTER ALL THIS?

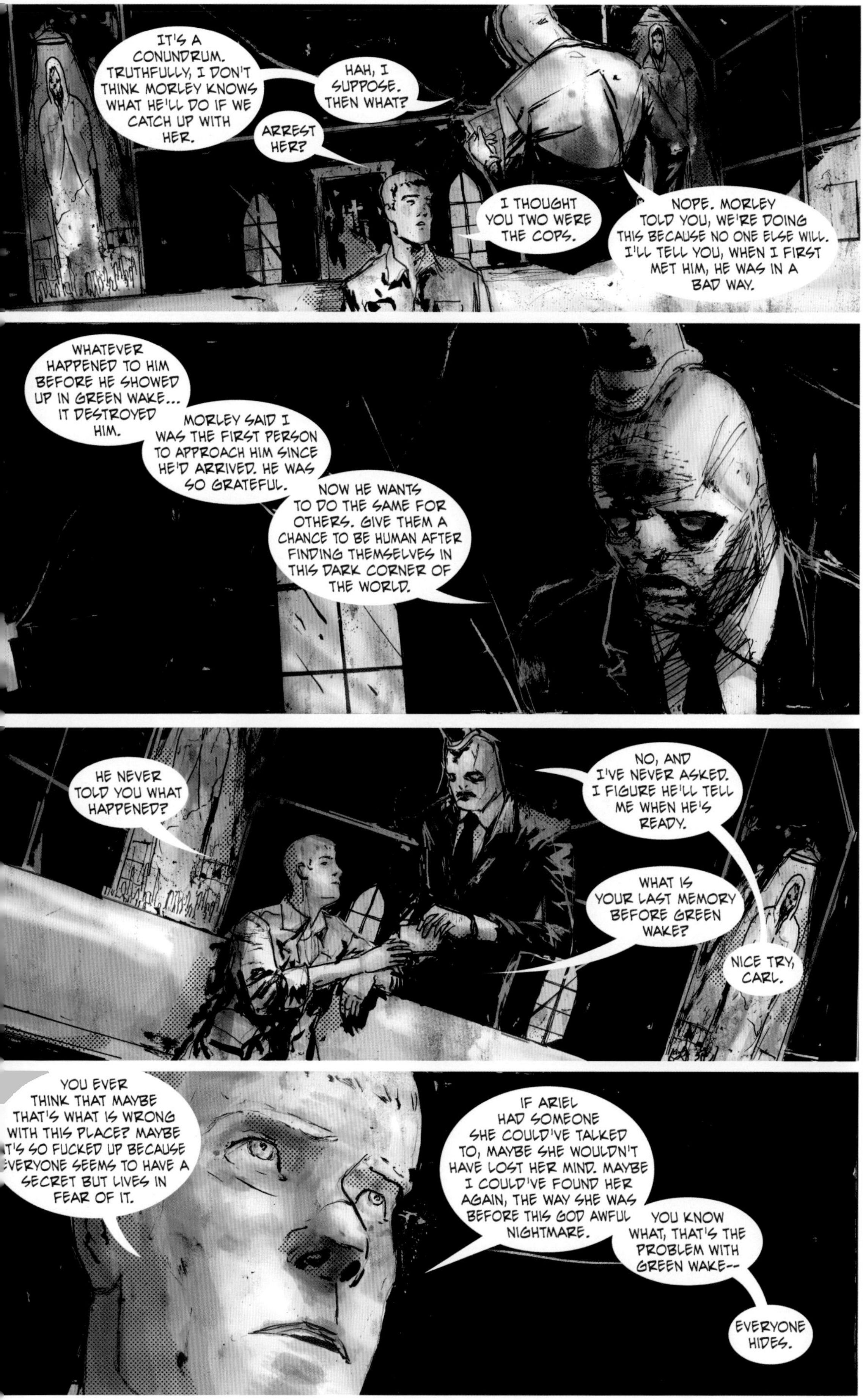
IT'S A CONUNDRUM. TRUTHFULLY, I DON'T THINK MORLEY KNOWS WHAT HE'LL DO IF WE CATCH UP WITH HER.
HAH, I SUPPOSE. THEN WHAT?
ARREST HER?
I THOUGHT YOU TWO WERE THE COPS.
NOPE. MORLEY TOLD YOU, WE'RE DOING THIS BECAUSE NO ONE ELSE WILL. I'LL TELL YOU, WHEN I FIRST MET HIM, HE WAS IN A BAD WAY.
WHATEVER HAPPENED TO HIM BEFORE HE SHOWED UP IN GREEN WAKE... IT DESTROYED HIM.
MORLEY SAID I WAS THE FIRST PERSON TO APPROACH HIM SINCE HE'D ARRIVED. HE WAS SO GRATEFUL.
NOW HE WANTS TO DO THE SAME FOR OTHERS. GIVE THEM A CHANCE TO BE HUMAN AFTER FINDING THEMSELVES IN THIS DARK CORNER OF THE WORLD.
HE NEVER TOLD YOU WHAT HAPPENED?
NO, AND I'VE NEVER ASKED. I FIGURE HE'LL TELL ME WHEN HE'S READY.
WHAT IS YOUR LAST MEMORY BEFORE GREEN WAKE?
NICE TRY, CARL.
YOU EVER THINK THAT MAYBE THAT'S WHAT IS WRONG WITH THIS PLACE? MAYBE IT'S SO FUCKED UP BECAUSE EVERYONE SEEMS TO HAVE A SECRET BUT LIVES IN FEAR OF IT.
IF ARIEL HAD SOMEONE SHE COULD'VE TALKED TO, MAYBE SHE WOULDN'T HAVE LOST HER MIND. MAYBE I COULD'VE FOUND HER AGAIN, THE WAY SHE WAS BEFORE THIS GOD AWFUL NIGHTMARE.
YOU KNOW WHAT, THAT'S THE PROBLEM WITH GREEN WAKE--
EVERYONE HIDES.

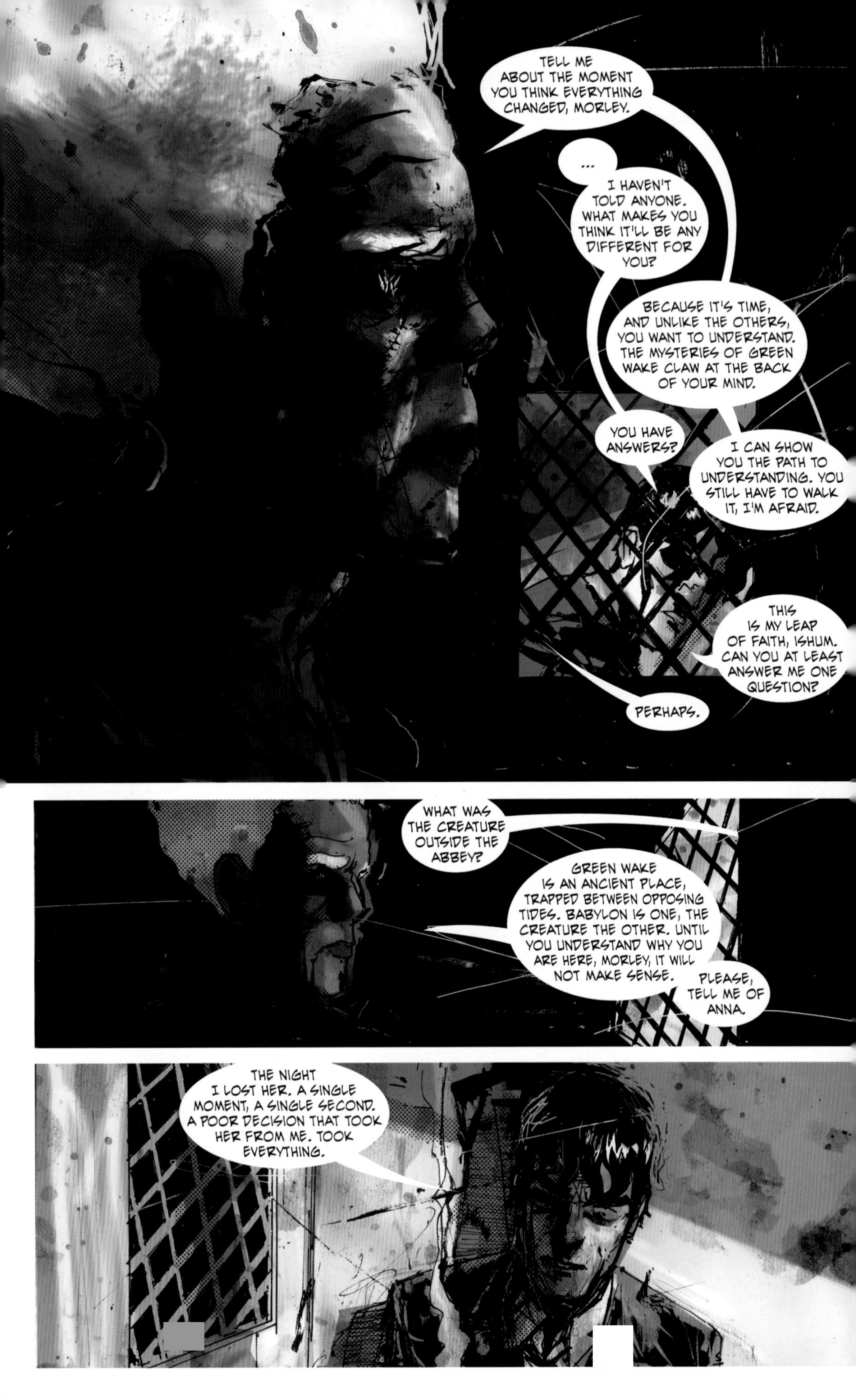
TELL ME ABOUT THE MOMENT YOU THINK EVERYTHING CHANGED, MORLEY.
...
I HAVEN'T TOLD ANYONE. WHAT MAKES YOU THINK IT'LL BE ANY DIFFERENT FOR YOU?
BECAUSE IT'S TIME, AND UNLIKE THE OTHERS, YOU WANT TO UNDERSTAND. THE MYSTERIES OF GREEN WAKE CLAW AT THE BACK OF YOUR MIND.
YOU HAVE ANSWERS?
I CAN SHOW YOU THE PATH TO UNDERSTANDING. YOU STILL HAVE TO WALK IT, I'M AFRAID.
THIS IS MY LEAP OF FAITH, ISHUM. CAN YOU AT LEAST ANSWER ME ONE QUESTION?
PERHAPS.
WHAT WAS THE CREATURE OUTSIDE THE ABBEY?
GREEN WAKE IS AN ANCIENT PLACE, TRAPPED BETWEEN OPPOSING TIDES. BABYLON IS ONE, THE CREATURE THE OTHER. UNTIL YOU UNDERSTAND WHY YOU ARE HERE, MORLEY, IT WILL NOT MAKE SENSE.
PLEASE, TELL ME OF ANNA.
THE NIGHT I LOST HER. A SINGLE MOMENT, A SINGLE SECOND. A POOR DECISION THAT TOOK HER FROM ME. TOOK EVERYTHING.

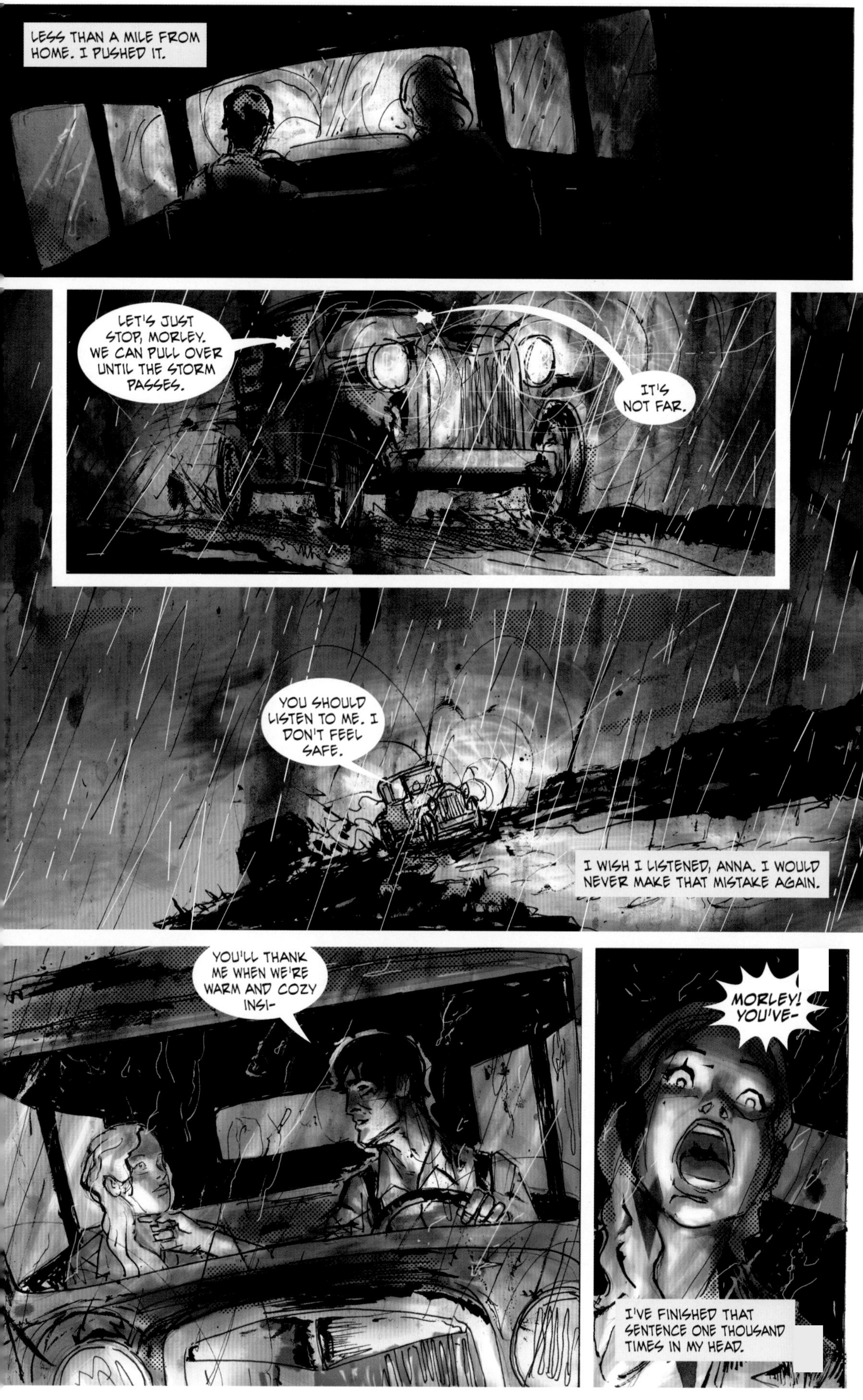
LESS THAN A MILE FROM HOME. I PUSHED IT.
LET'S JUST STOP, MORLEY. WE CAN PULL OVER UNTIL THE STORM PASSES.
IT'S NOT FAR.
YOU SHOULD LISTEN TO ME. I DON'T FEEL SAFE.
I WISH I LISTENED, ANNA. I WOULD NEVER MAKE THAT MISTAKE AGAIN.
YOU'LL THANK ME WHEN WE'RE WARM AND COZY INSI-
MORLEY! YOU'VE-
I'VE FINISHED THAT SENTENCE ONE THOUSAND TIMES IN MY HEAD.

WHAT DOES SHE SAY?

YOU'VE KILLED US.

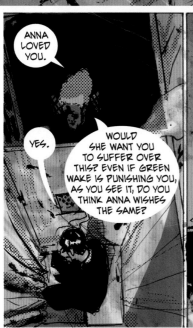

ANNA LOVED YOU.

YES.

WOULD SHE WANT YOU TO SUFFER OVER THIS? EVEN IF GREEN WAKE IS PUNISHING YOU, AS YOU SEE IT, DO YOU THINK ANNA WISHES THE SAME?

I--

I'VE NEVER CONSIDERED THAT.

BRACE YOURSELF.

RAHHHHH!

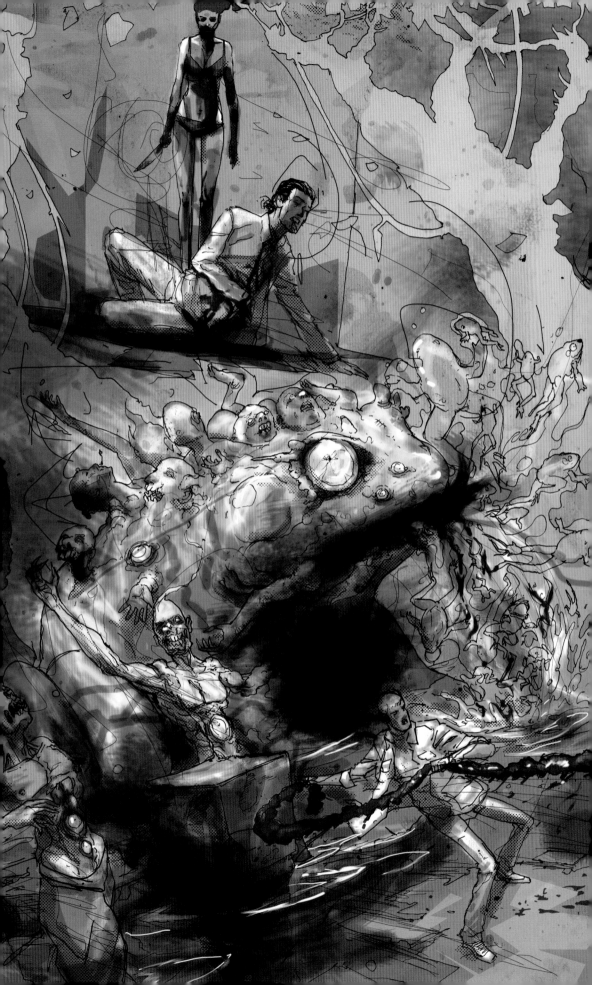

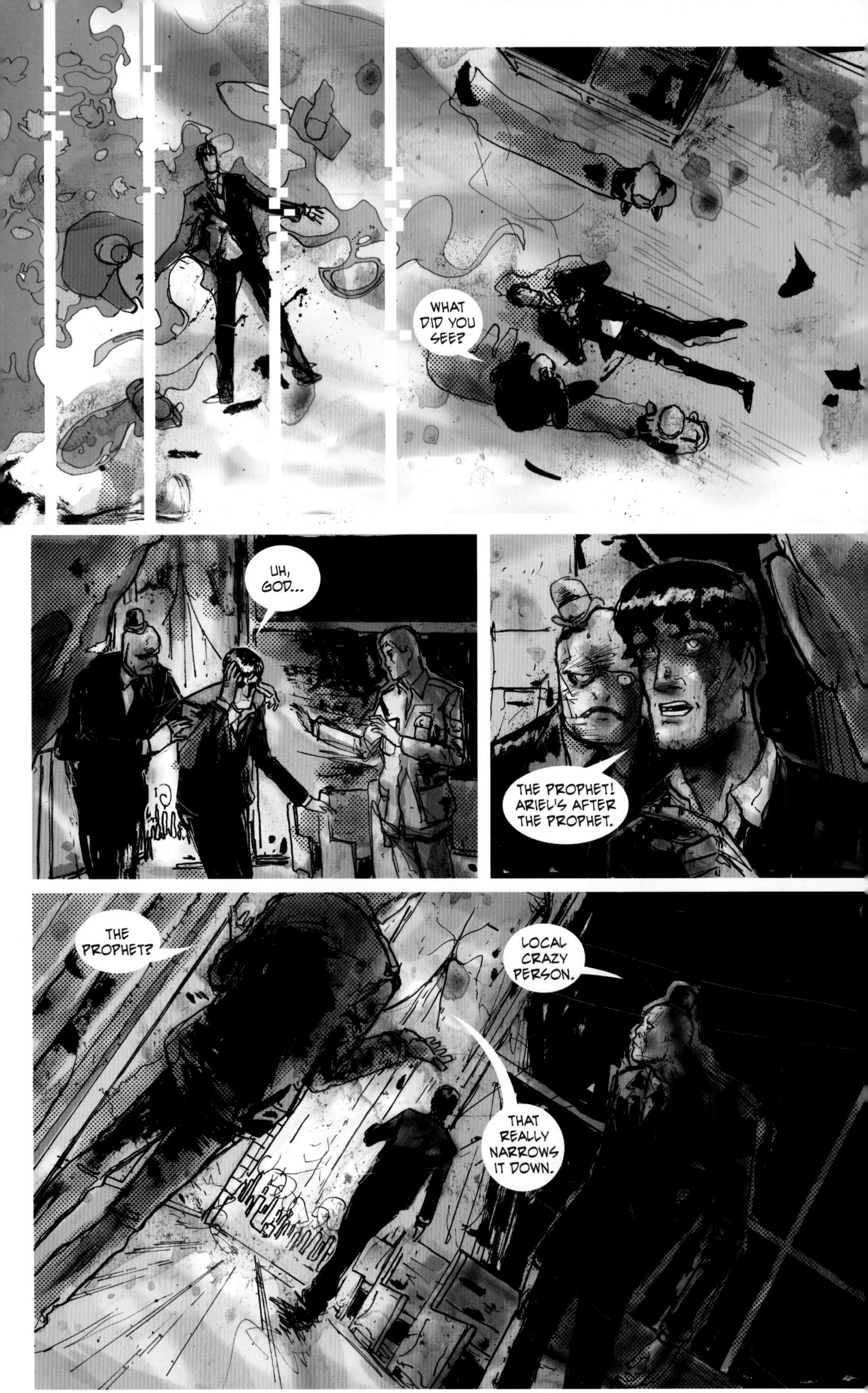
WHAT DID YOU SEE?
UH, GOD...
THE PROPHET! ARIEL'S AFTER THE PROPHET.
THE PROPHET?
LOCAL CRAZY PERSON.
THAT REALLY NARROWS IT DOWN.

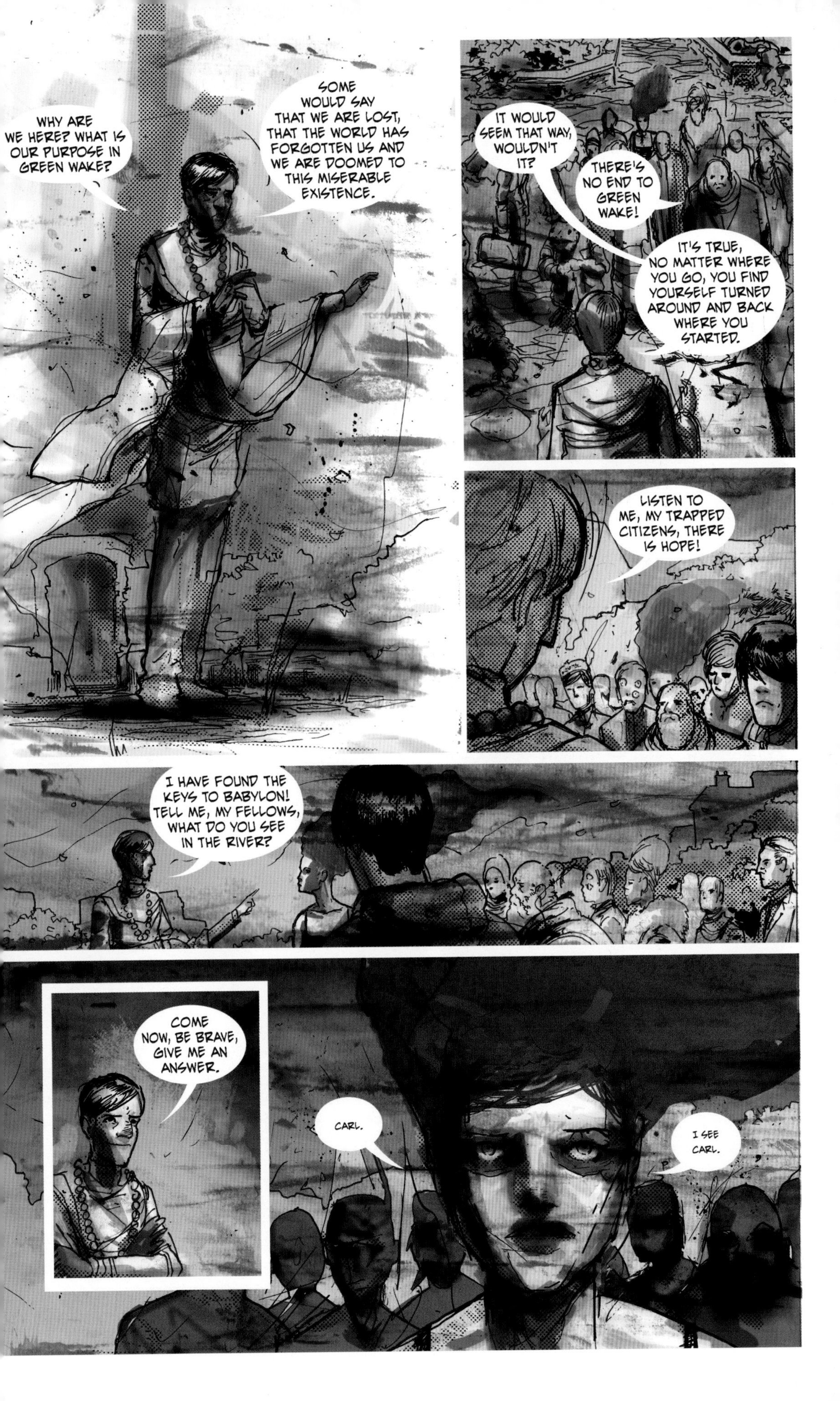
WHY ARE WE HERE? WHAT IS OUR PURPOSE IN GREEN WAKE?
SOME WOULD SAY THAT WE ARE LOST, THAT THE WORLD HAS FORGOTTEN US AND WE ARE DOOMED TO THIS MISERABLE EXISTENCE.
IT WOULD SEEM THAT WAY, WOULDN'T IT?
THERE'S NO END TO GREEN WAKE!
IT'S TRUE, NO MATTER WHERE YOU GO, YOU FIND YOURSELF TURNED AROUND AND BACK WHERE YOU STARTED.
LISTEN TO ME, MY TRAPPED CITIZENS, THERE IS HOPE!
I HAVE FOUND THE KEYS TO BABYLON! TELL ME, MY FELLOWS, WHAT DO YOU SEE IN THE RIVER?
COME NOW, BE BRAVE, GIVE ME AN ANSWER.
CARL.
I SEE CARL.

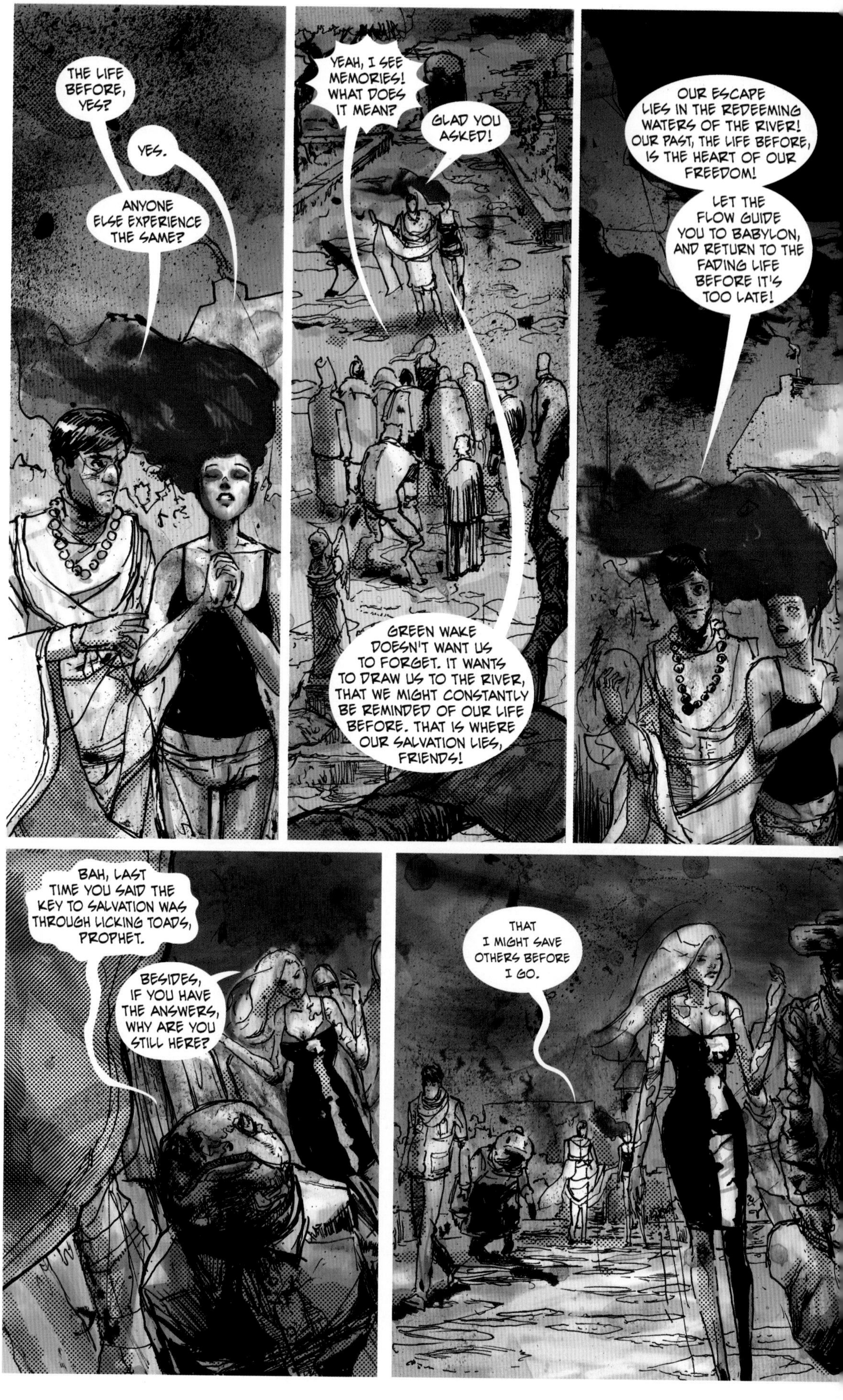
THE LIFE BEFORE, YES?
YES.
ANYONE ELSE EXPERIENCE THE SAME?
YEAH, I SEE MEMORIES! WHAT DOES IT MEAN?
GLAD YOU ASKED!
GREEN WAKE DOESN'T WANT US TO FORGET. IT WANTS TO DRAW US TO THE RIVER, THAT WE MIGHT CONSTANTLY BE REMINDED OF OUR LIFE BEFORE. THAT IS WHERE OUR SALVATION LIES, FRIENDS!
OUR ESCAPE LIES IN THE REDEEMING WATERS OF THE RIVER! OUR PAST, THE LIFE BEFORE, IS THE HEART OF OUR FREEDOM!
LET THE FLOW GUIDE YOU TO BABYLON, AND RETURN TO THE FADING LIFE BEFORE IT'S TOO LATE!
BAH, LAST TIME YOU SAID THE KEY TO SALVATION WAS THROUGH LICKING TOADS, PROPHET.
BESIDES, IF YOU HAVE THE ANSWERS, WHY ARE YOU STILL HERE?
THAT I MIGHT SAVE OTHERS BEFORE I GO.

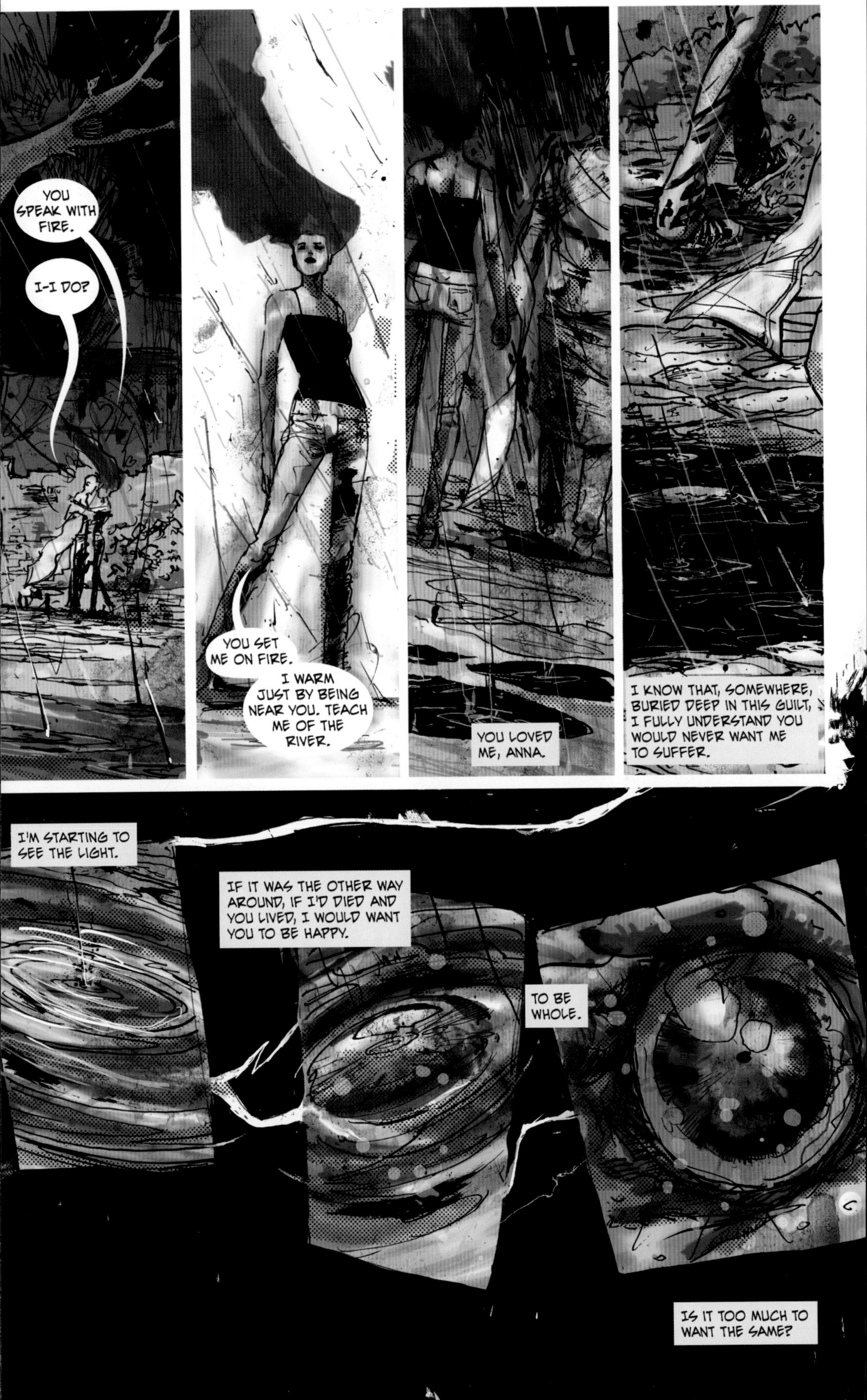
YOU SPEAK WITH FIRE.
I-I DO?
YOU SET ME ON FIRE.
I WARM JUST BY BEING NEAR YOU. TEACH ME OF THE RIVER.
YOU LOVED ME, ANNA.
I KNOW THAT, SOMEWHERE, BURIED DEEP IN THIS GUILT, I FULLY UNDERSTAND YOU WOULD NEVER WANT ME TO SUFFER.
I'M STARTING TO SEE THE LIGHT.
IF IT WAS THE OTHER WAY AROUND, IF I'D DIED AND YOU LIVED, I WOULD WANT YOU TO BE HAPPY.
TO BE WHOLE.
IS IT TOO MUCH TO WANT THE SAME?

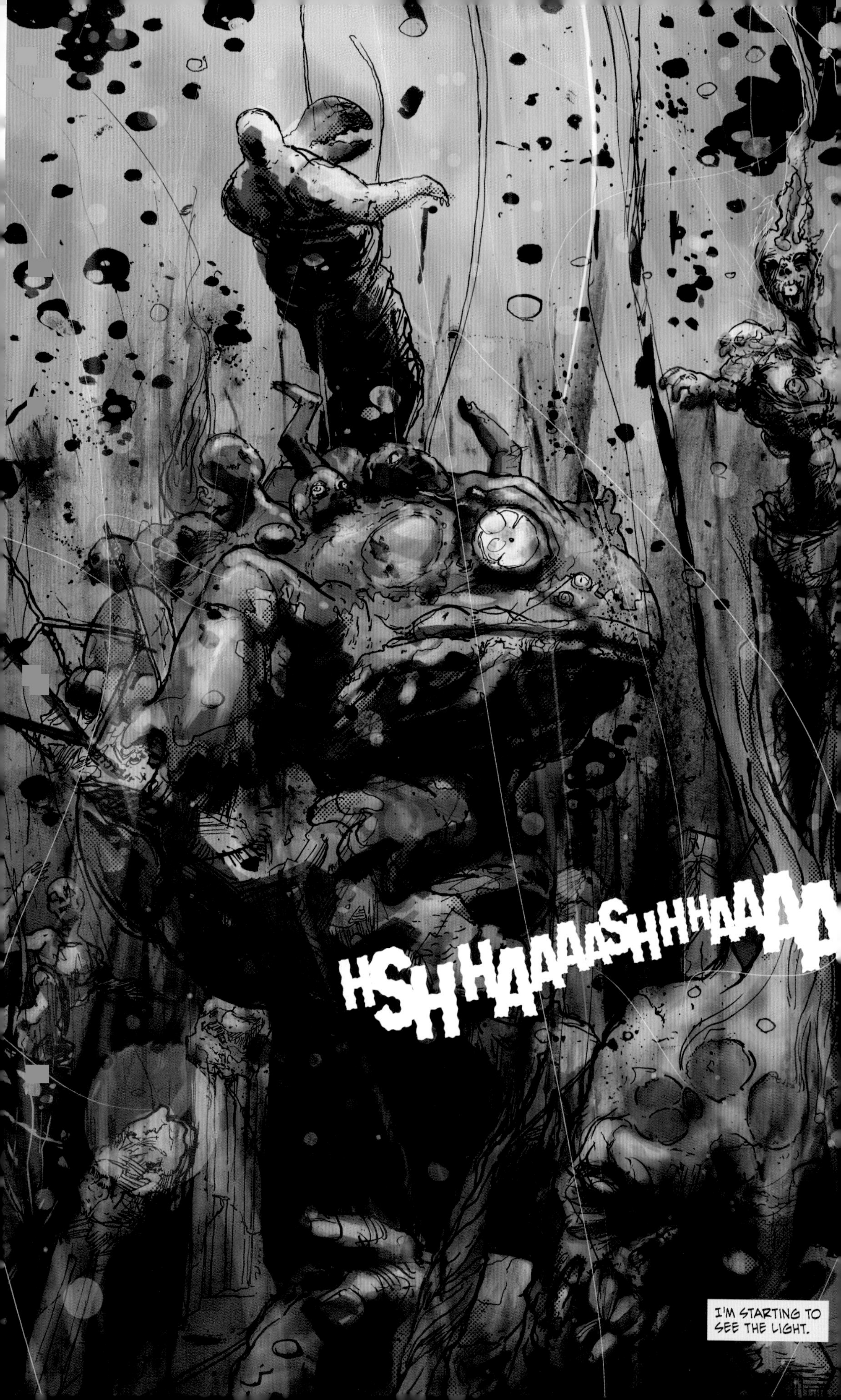
HSH HAAAASHHHAAAA
I'M STARTING TO SEE THE LIGHT.

een Wake #4 cover

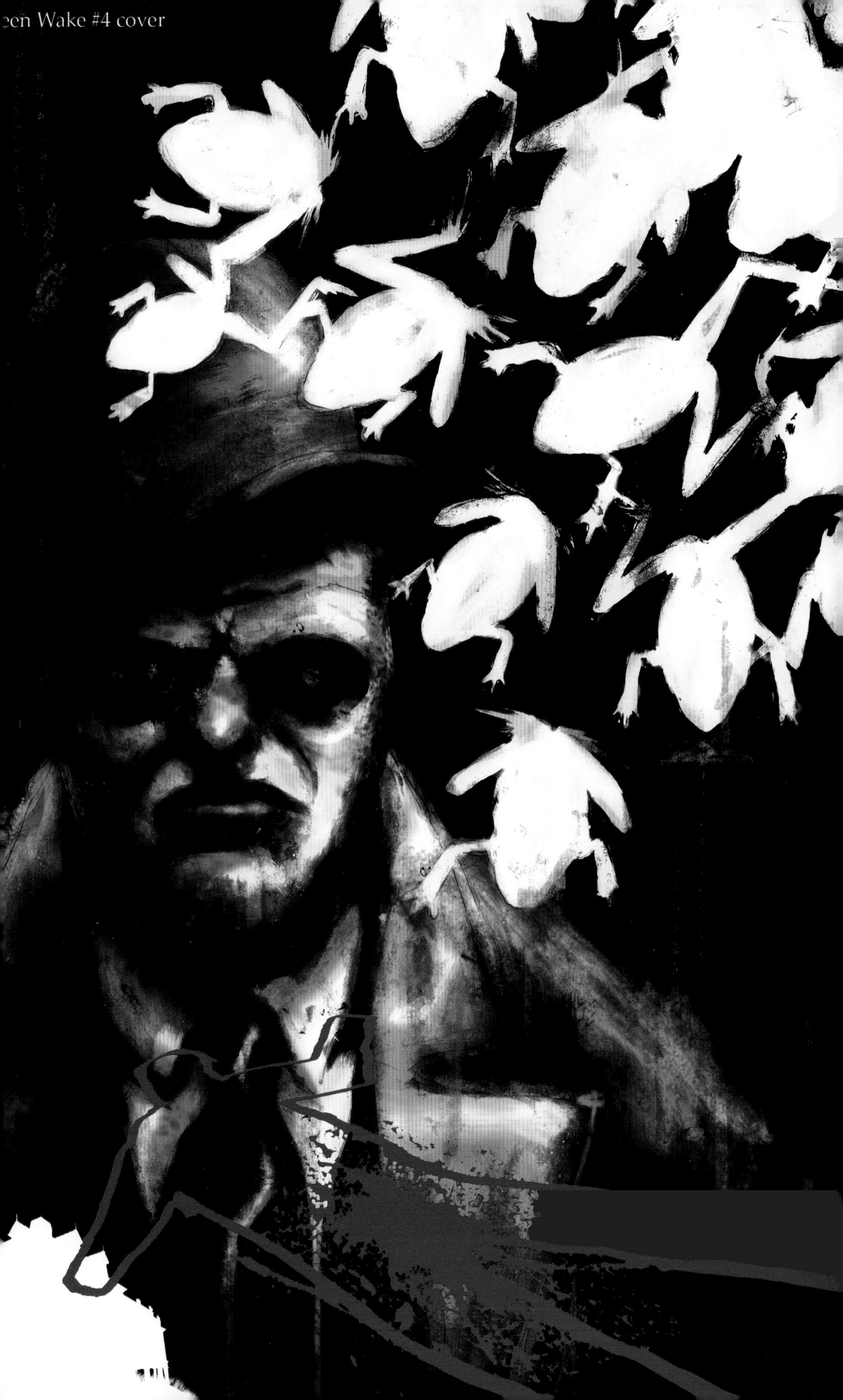

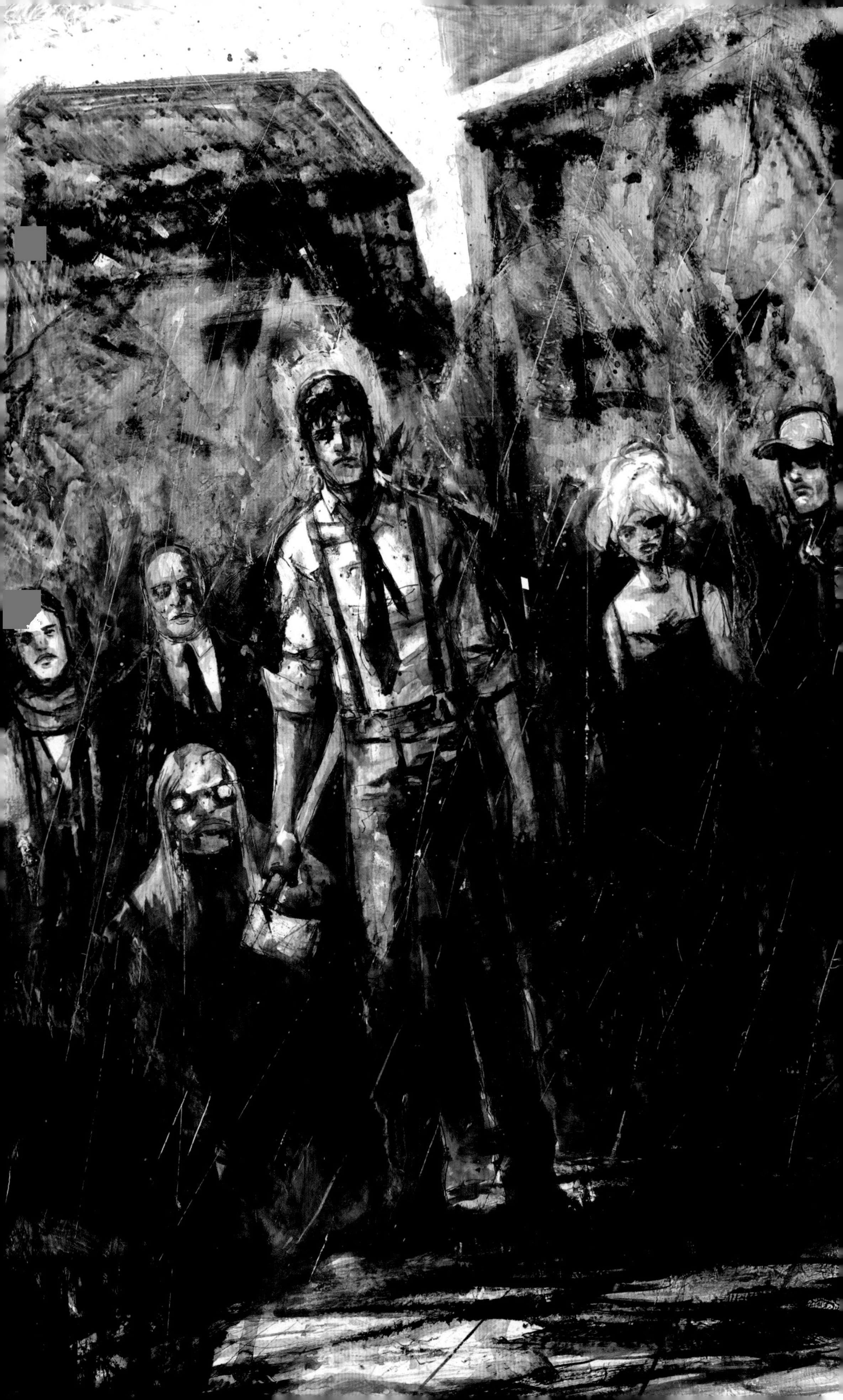

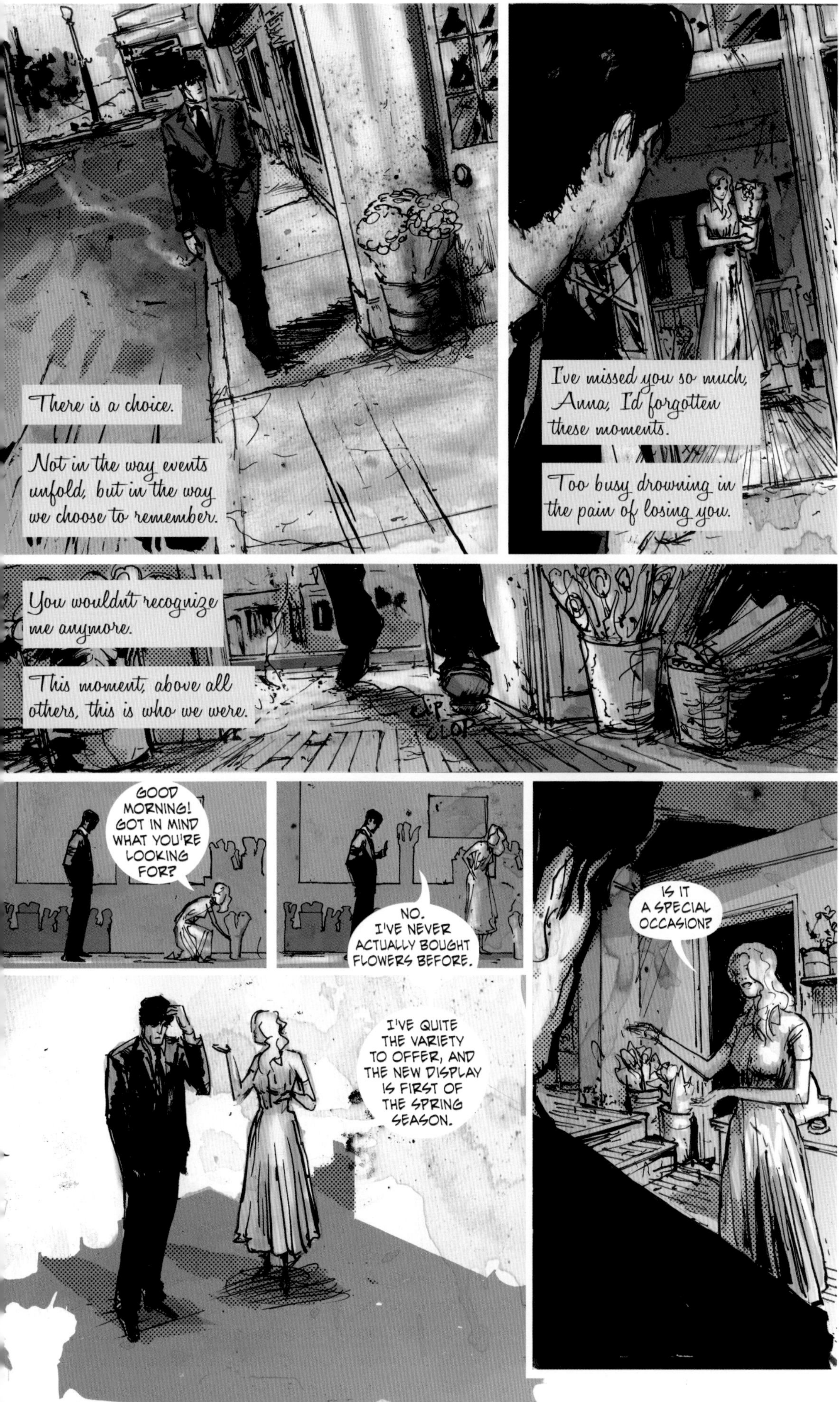
There is a choice.
Not in the way events unfold, but in the way we choose to remember.
I've missed you so much, Anna, I'd forgotten these moments.
Too busy drowning in the pain of losing you.
You wouldn't recognize me anymore.
This moment, above all others, this is who we were.
GOOD MORNING! GOT IN MIND WHAT YOU'RE LOOKING FOR?
NO. I'VE NEVER ACTUALLY BOUGHT FLOWERS BEFORE.
IS IT A SPECIAL OCCASION?
I'VE QUITE THE VARIETY TO OFFER, AND THE NEW DISPLAY IS FIRST OF THE SPRING SEASON.

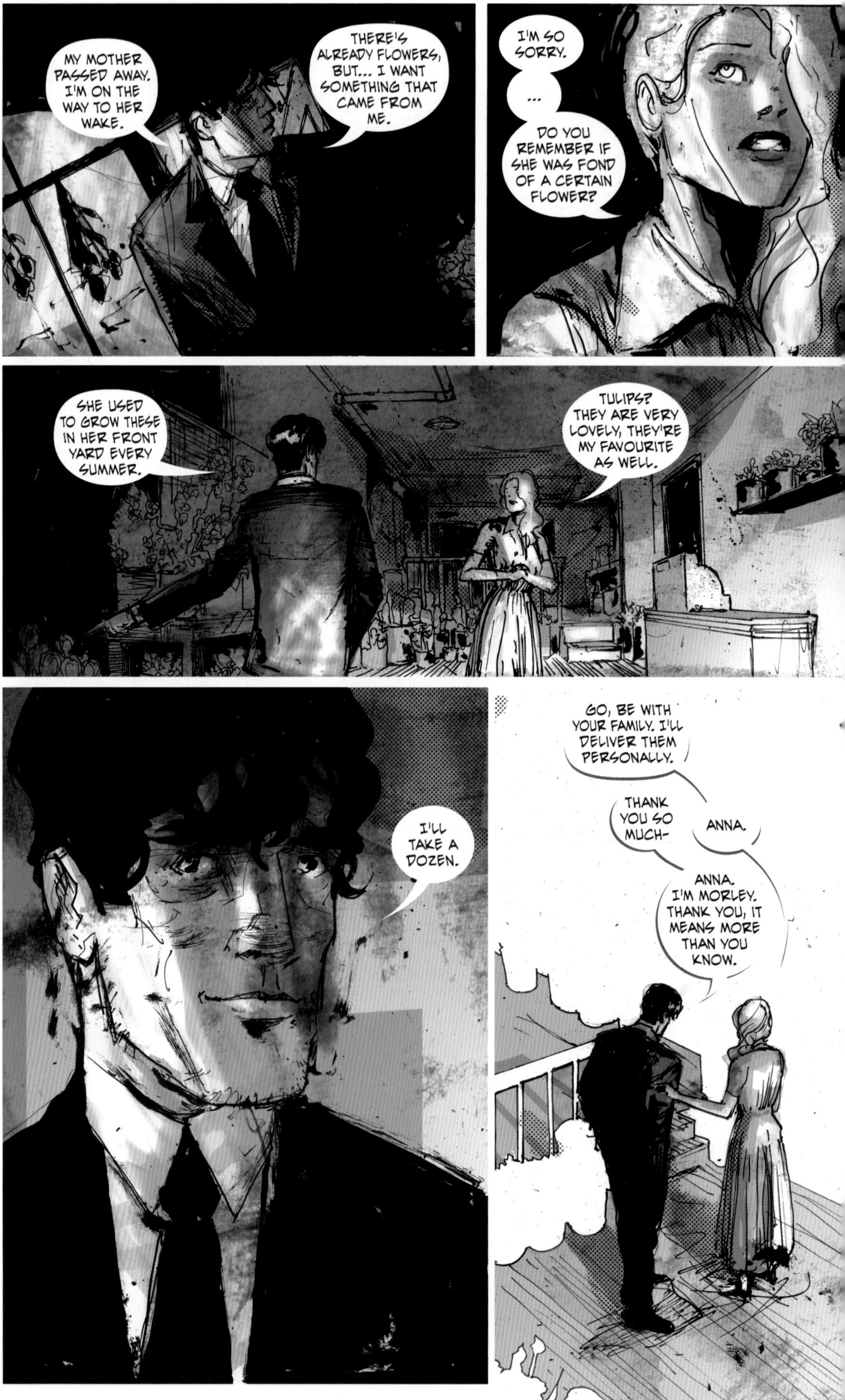
MY MOTHER PASSED AWAY. I'M ON THE WAY TO HER WAKE.
THERE'S ALREADY FLOWERS, BUT... I WANT SOMETHING THAT CAME FROM ME.
I'M SO SORRY.
...
DO YOU REMEMBER IF SHE WAS FOND OF A CERTAIN FLOWER?
SHE USED TO GROW THESE IN HER FRONT YARD EVERY SUMMER.
TULIPS? THEY ARE VERY LOVELY, THEY'RE MY FAVOURITE AS WELL.
I'LL TAKE A DOZEN.
GO, BE WITH YOUR FAMILY. I'LL DELIVER THEM PERSONALLY.
THANK YOU SO MUCH-
ANNA.
ANNA. I'M MORLEY. THANK YOU, IT MEANS MORE THAN YOU KNOW.

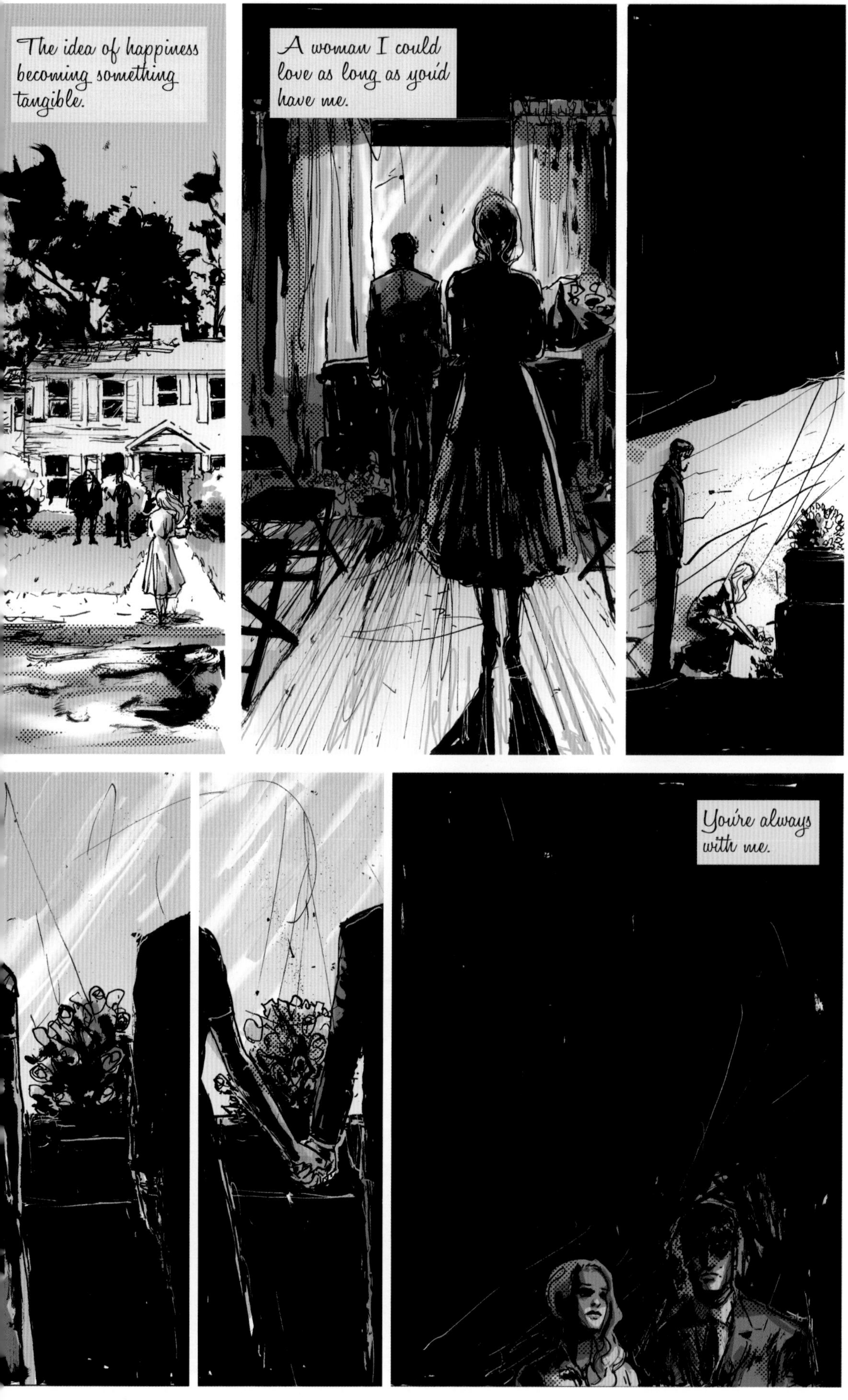
The idea of happiness becoming something tangible.
A woman I could love as long as you'd have me.
You're always with me.

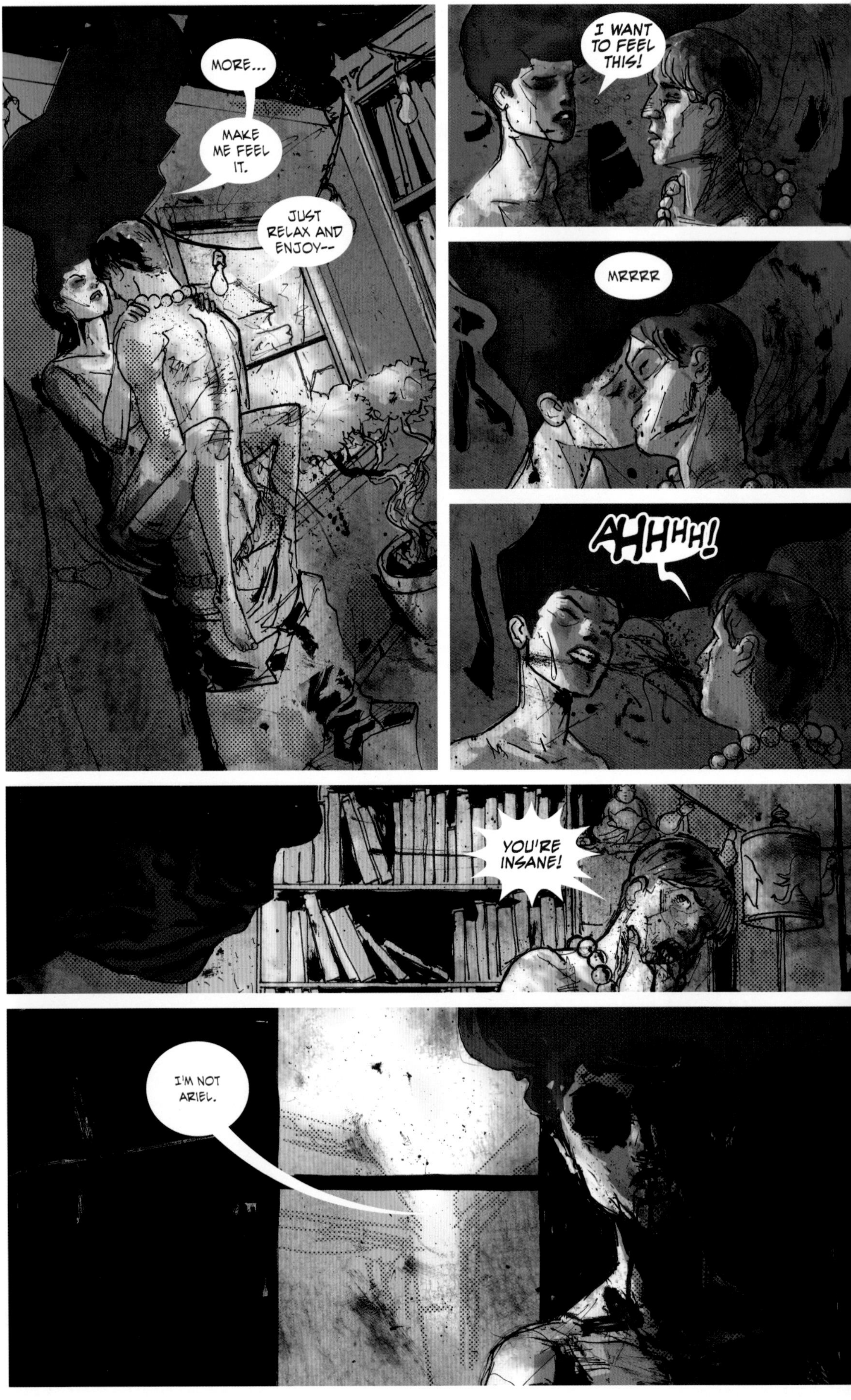
MORE...
MAKE ME FEEL IT.
JUST RELAX AND ENJOY--
I WANT TO FEEL THIS!
MRRRR
AHHHH!
YOU'RE INSANE!
I'M NOT ARIEL.

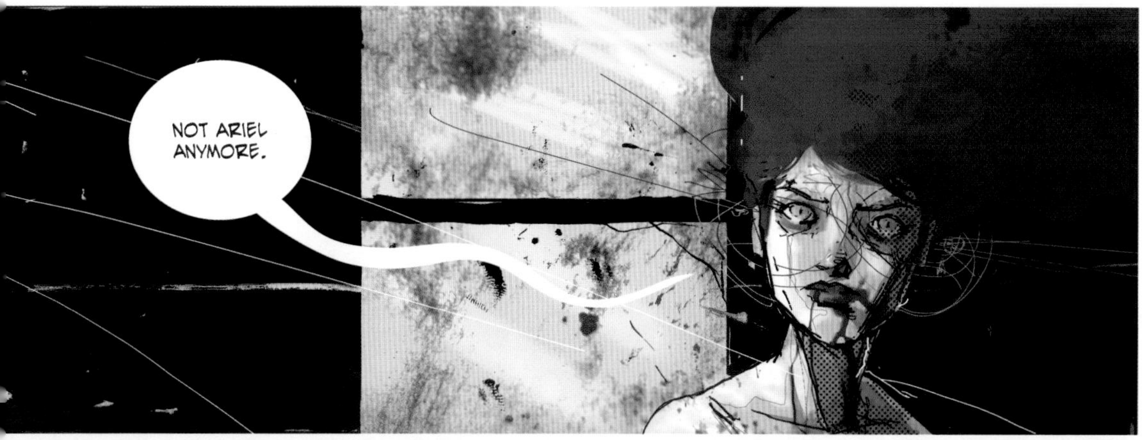
NOT ARIEL
ANYMORE.

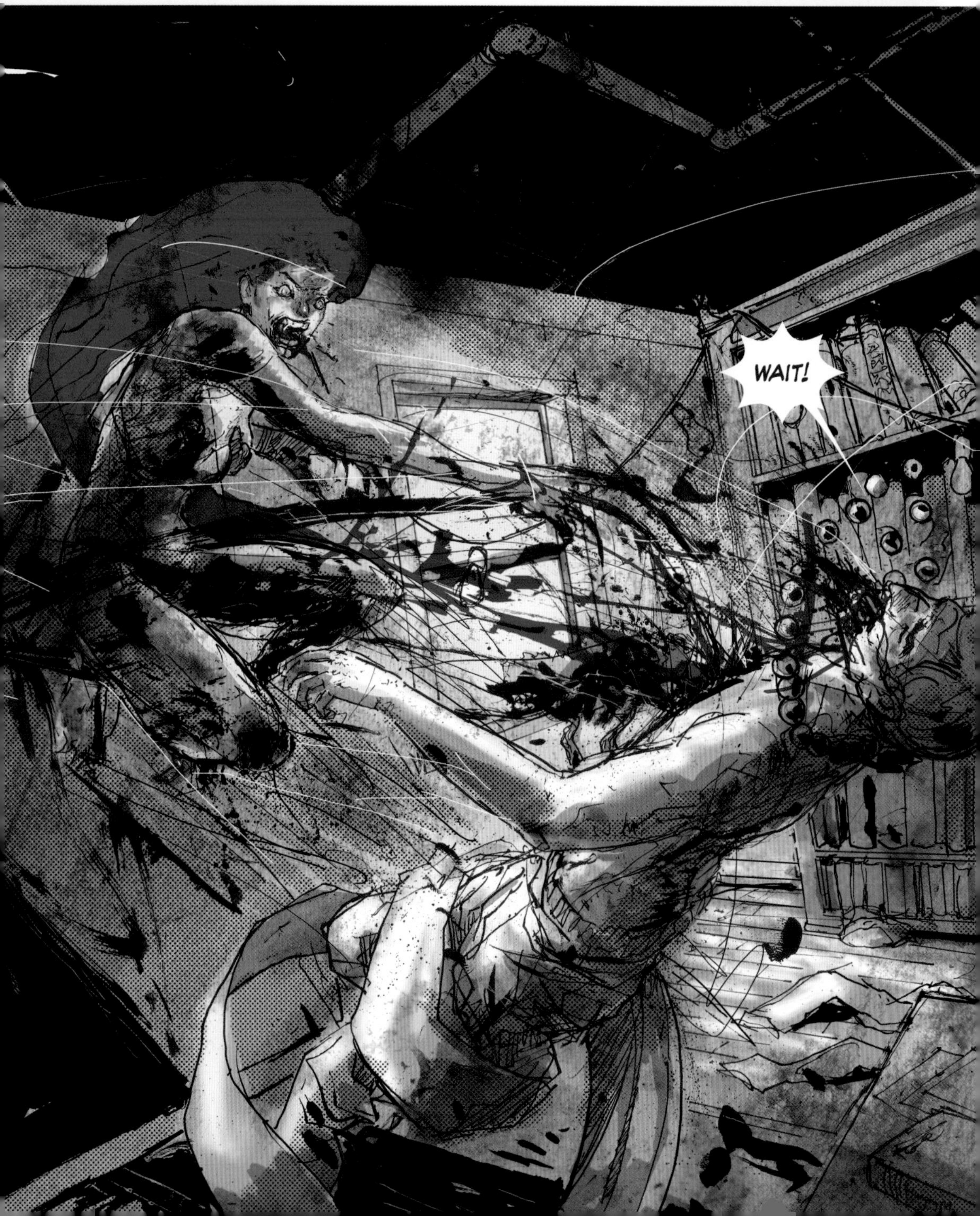
WAIT!

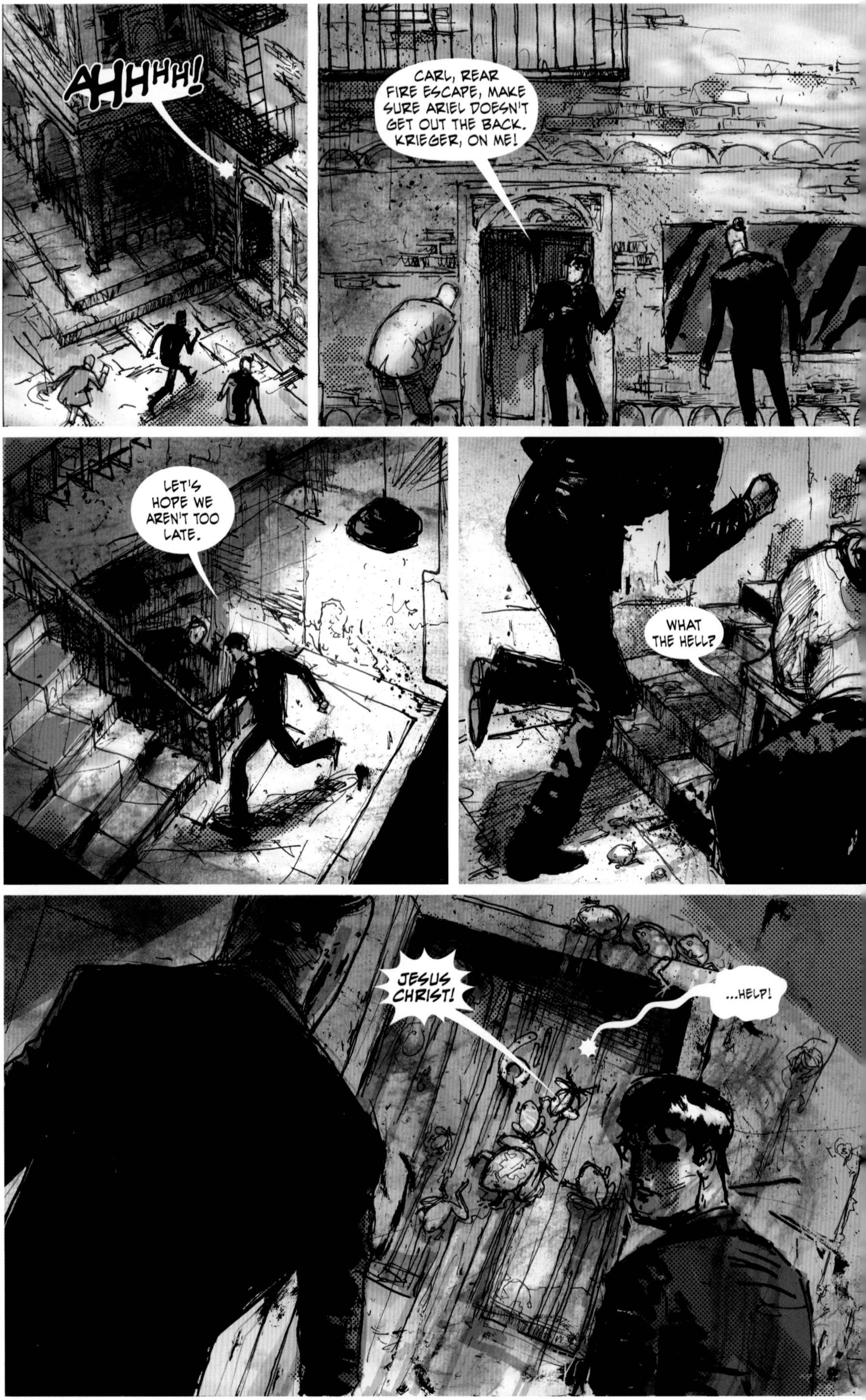
AHHHH!
CARL, REAR FIRE ESCAPE, MAKE SURE ARIEL DOESN'T GET OUT THE BACK. KRIEGER, ON ME!
LET'S HOPE WE AREN'T TOO LATE.
WHAT THE HELL?
JESUS CHRIST!
...HELP!

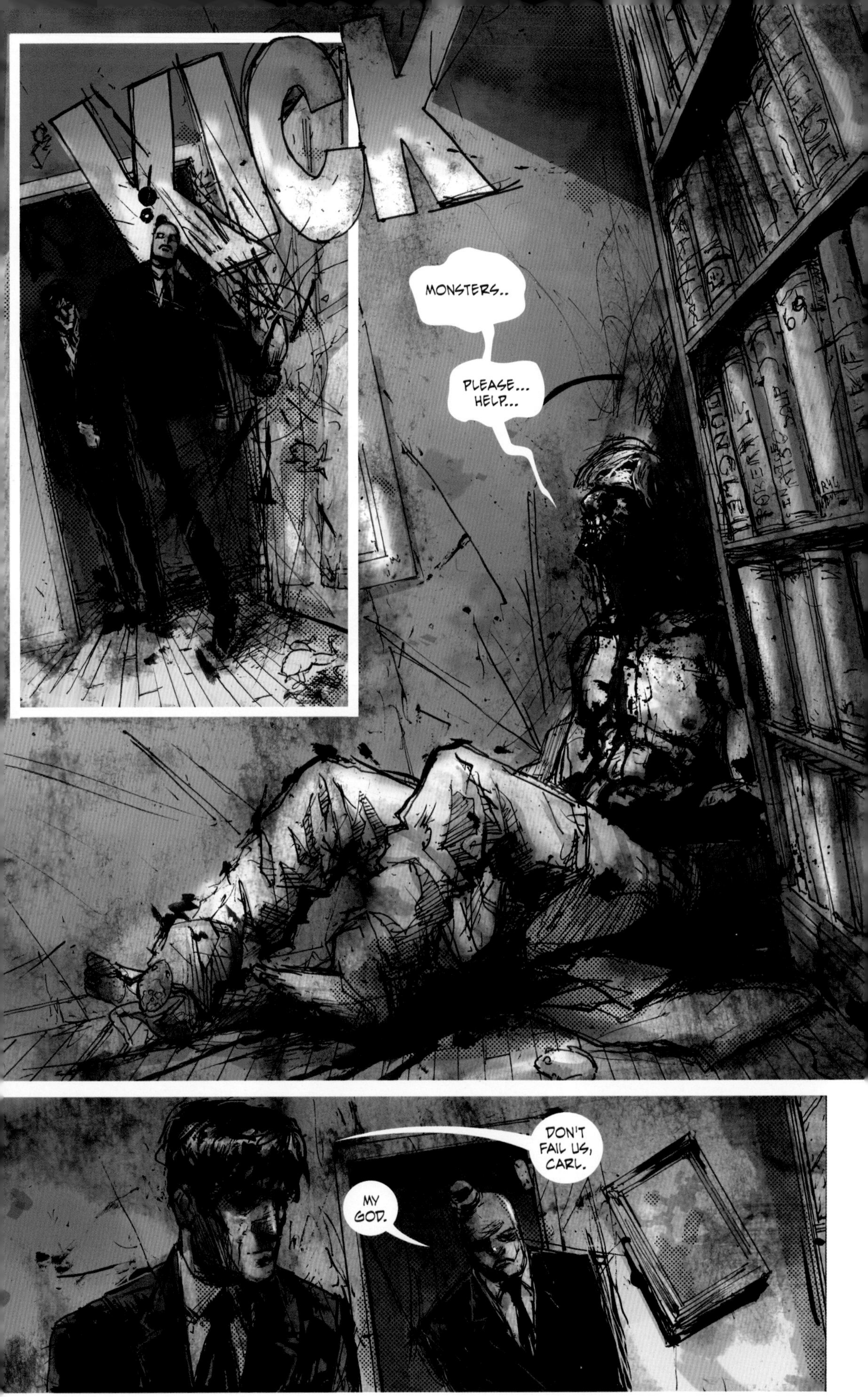
KRACK
MONSTERS..
PLEASE... HELP...
DON'T FAIL US, CARL.
MY GOD.

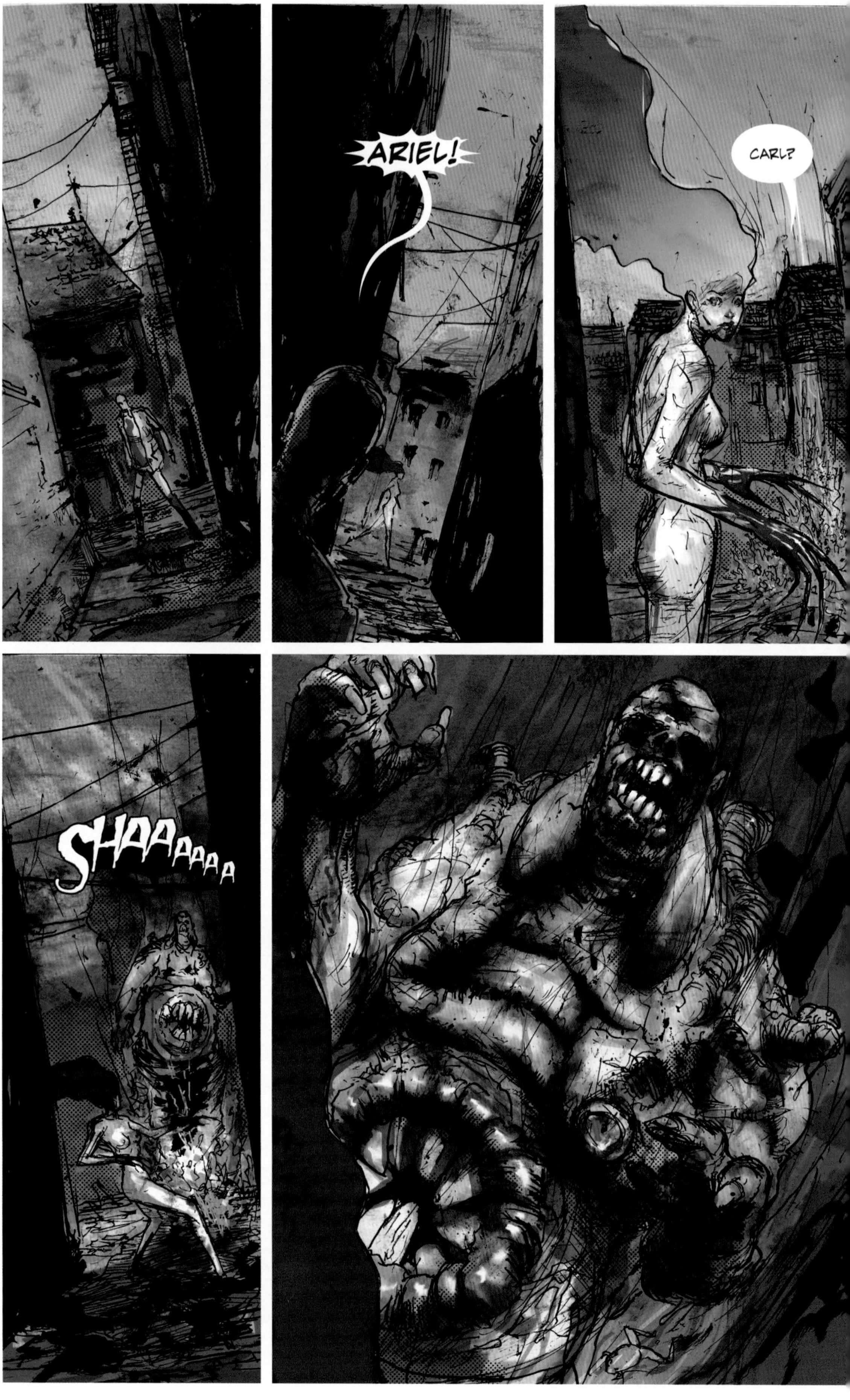
ARIEL!
CARL?
SHAAAAAA

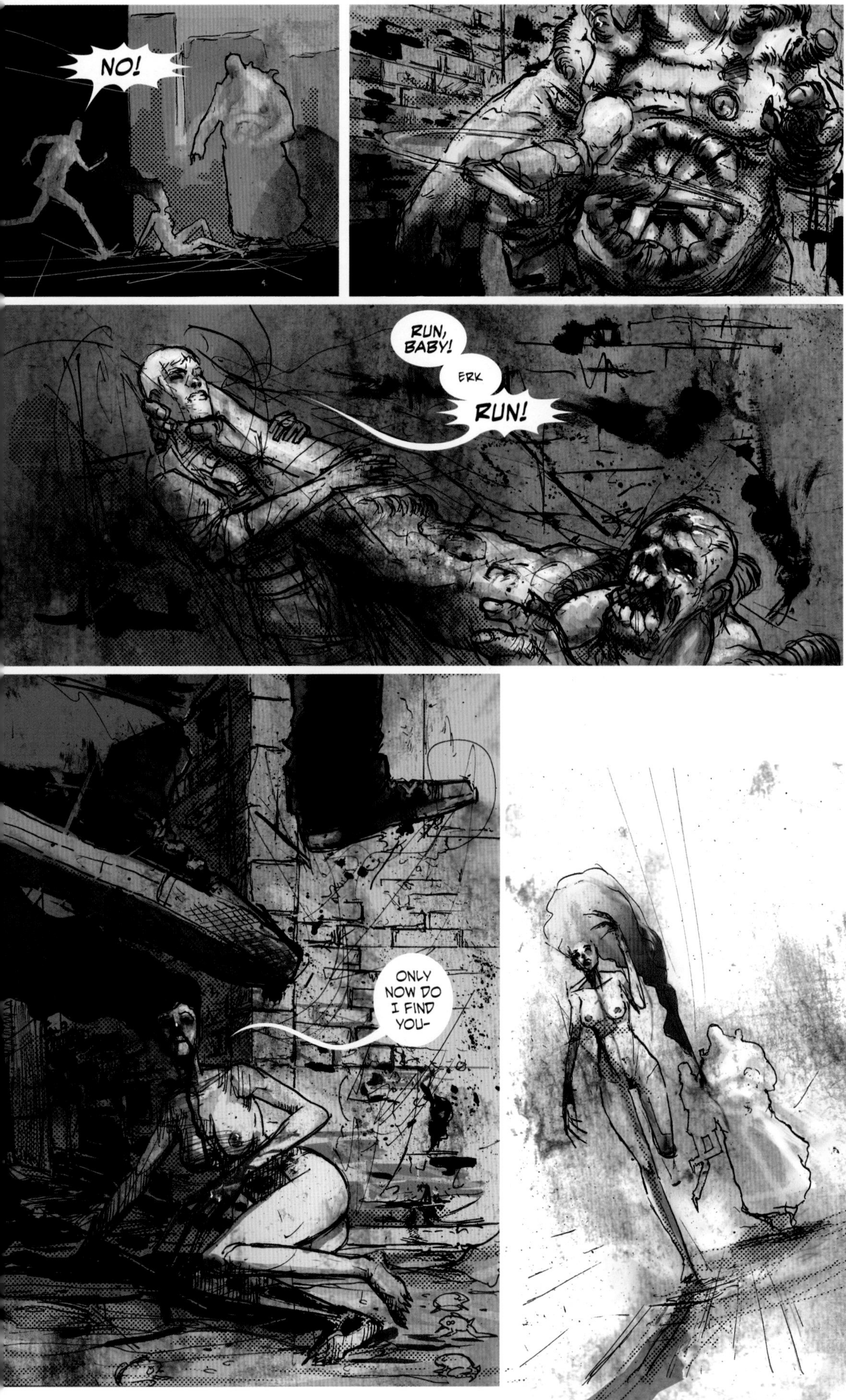

NO!
RUN, BABY!
ERK
RUN!
ONLY NOW DO I FIND YOU-

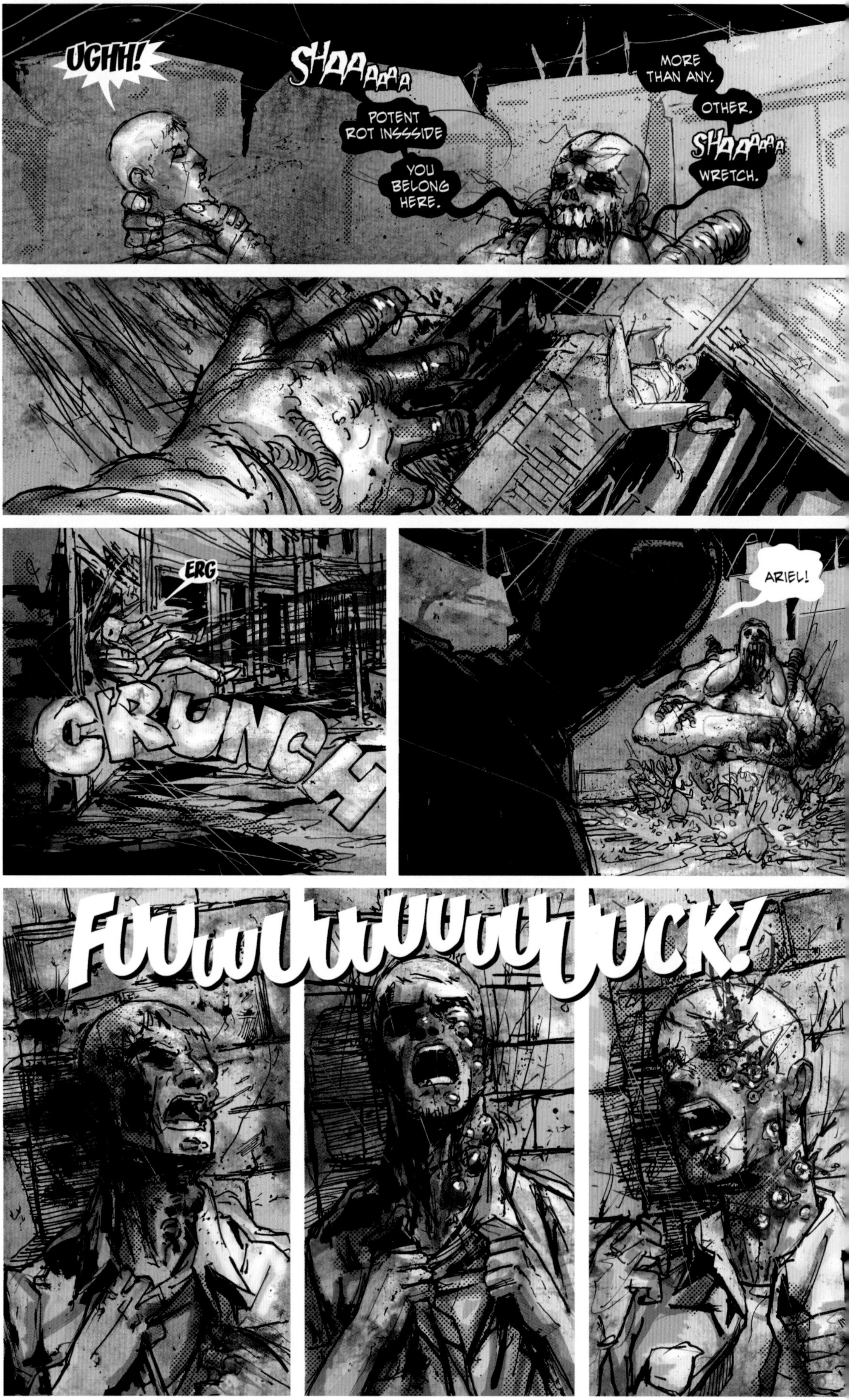
UGHH!
SHAAAAAA
POTENT ROT INSSSIDE
YOU BELONG HERE.
MORE THAN ANY.
OTHER.
SHAAAAAA
WRETCH.
ERG
CRUNCH
ARIEL!
FUUUUUUUUUUUUUCK!

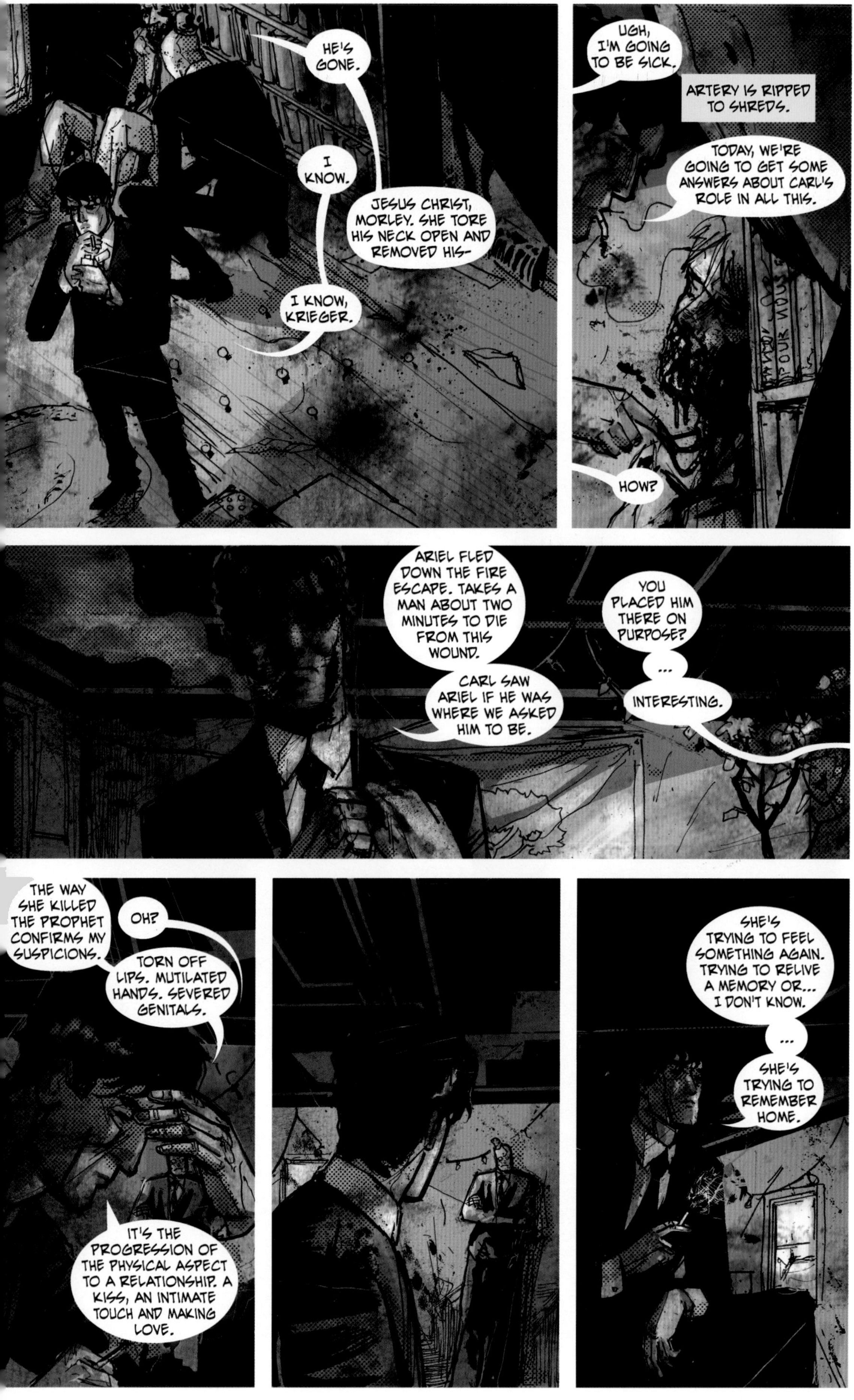
HE'S GONE.
I KNOW.
JESUS CHRIST, MORLEY. SHE TORE HIS NECK OPEN AND REMOVED HIS-
I KNOW, KRIEGER.
UGH, I'M GOING TO BE SICK.
ARTERY IS RIPPED TO SHREDS.
TODAY, WE'RE GOING TO GET SOME ANSWERS ABOUT CARL'S ROLE IN ALL THIS.
HOW?
ARIEL FLED DOWN THE FIRE ESCAPE. TAKES A MAN ABOUT TWO MINUTES TO DIE FROM THIS WOUND.
CARL SAW ARIEL IF HE WAS WHERE WE ASKED HIM TO BE.
YOU PLACED HIM THERE ON PURPOSE?
...
INTERESTING.
THE WAY SHE KILLED THE PROPHET CONFIRMS MY SUSPICIONS.
OH?
TORN OFF LIPS. MUTILATED HANDS. SEVERED GENITALS.
IT'S THE PROGRESSION OF THE PHYSICAL ASPECT TO A RELATIONSHIP. A KISS, AN INTIMATE TOUCH AND MAKING LOVE.
SHE'S TRYING TO FEEL SOMETHING AGAIN. TRYING TO RELIVE A MEMORY OR... I DON'T KNOW.
...
SHE'S TRYING TO REMEMBER HOME.

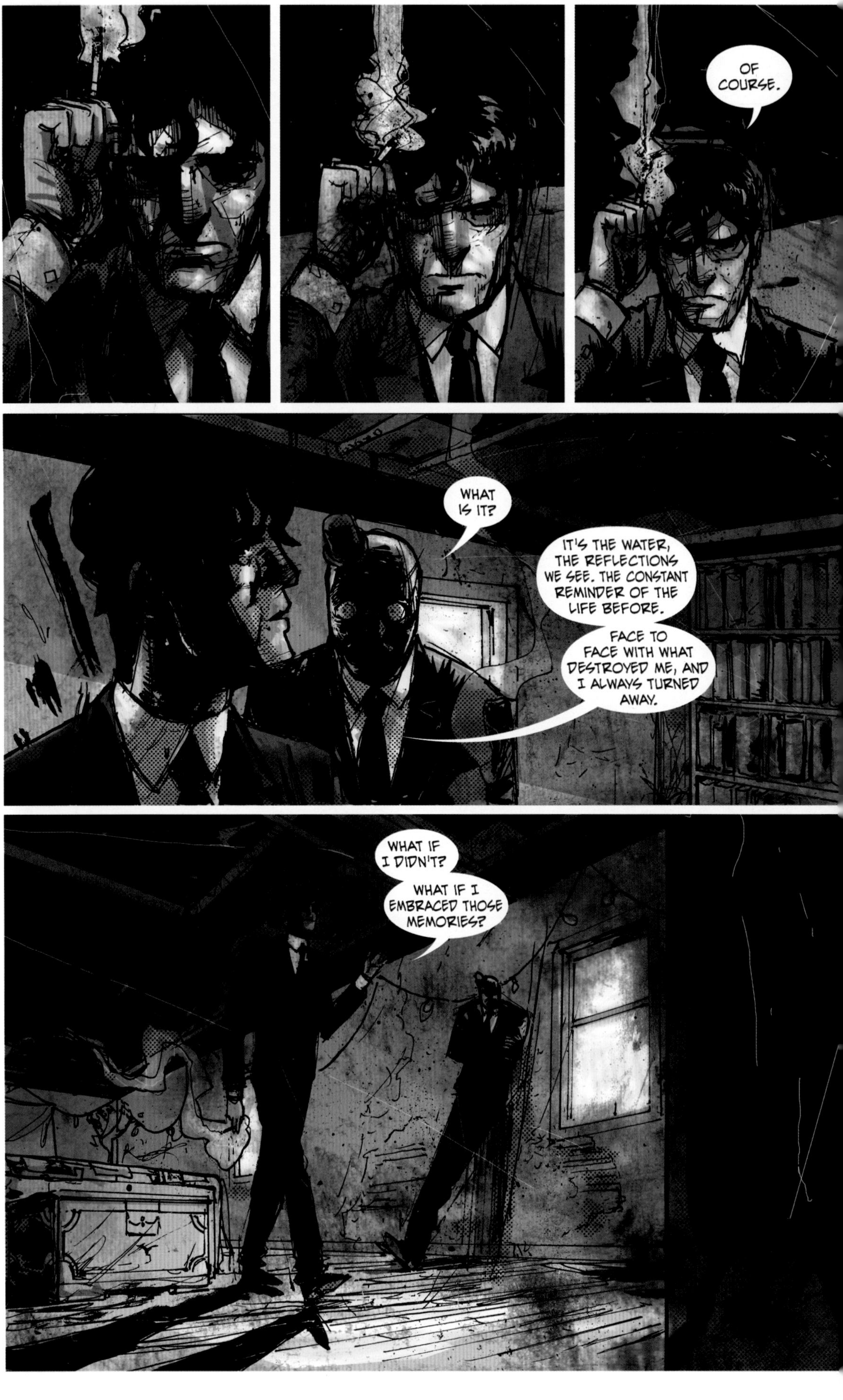
OF COURSE.
WHAT IS IT?
IT'S THE WATER, THE REFLECTIONS WE SEE. THE CONSTANT REMINDER OF THE LIFE BEFORE.
FACE TO FACE WITH WHAT DESTROYED ME, AND I ALWAYS TURNED AWAY.
WHAT IF I DIDN'T?
WHAT IF I EMBRACED THOSE MEMORIES?

MAYBE THE RIVER IS THE WAY TO BABYLON.

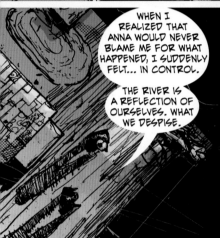

WHEN I REALIZED THAT ANNA WOULD NEVER BLAME ME FOR WHAT HAPPENED, I SUDDENLY FELT... IN CONTROL.

THE RIVER IS A REFLECTION OF OURSELVES. WHAT WE DESPISE.

AND WHAT STANDS ABOVE THE RIVER?

...

YOU THINK THE BLOOD SMEARS REPRESENT THE BRIDGE?

I MADE A MONSTER OF HER MEMORY.

THAT'S WHAT GREEN WAKE IS. IT'S A MONSTER THAT FEEDS ON THE GUILT OF OUR PAST.

NOTHING IN LIFE IS COINCIDENCE.

...

KRIEGER, BEFORE I CAME TO GREEN WAKE, MY WIFE DIED.

MORLEY, I'M SO SORRY.

FOR THE LONGEST TIME, I THOUGHT IT WAS MY FAULT. THAT, SOMEHOW, IN HER FINAL MOMENTS ANNA BLAMED ME.

I PUT THAT ON HER. I MADE ANNA INTO SOMETHING SHE NEVER WAS.

WHAT?

THE LAST THING YOU REMEMBER, KRIEGER! TELL ME!

...

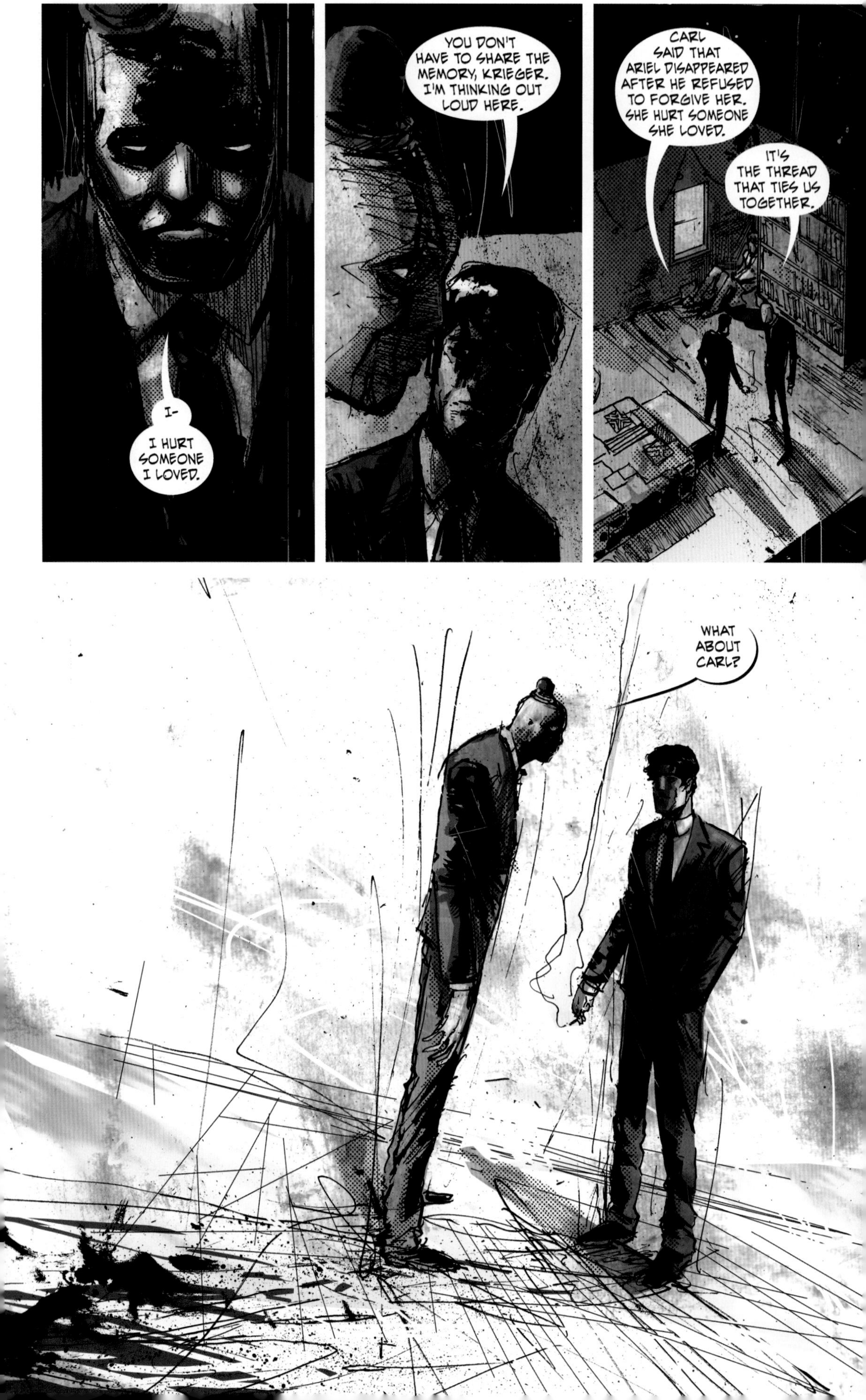
I-
I HURT SOMEONE I LOVED.
YOU DON'T HAVE TO SHARE THE MEMORY, KRIEGER. I'M THINKING OUT LOUD HERE.
CARL SAID THAT ARIEL DISAPPEARED AFTER HE REFUSED TO FORGIVE HER. SHE HURT SOMEONE SHE LOVED.
IT'S THE THREAD THAT TIES US TOGETHER.
WHAT ABOUT CARL?

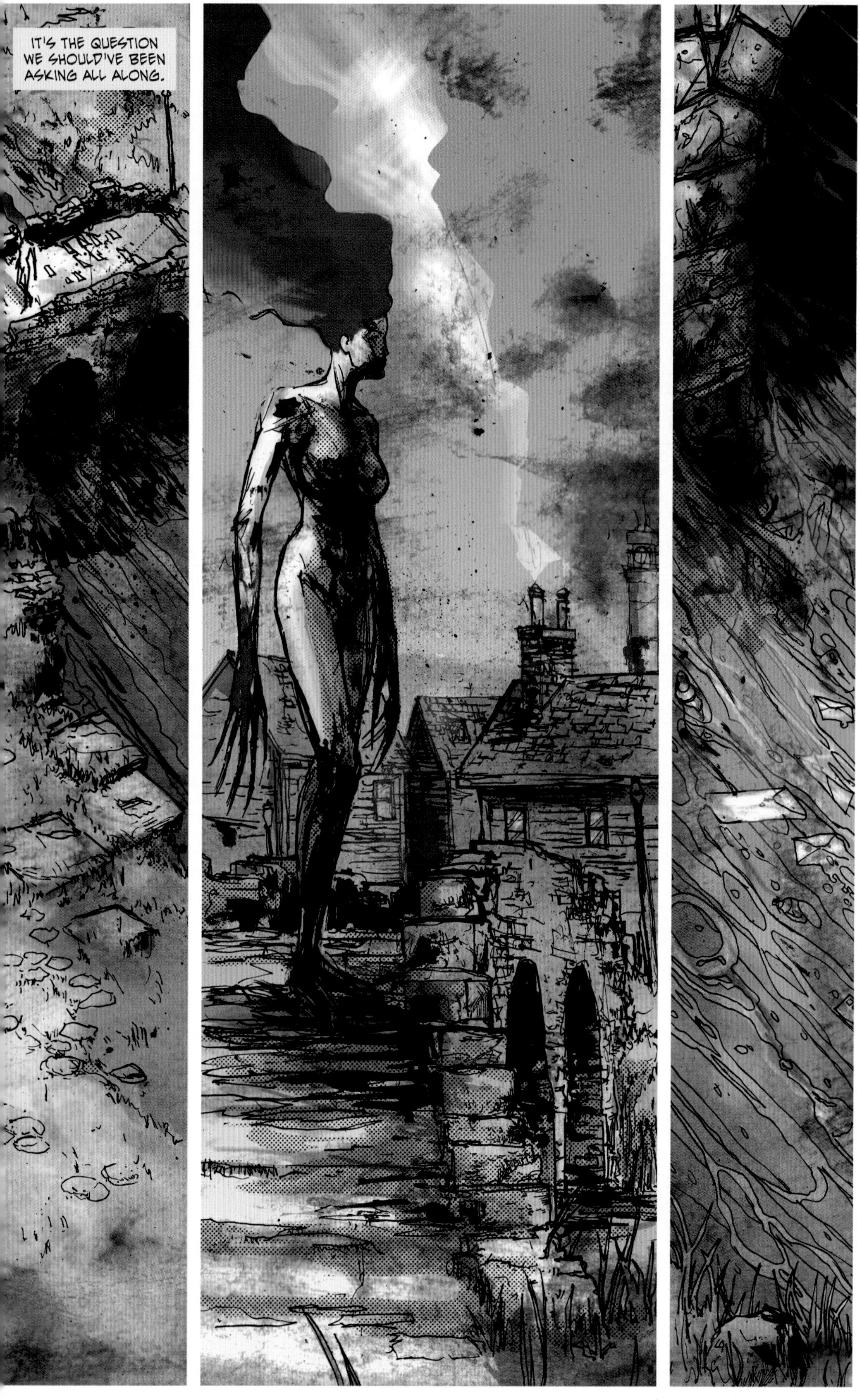
IT'S THE QUESTION WE SHOULD'VE BEEN ASKING ALL ALONG.

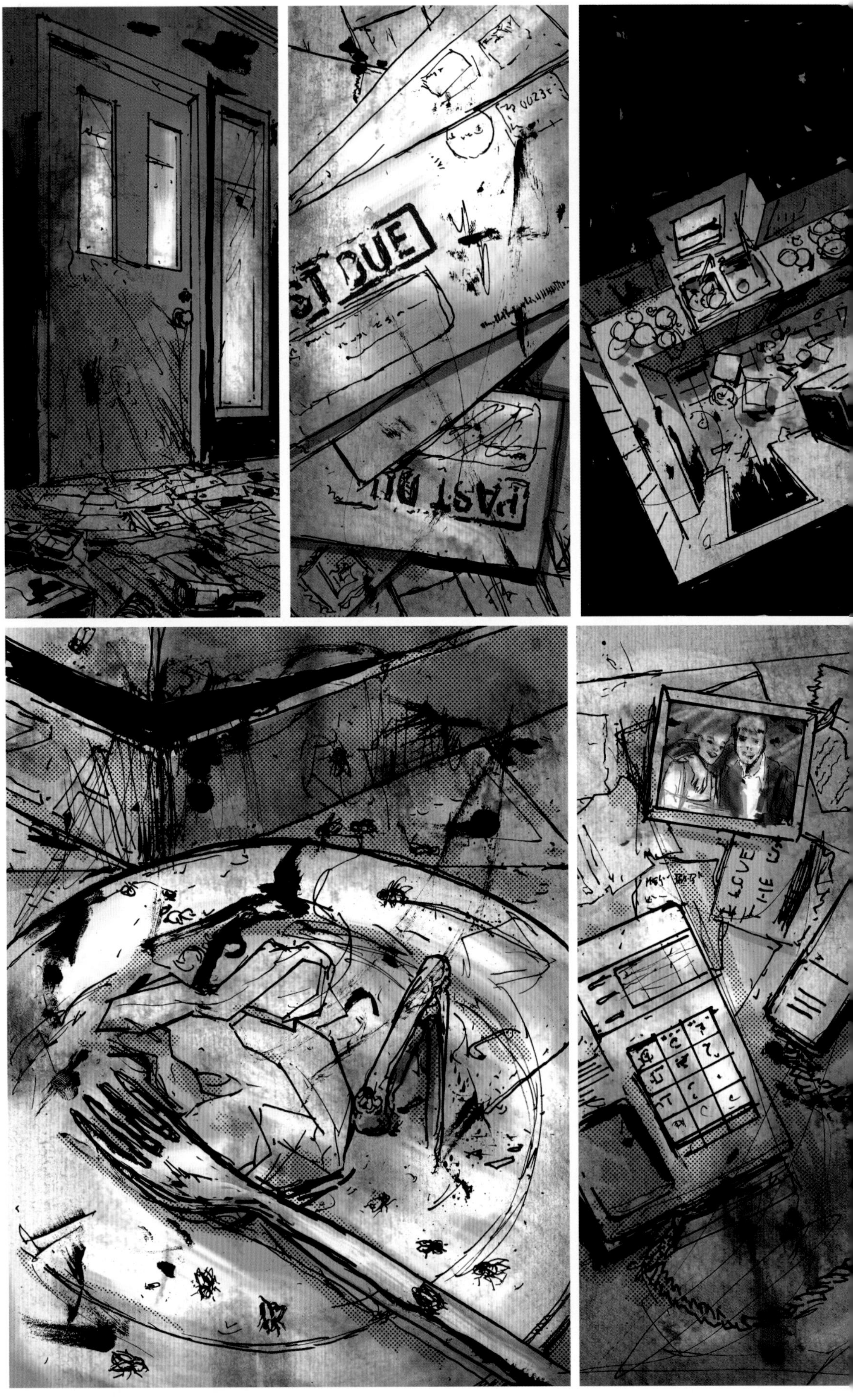
ST DUE

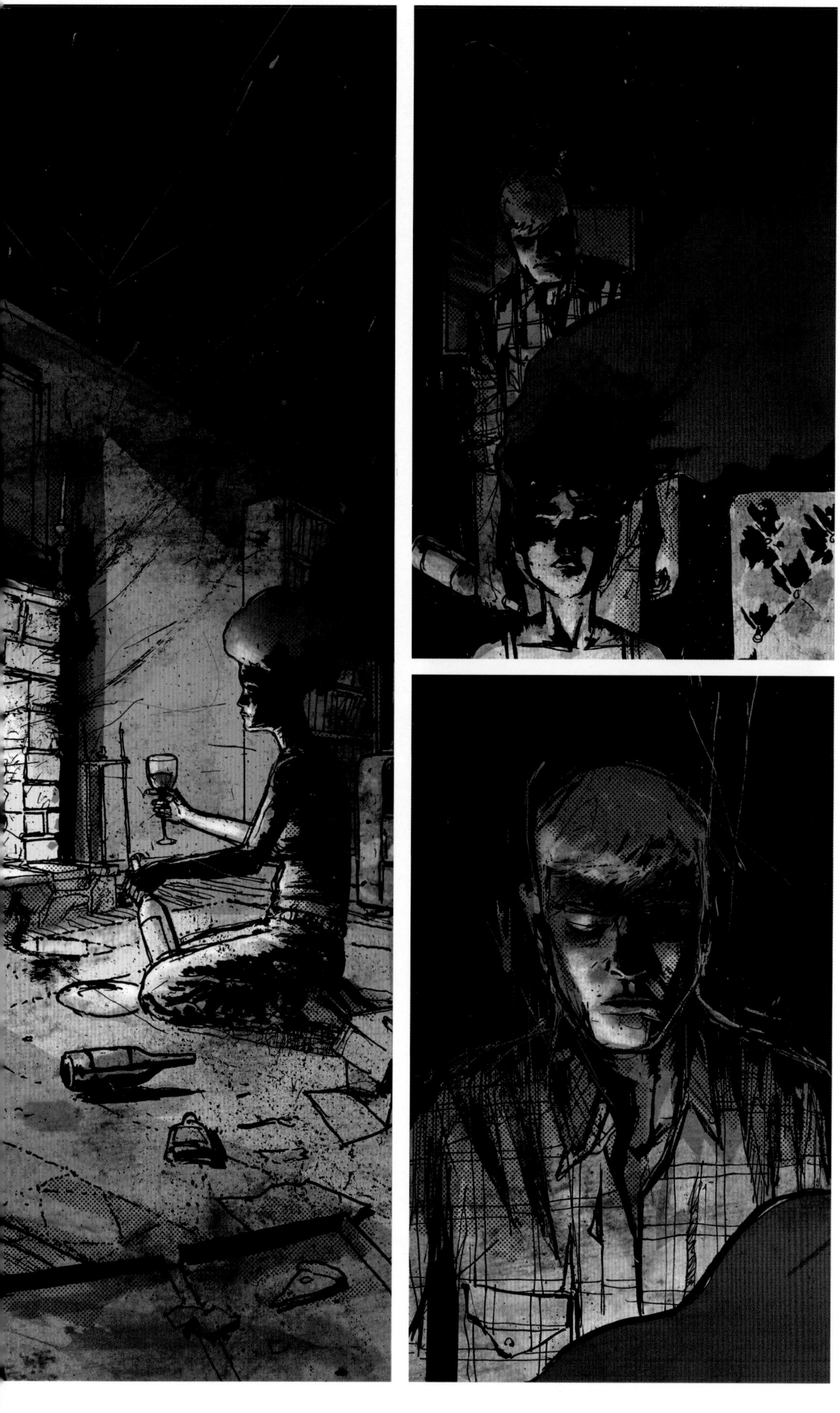

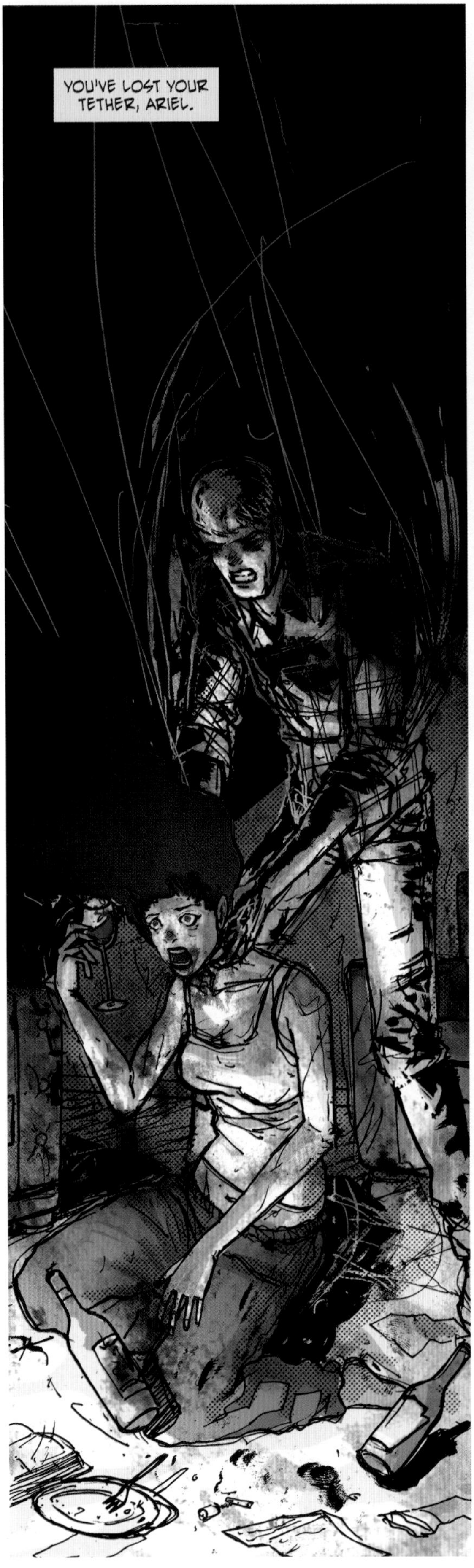
YOU'VE LOST YOUR
TETHER, ARIEL.

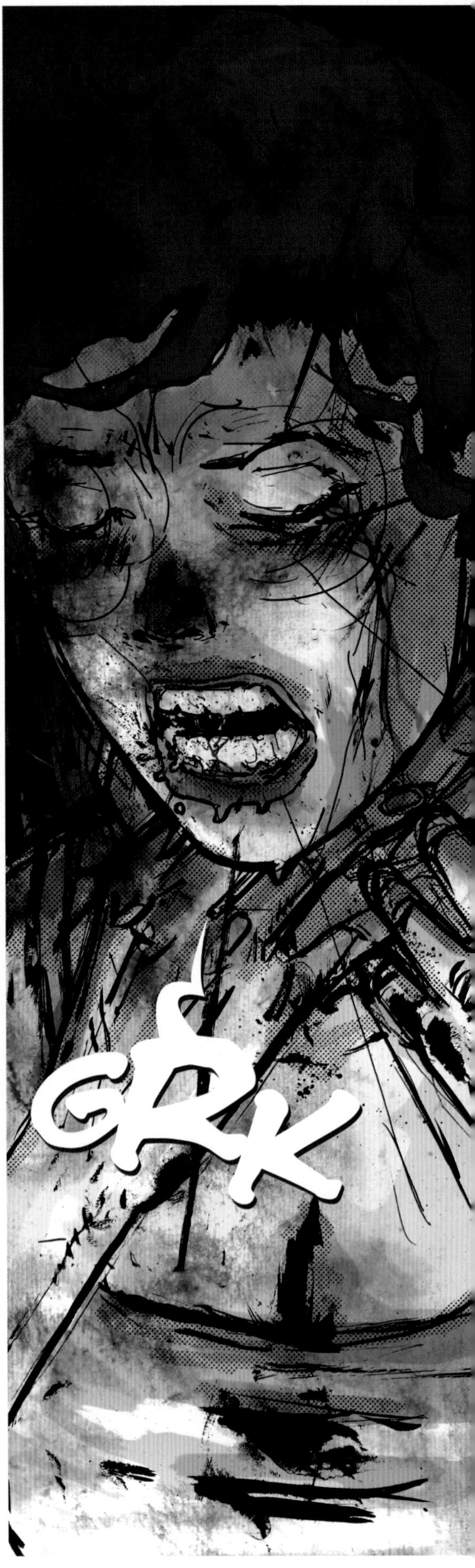
GRK

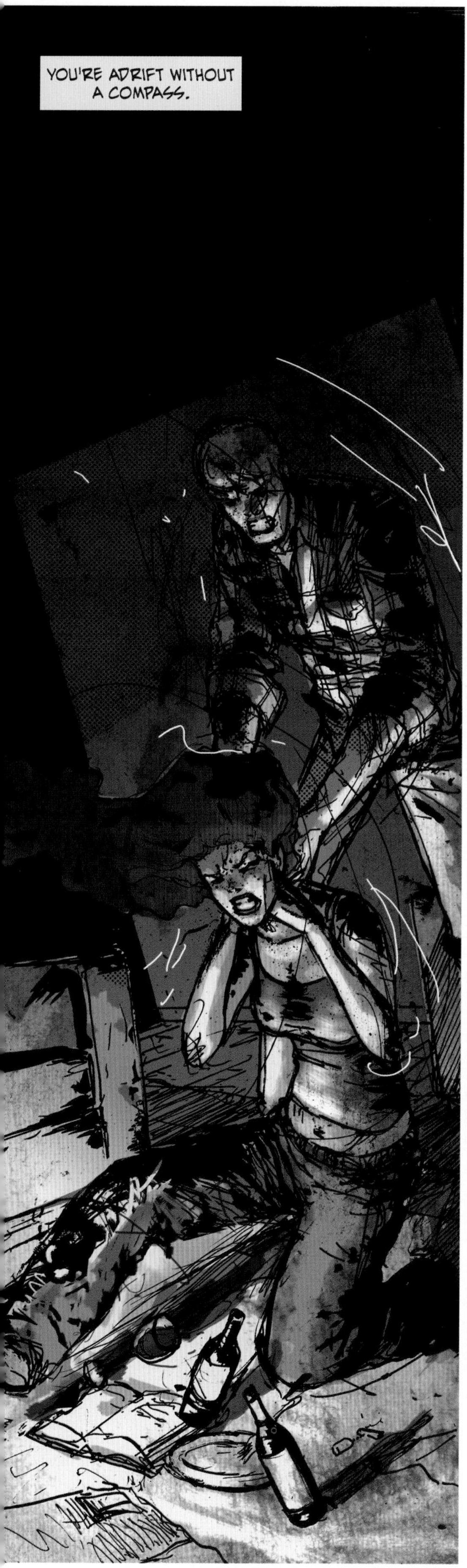
YOU'RE ADRIFT WITHOUT A COMPASS.

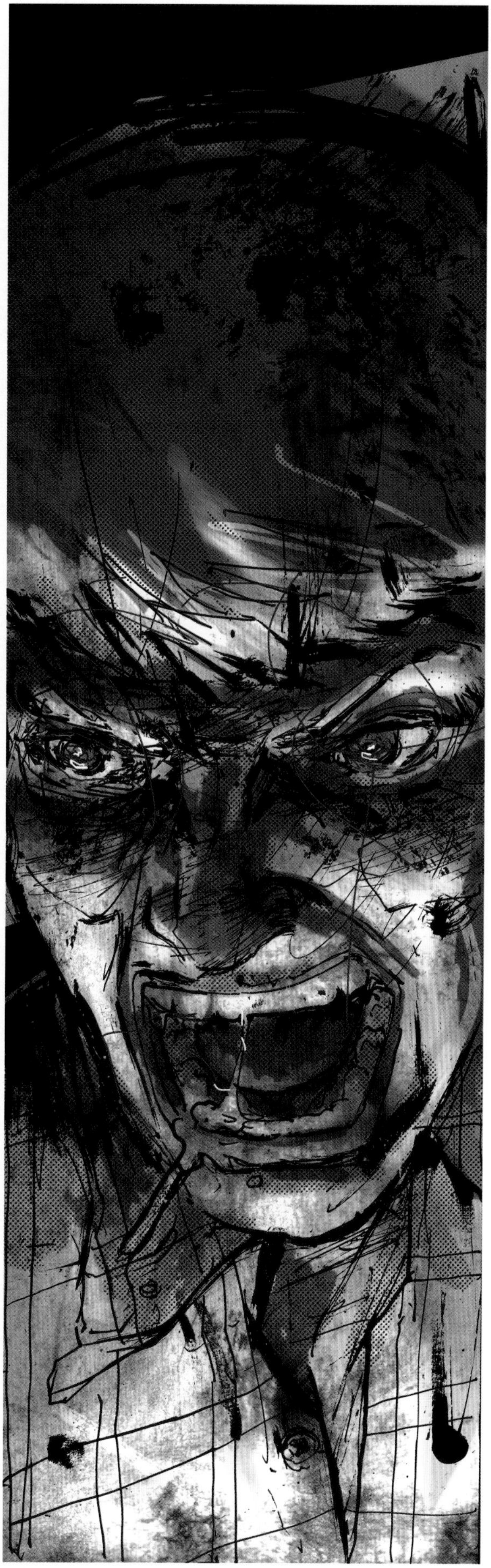

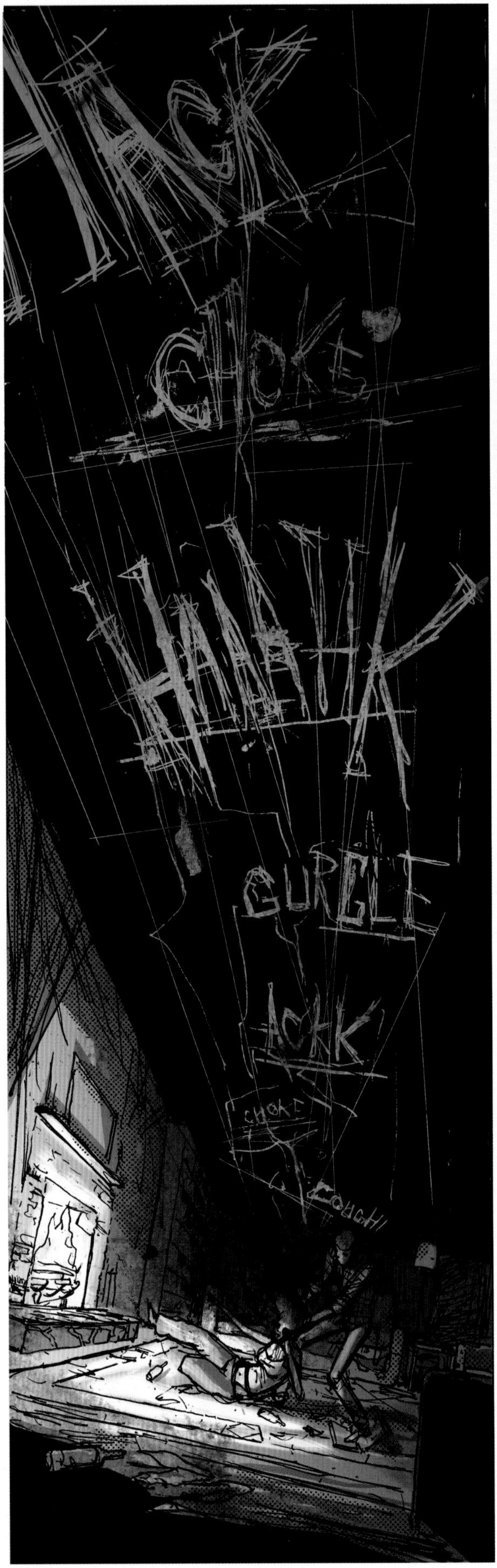
CHOKE
GURGLE
ACKK
CHOKE
COUGH

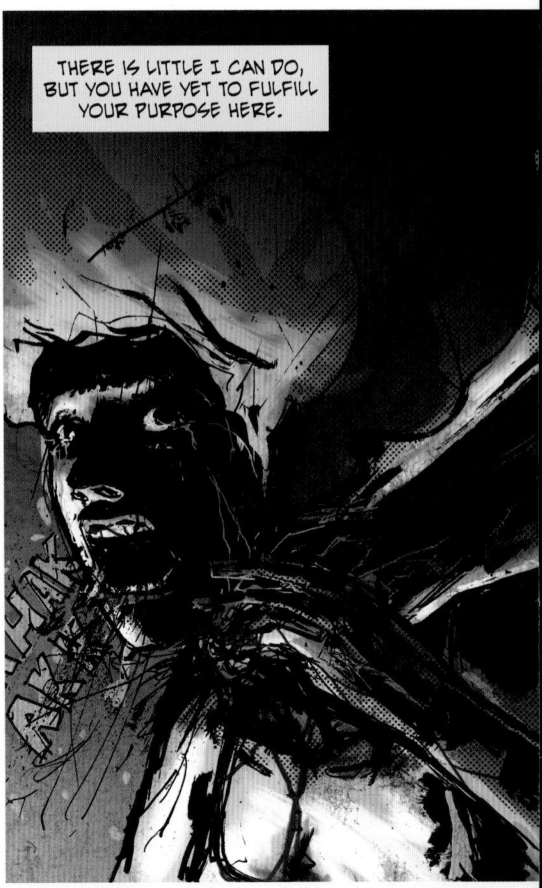
THERE IS LITTLE I CAN DO, BUT YOU HAVE YET TO FULFILL YOUR PURPOSE HERE.

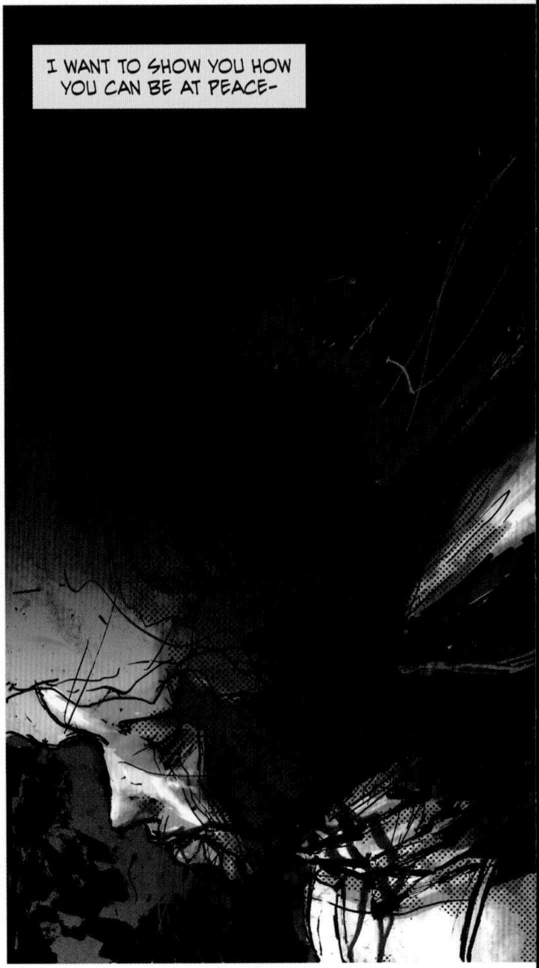
I WANT TO SHOW YOU HOW YOU CAN BE AT PEACE-

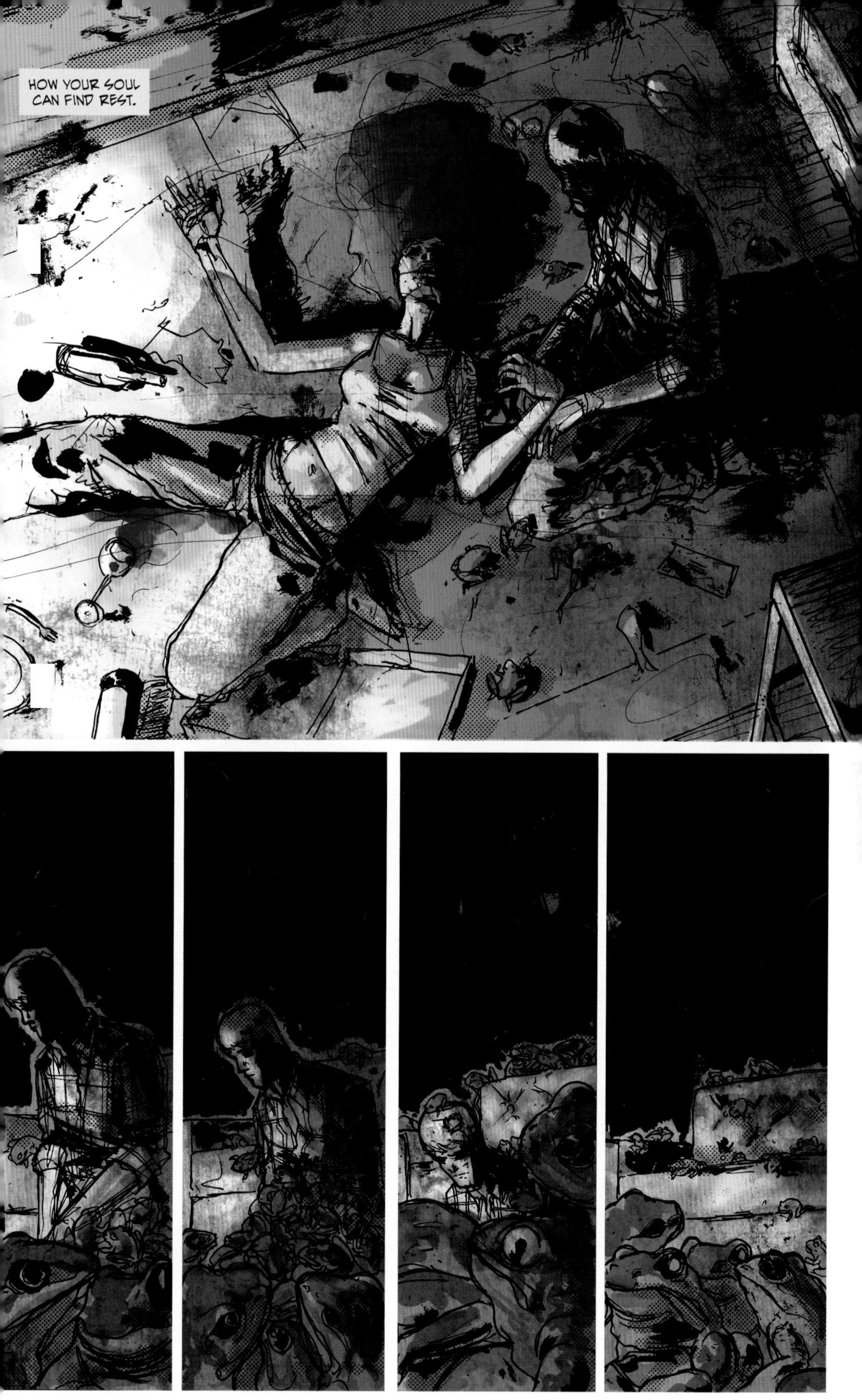
HOW YOUR SOUL
CAN FIND REST.

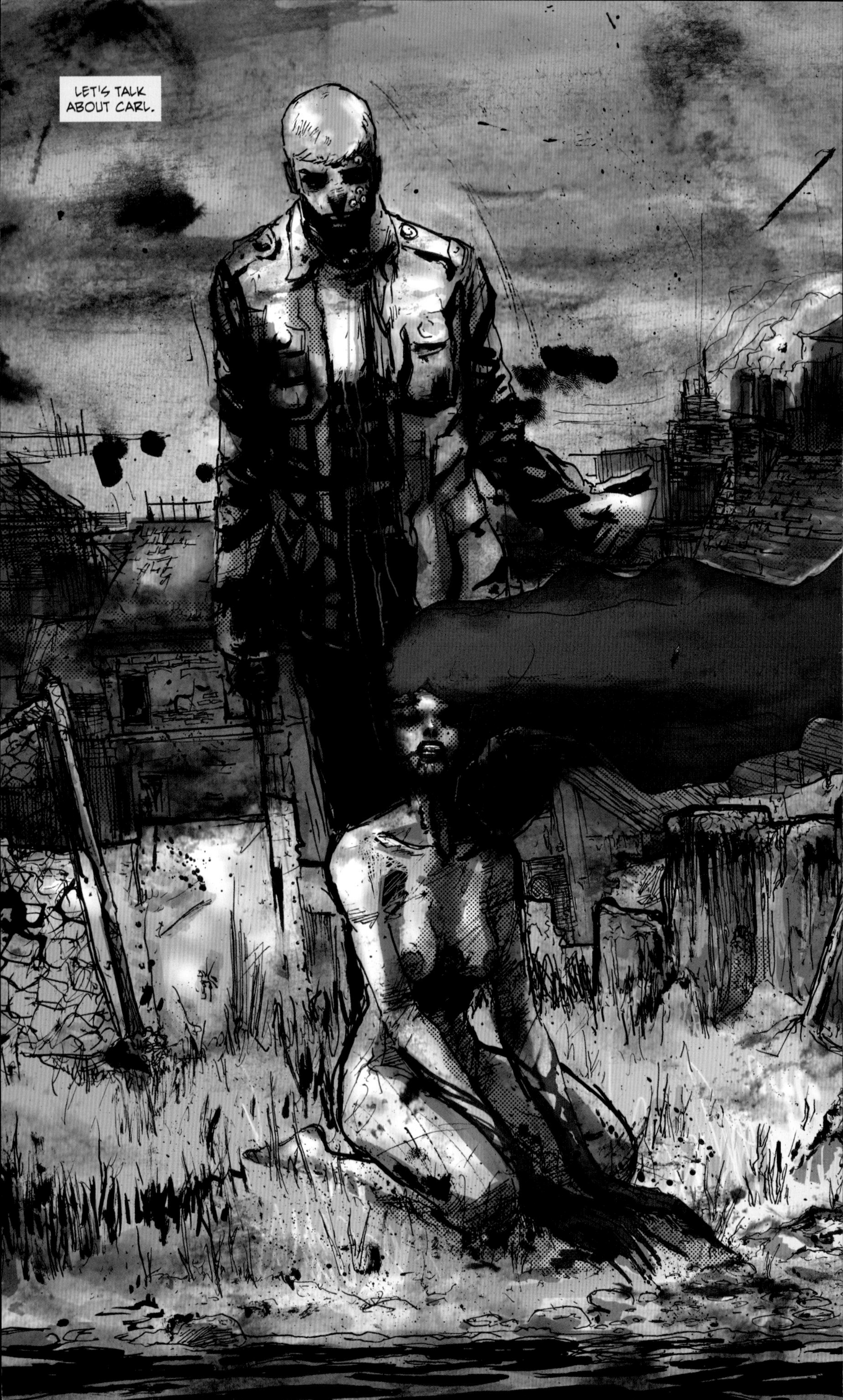
LET'S TALK ABOUT CARL.

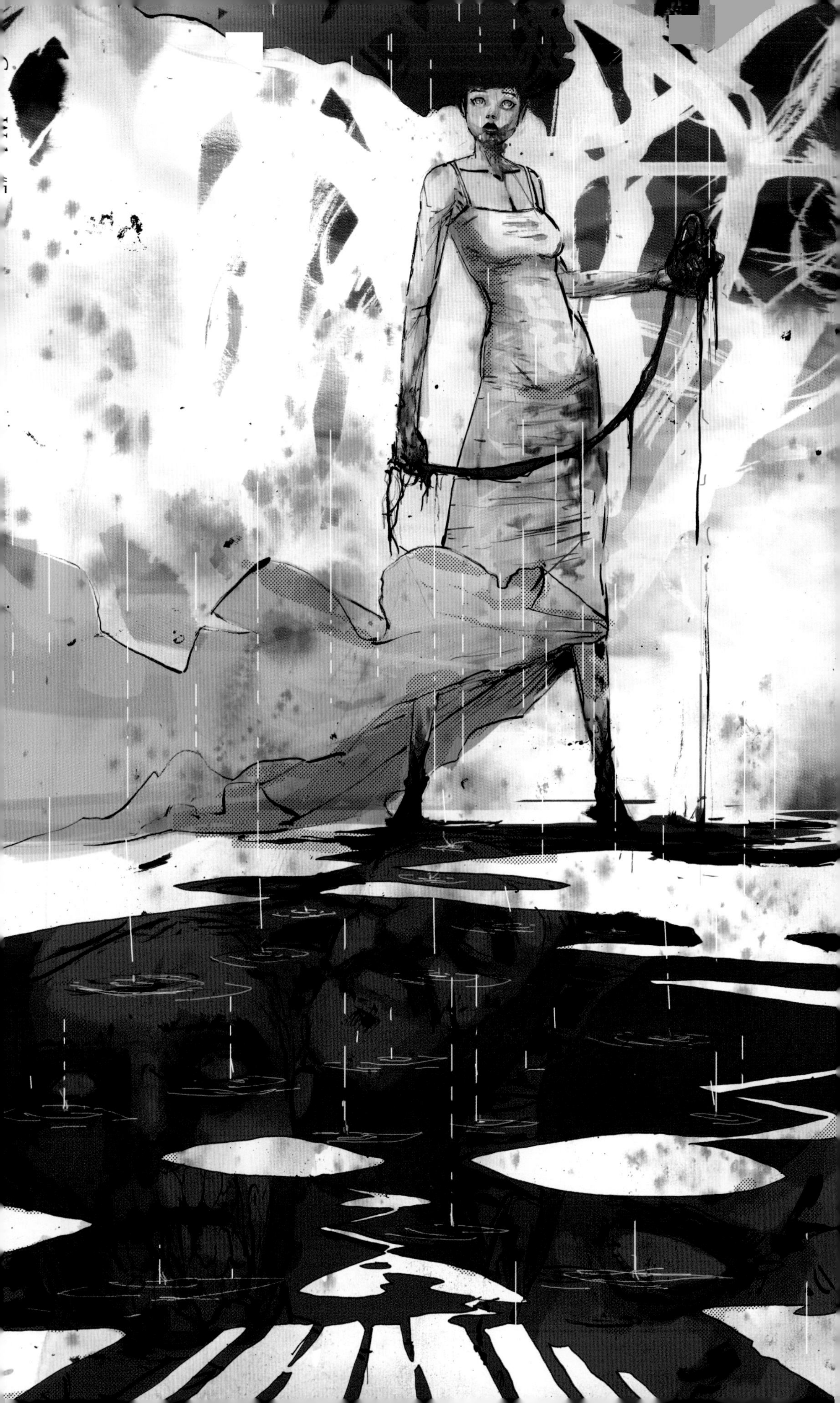

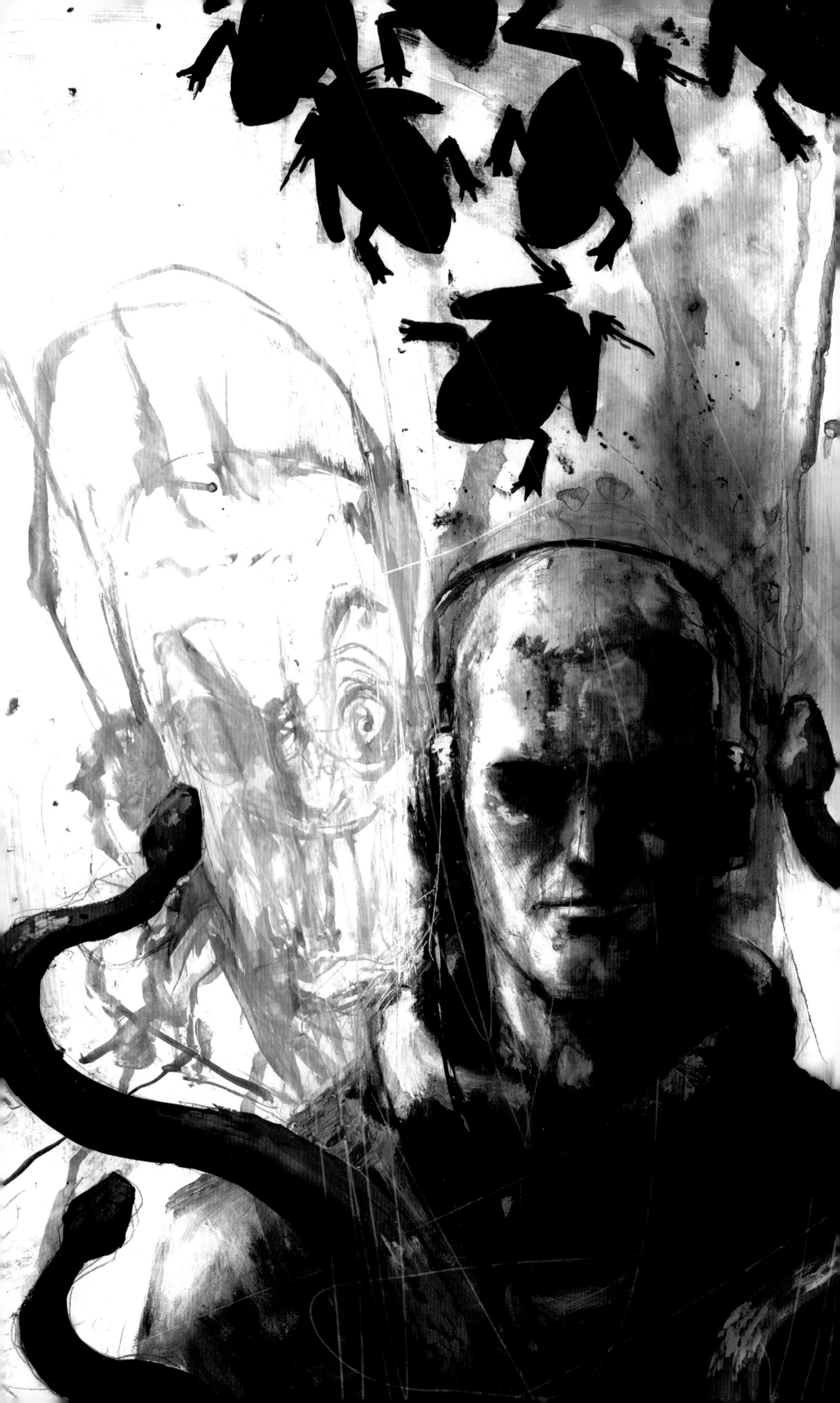

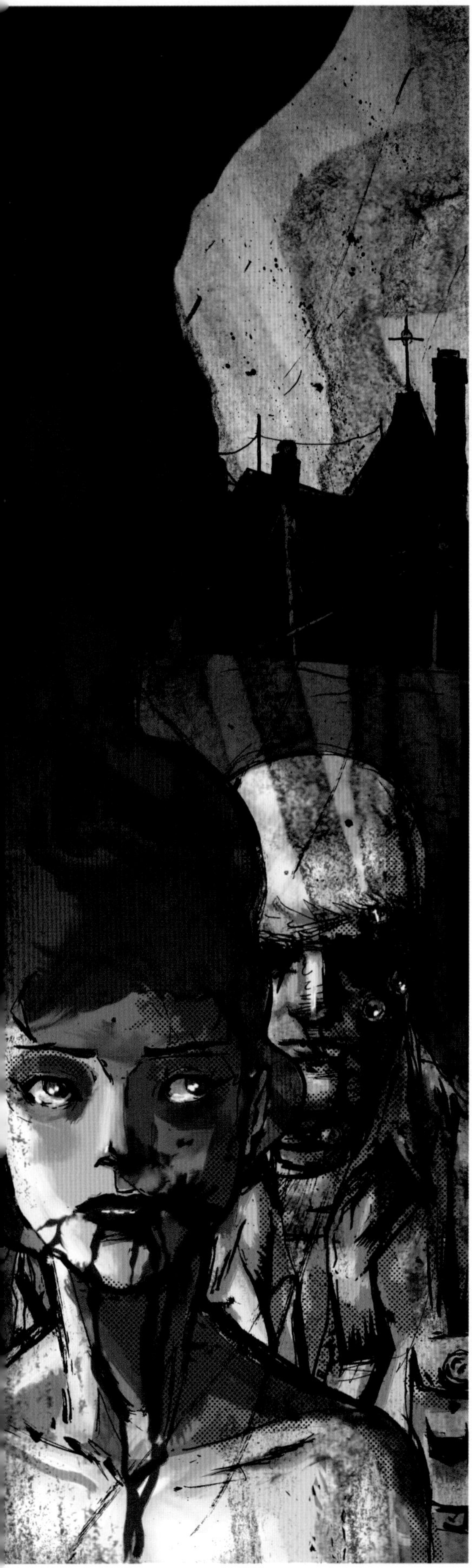

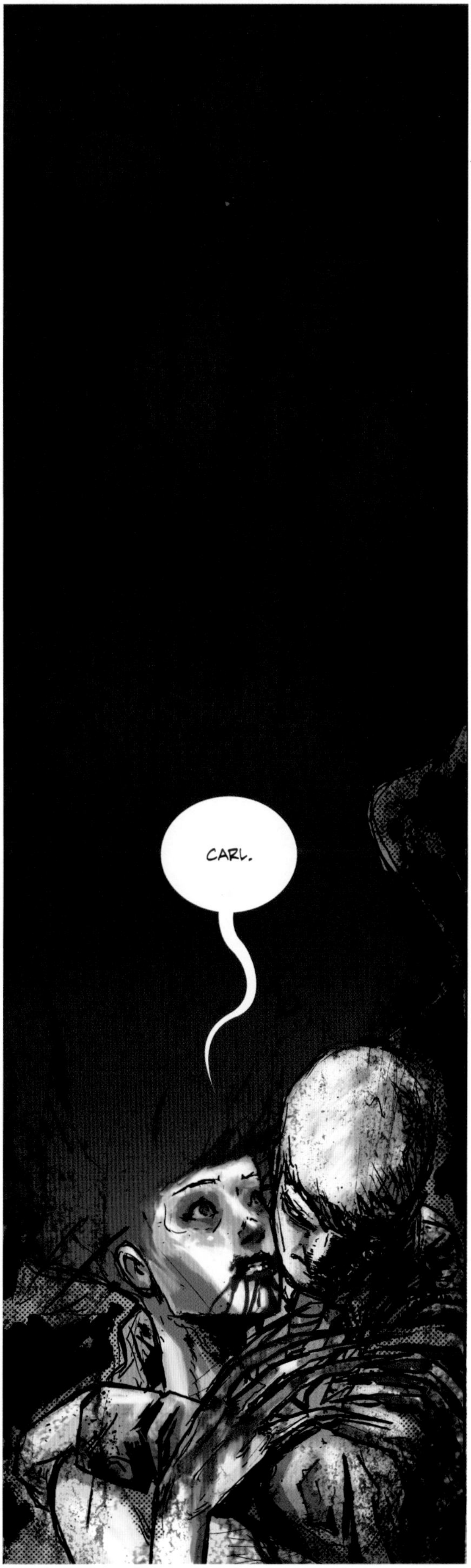
CARL.

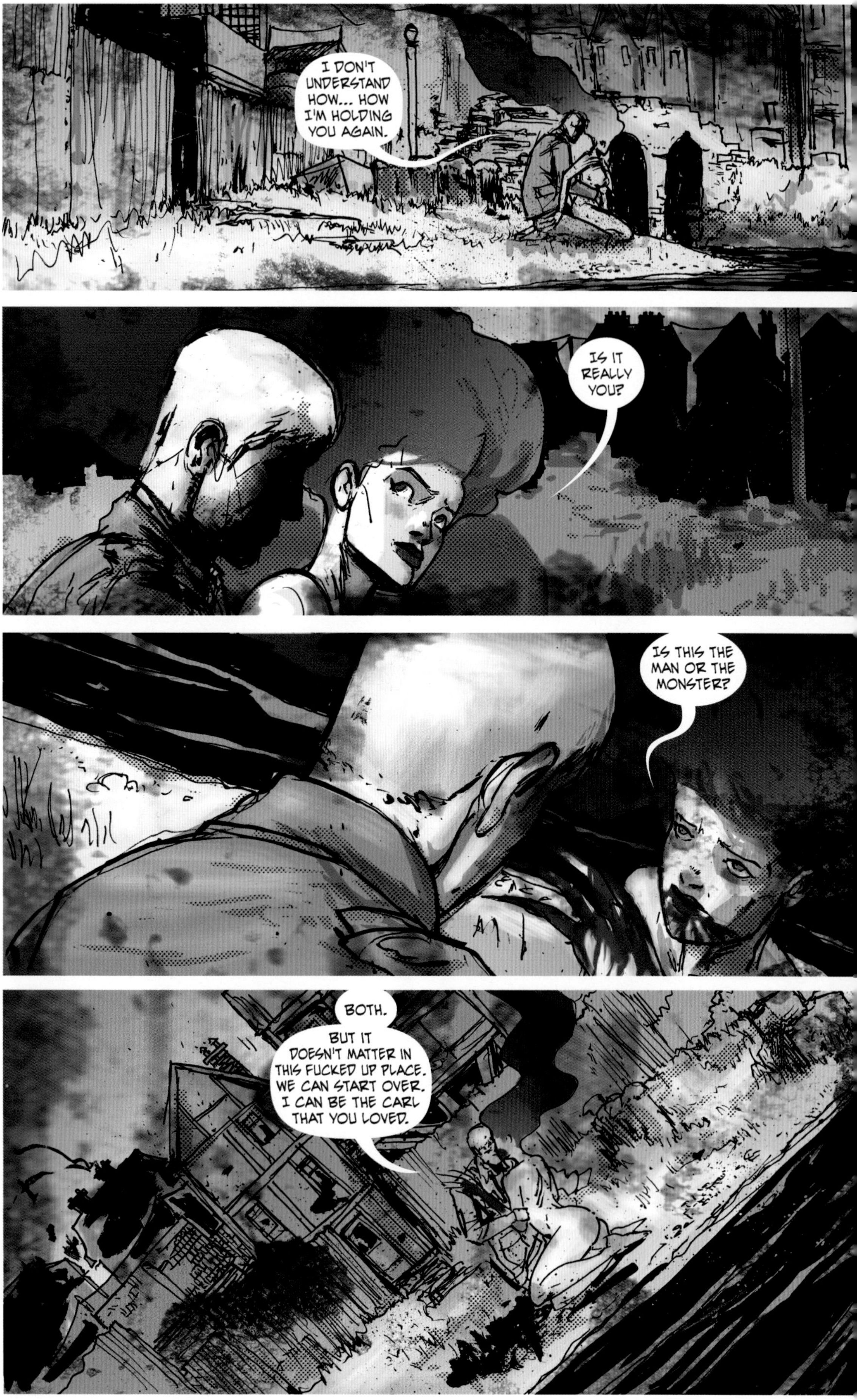
I DON'T UNDERSTAND HOW... HOW I'M HOLDING YOU AGAIN.
IS IT REALLY YOU?
IS THIS THE MAN OR THE MONSTER?
BOTH.
BUT IT DOESN'T MATTER IN THIS FUCKED UP PLACE. WE CAN START OVER. I CAN BE THE CARL THAT YOU LOVED.

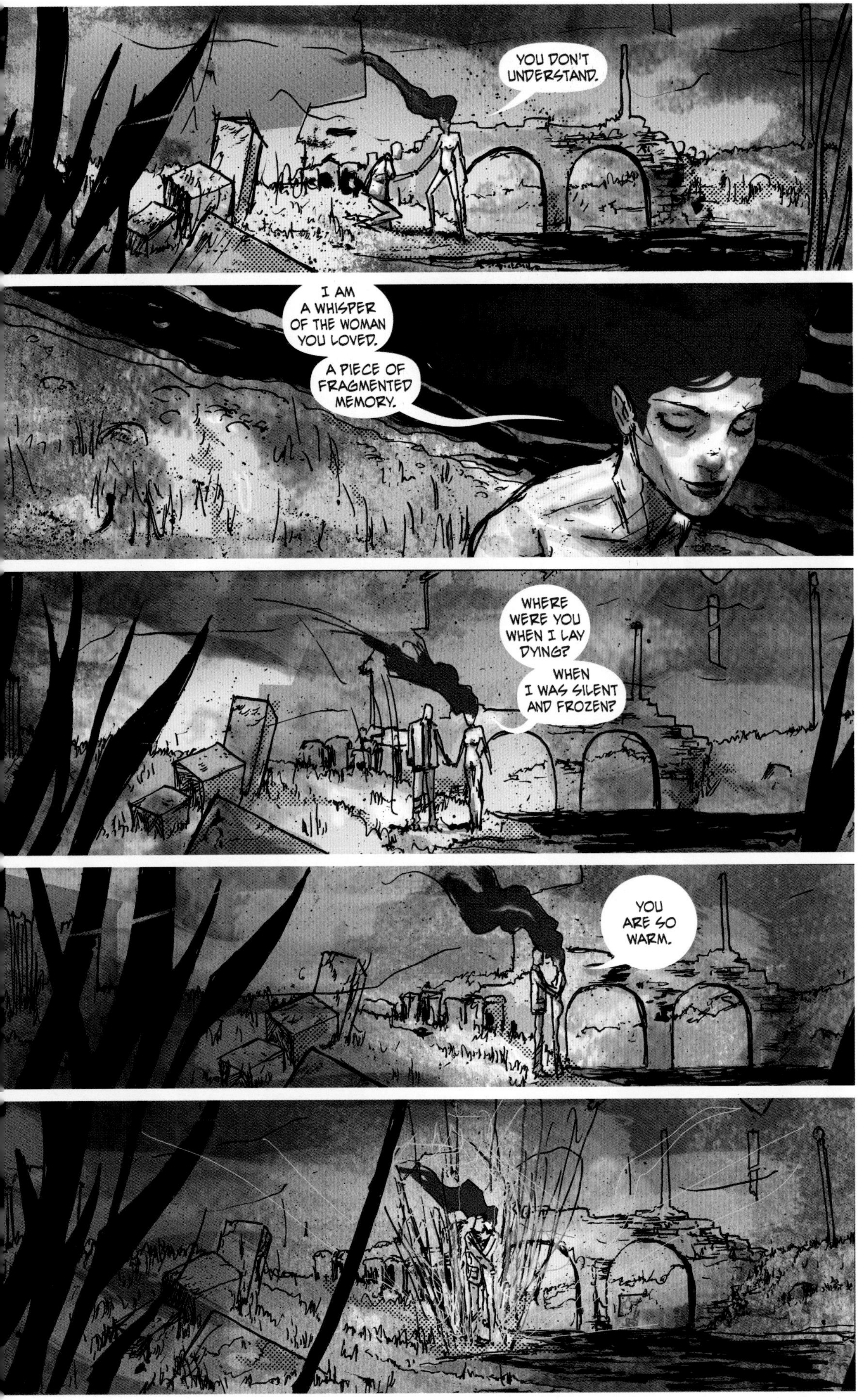
YOU DON'T UNDERSTAND.
I AM A WHISPER OF THE WOMAN YOU LOVED.
A PIECE OF FRAGMENTED MEMORY.
WHERE WERE YOU WHEN I LAY DYING?
WHEN I WAS SILENT AND FROZEN?
YOU ARE SO WARM.

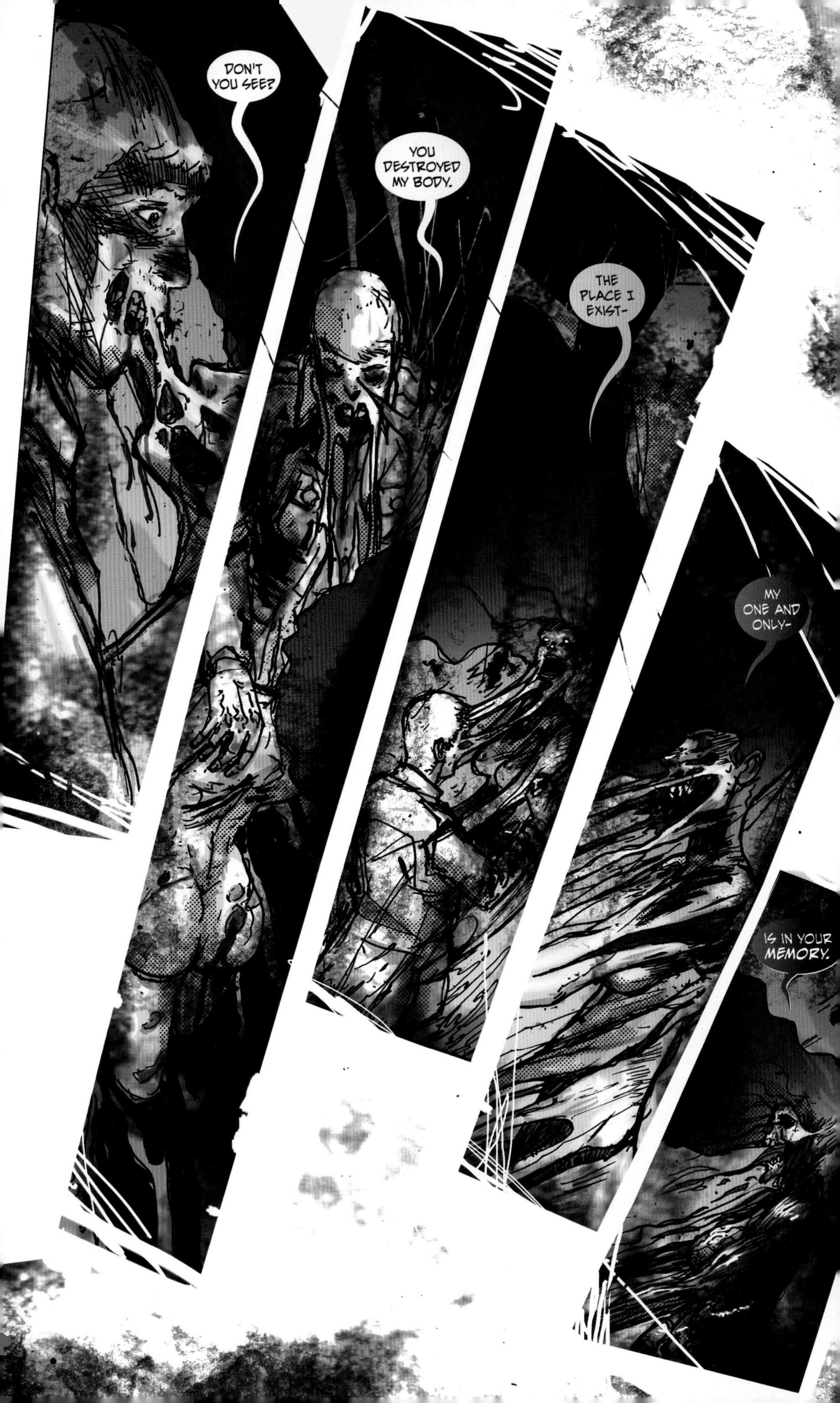

DON'T YOU SEE?
YOU DESTROYED MY BODY.
THE PLACE I EXIST-
MY ONE AND ONLY-
IS IN YOUR MEMORY.

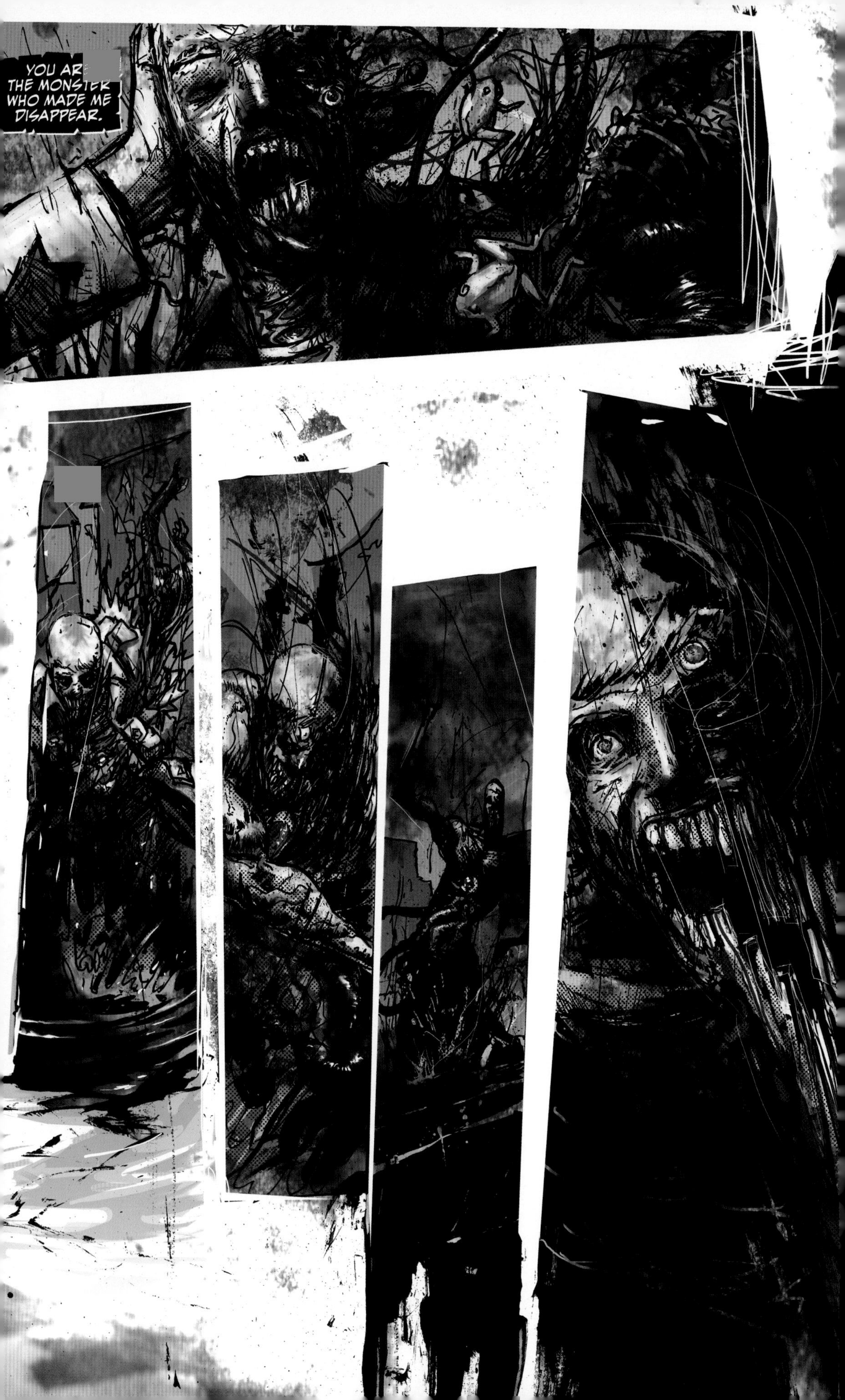
YOU AR
THE MONSTER
WHO MADE ME
DISAPPEAR.

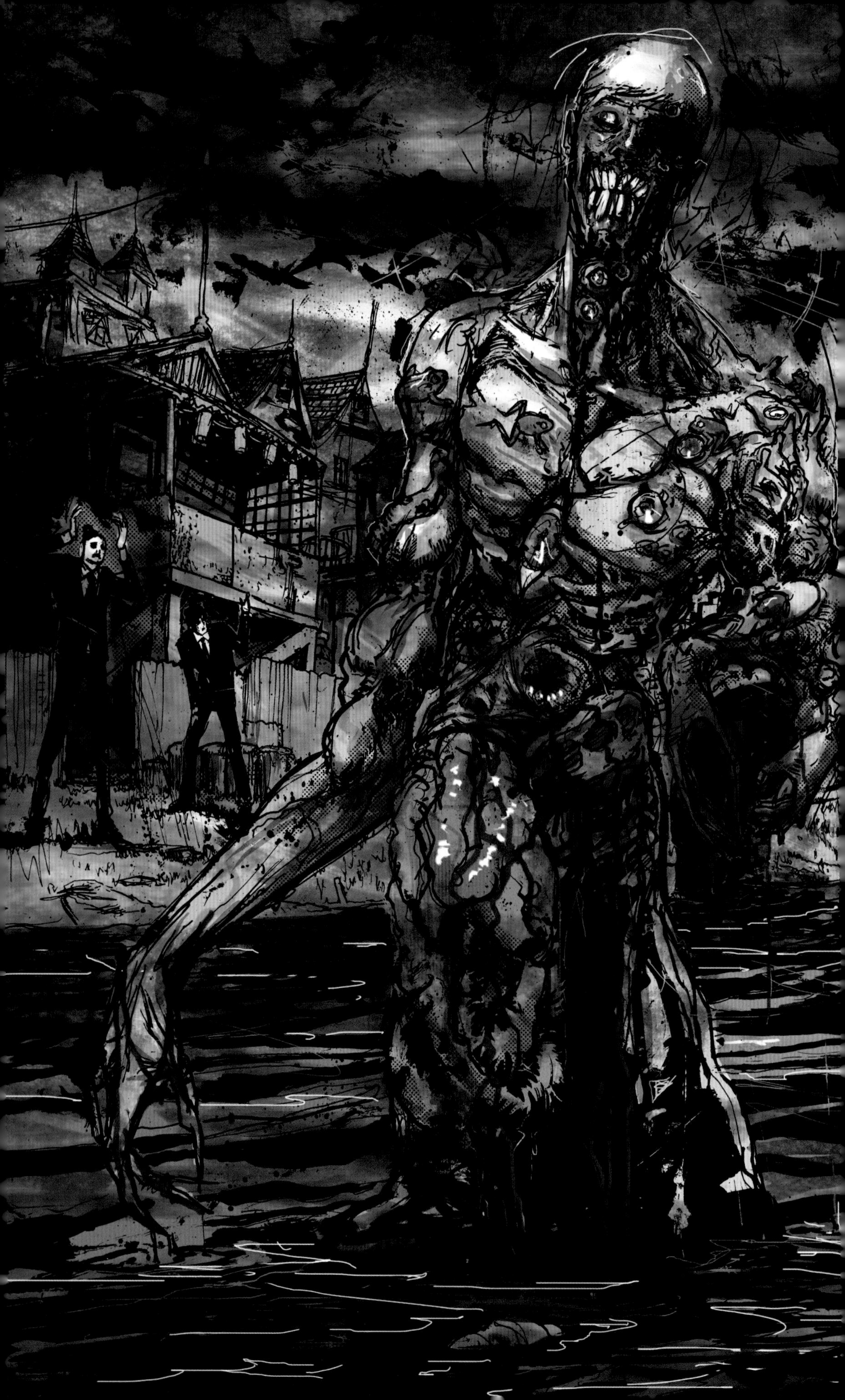

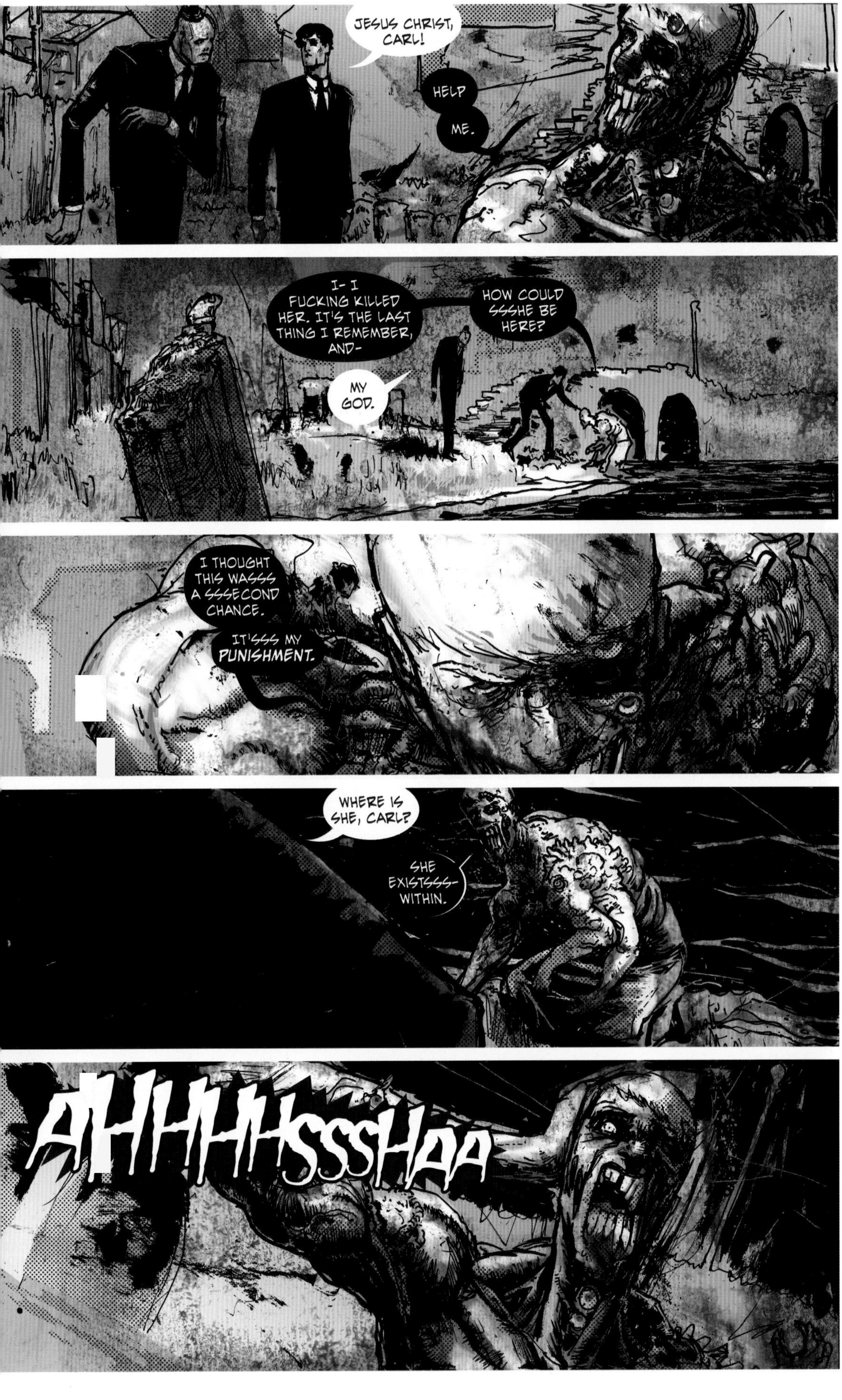

JESUS CHRIST, CARL!
HELP
ME.
I- I FUCKING KILLED HER. IT'S THE LAST THING I REMEMBER, AND-
HOW COULD SSSHE BE HERE?
MY GOD.
I THOUGHT THIS WASSS A SSSECOND CHANCE.
IT'SSS MY PUNISHMENT.
WHERE IS SHE, CARL?
SHE EXISTSSS- WITHIN.
AHHHHSSSHAA

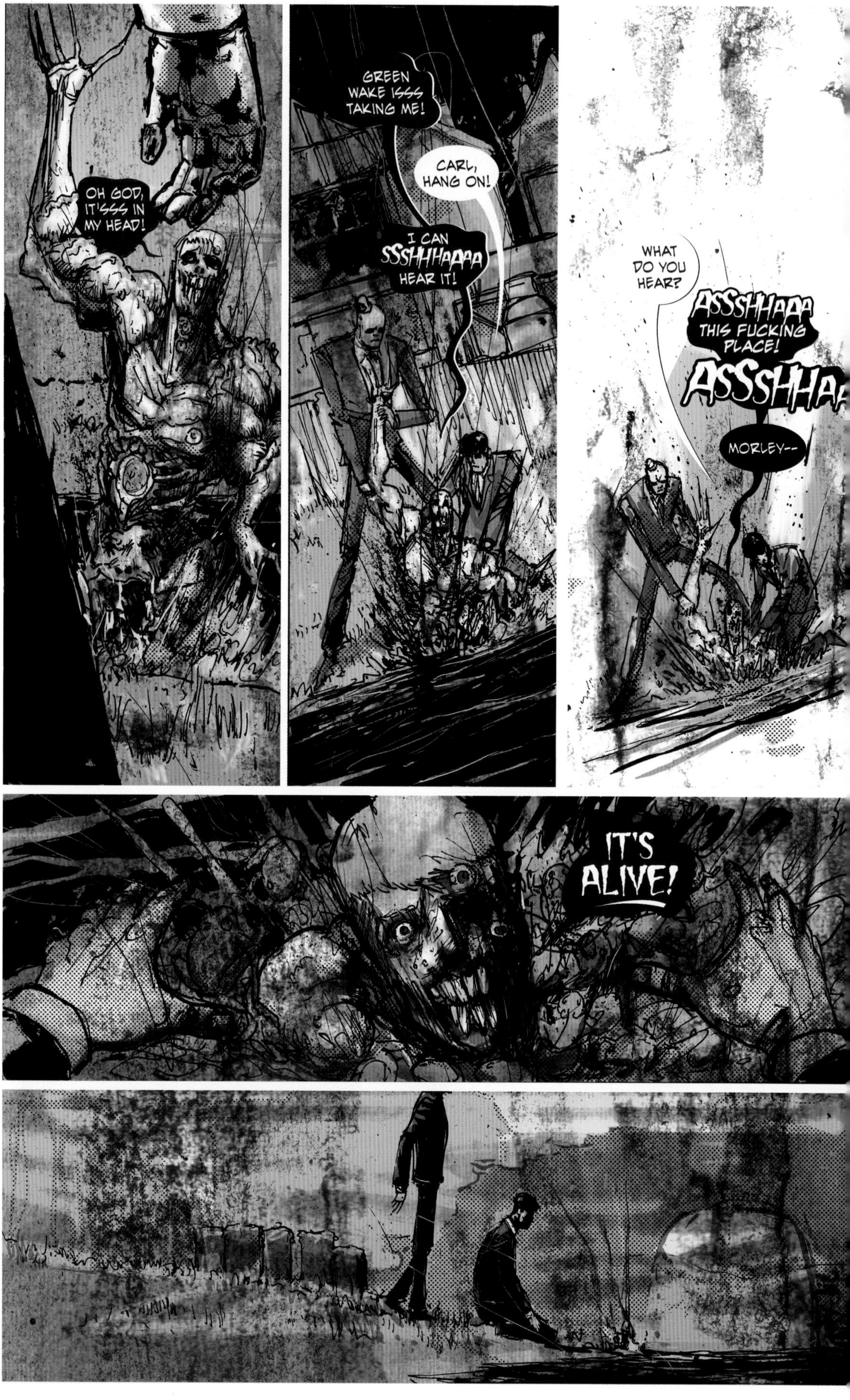
OH GOD, IT'SSS IN MY HEAD!
GREEN WAKE ISSS TAKING ME!
CARL, HANG ON!
I CAN SSSHHAAAA HEAR IT!
WHAT DO YOU HEAR?
ASSSHHAAA THIS FUCKING PLACE! ASSSHHA
MORLEY--
IT'S ALIVE!

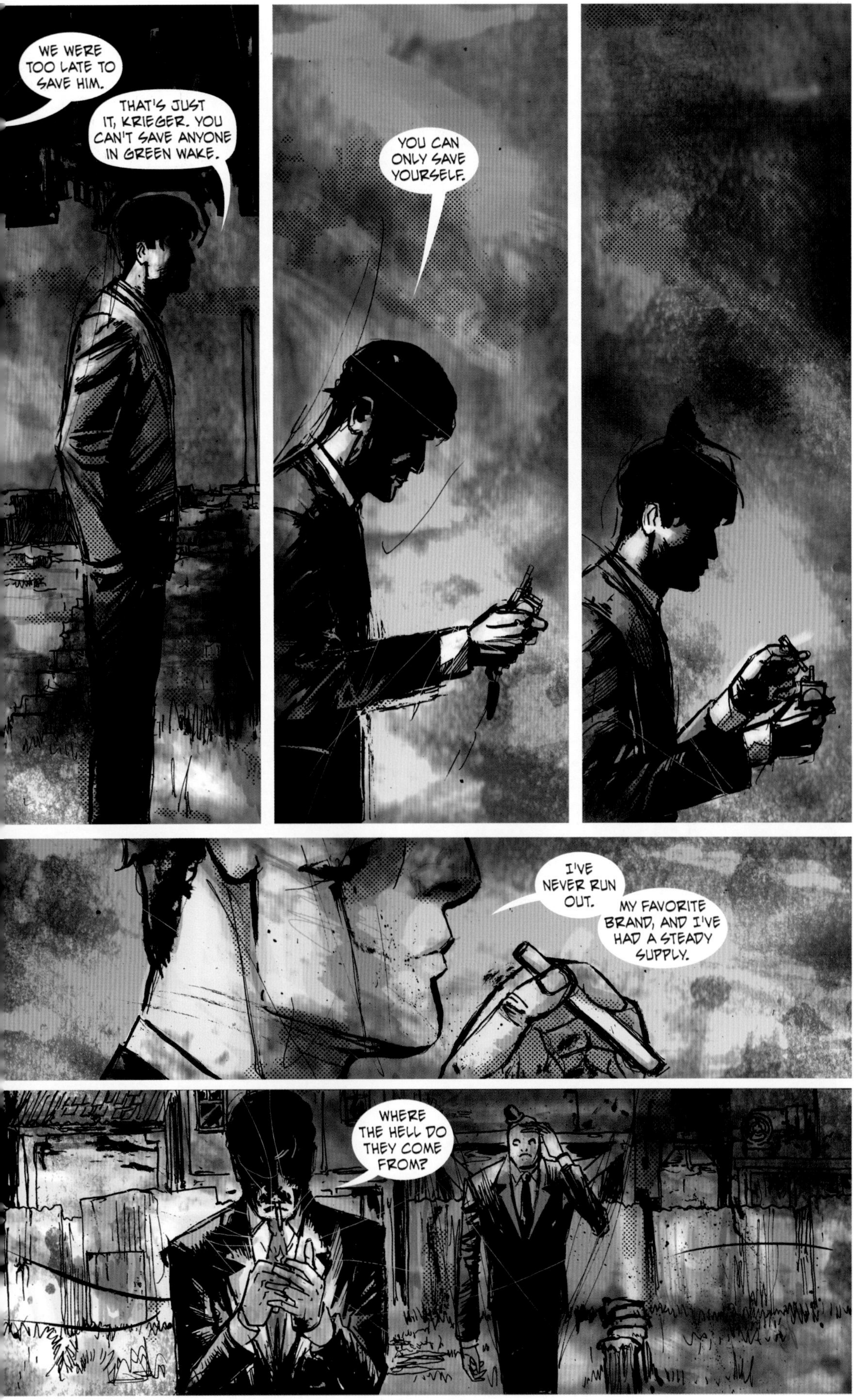
WE WERE TOO LATE TO SAVE HIM.
THAT'S JUST IT, KRIEGER. YOU CAN'T SAVE ANYONE IN GREEN WAKE.
YOU CAN ONLY SAVE YOURSELF.
I'VE NEVER RUN OUT.
MY FAVORITE BRAND, AND I'VE HAD A STEADY SUPPLY.
WHERE THE HELL DO THEY COME FROM?

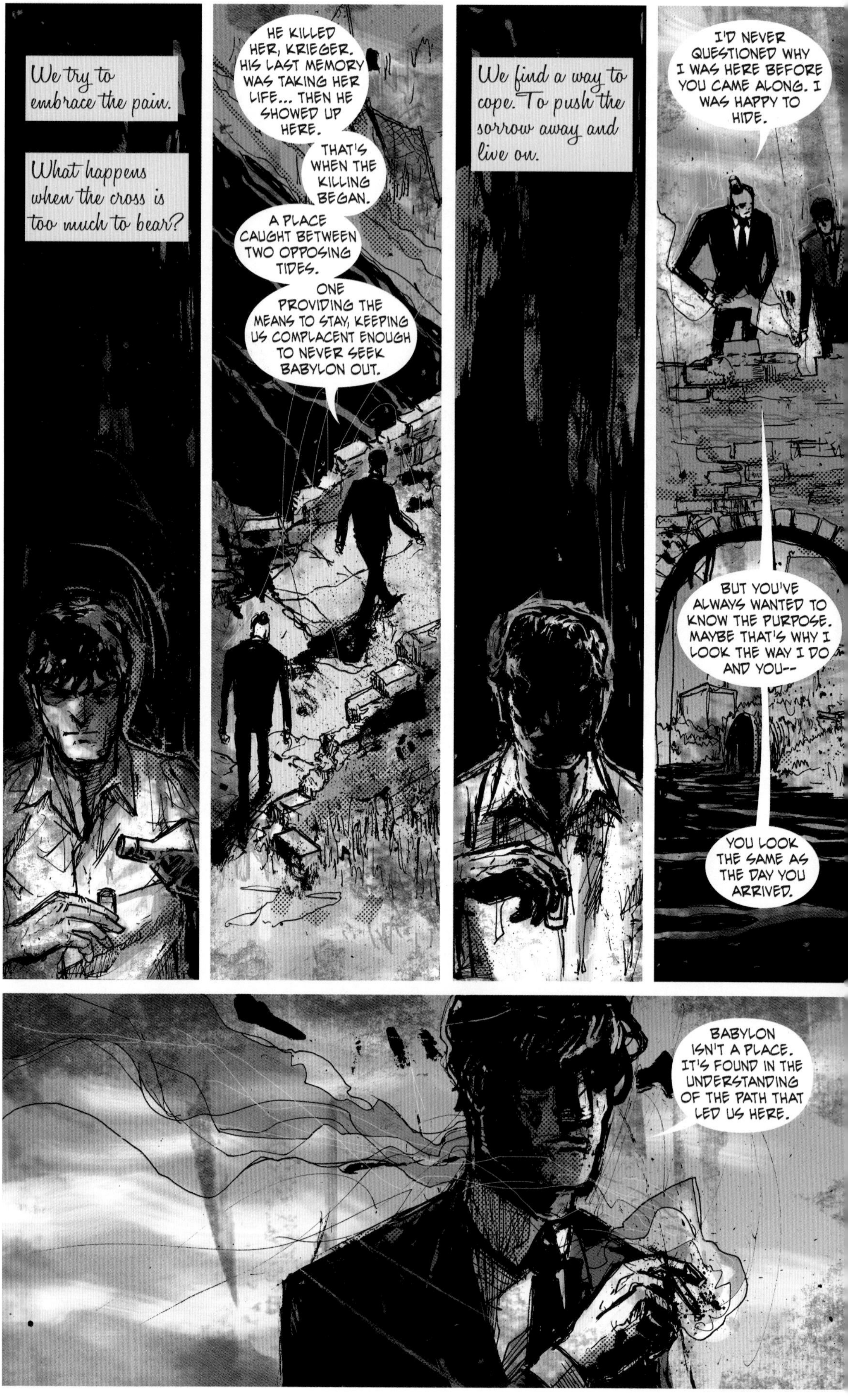

We try to embrace the pain.
What happens when the cross is too much to bear?
HE KILLED HER, KRIEGER. HIS LAST MEMORY WAS TAKING HER LIFE... THEN HE SHOWED UP HERE.
THAT'S WHEN THE KILLING BEGAN.
A PLACE CAUGHT BETWEEN TWO OPPOSING TIDES.
ONE PROVIDING THE MEANS TO STAY, KEEPING US COMPLACENT ENOUGH TO NEVER SEEK BABYLON OUT.
We find a way to cope. To push the sorrow away and live on.
I'D NEVER QUESTIONED WHY I WAS HERE BEFORE YOU CAME ALONG. I WAS HAPPY TO HIDE.
BUT YOU'VE ALWAYS WANTED TO KNOW THE PURPOSE. MAYBE THAT'S WHY I LOOK THE WAY I DO AND YOU--
YOU LOOK THE SAME AS THE DAY YOU ARRIVED.
BABYLON ISN'T A PLACE. IT'S FOUND IN THE UNDERSTANDING OF THE PATH THAT LED US HERE.

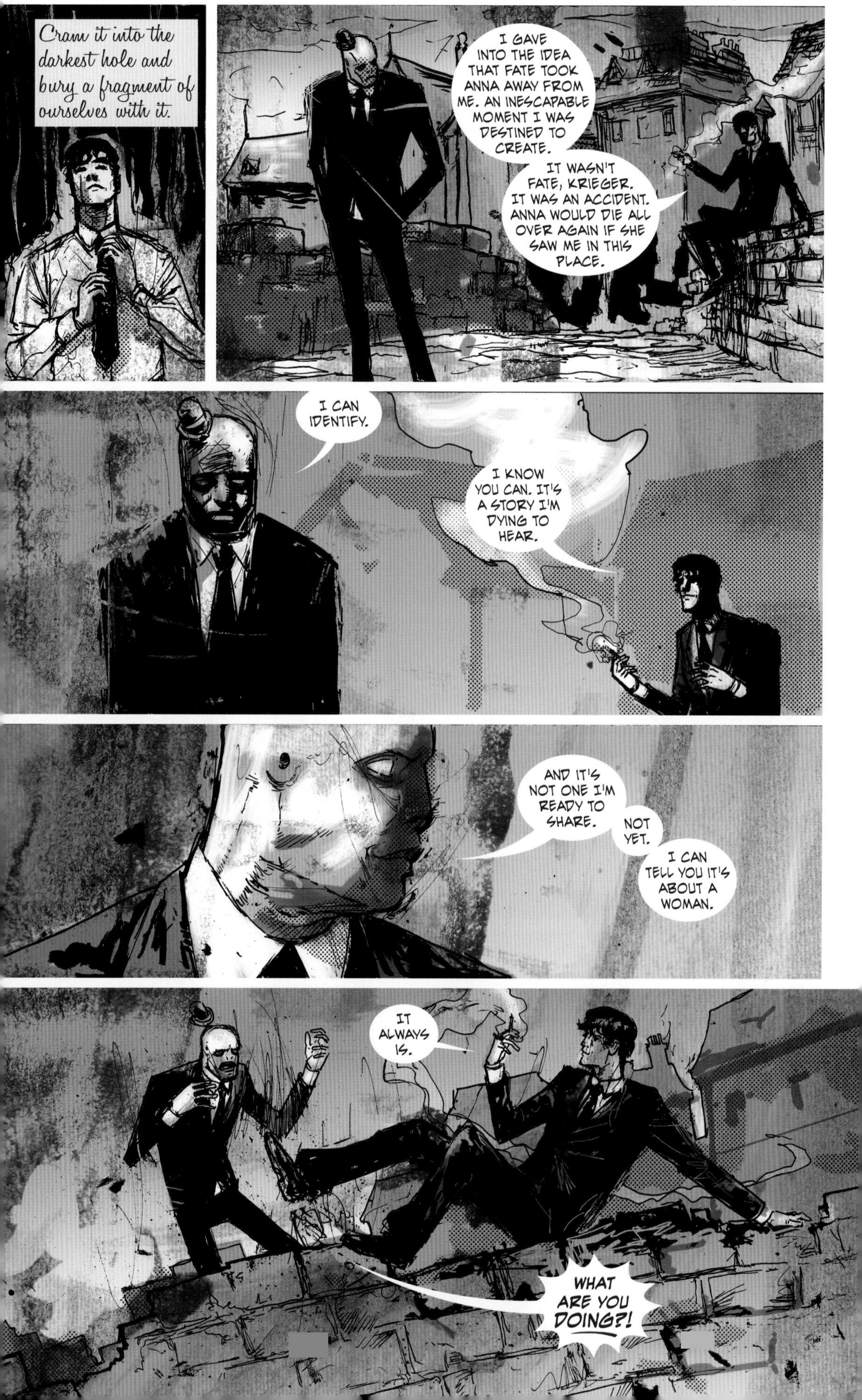
Cram it into the darkest hole and bury a fragment of ourselves with it.
I GAVE INTO THE IDEA THAT FATE TOOK ANNA AWAY FROM ME. AN INESCAPABLE MOMENT I WAS DESTINED TO CREATE.
IT WASN'T FATE, KRIEGER. IT WAS AN ACCIDENT. ANNA WOULD DIE ALL OVER AGAIN IF SHE SAW ME IN THIS PLACE.
I CAN IDENTIFY.
I KNOW YOU CAN. IT'S A STORY I'M DYING TO HEAR.
AND IT'S NOT ONE I'M READY TO SHARE.
NOT YET.
I CAN TELL YOU IT'S ABOUT A WOMAN.
IT ALWAYS IS.
WHAT ARE YOU DOING?!

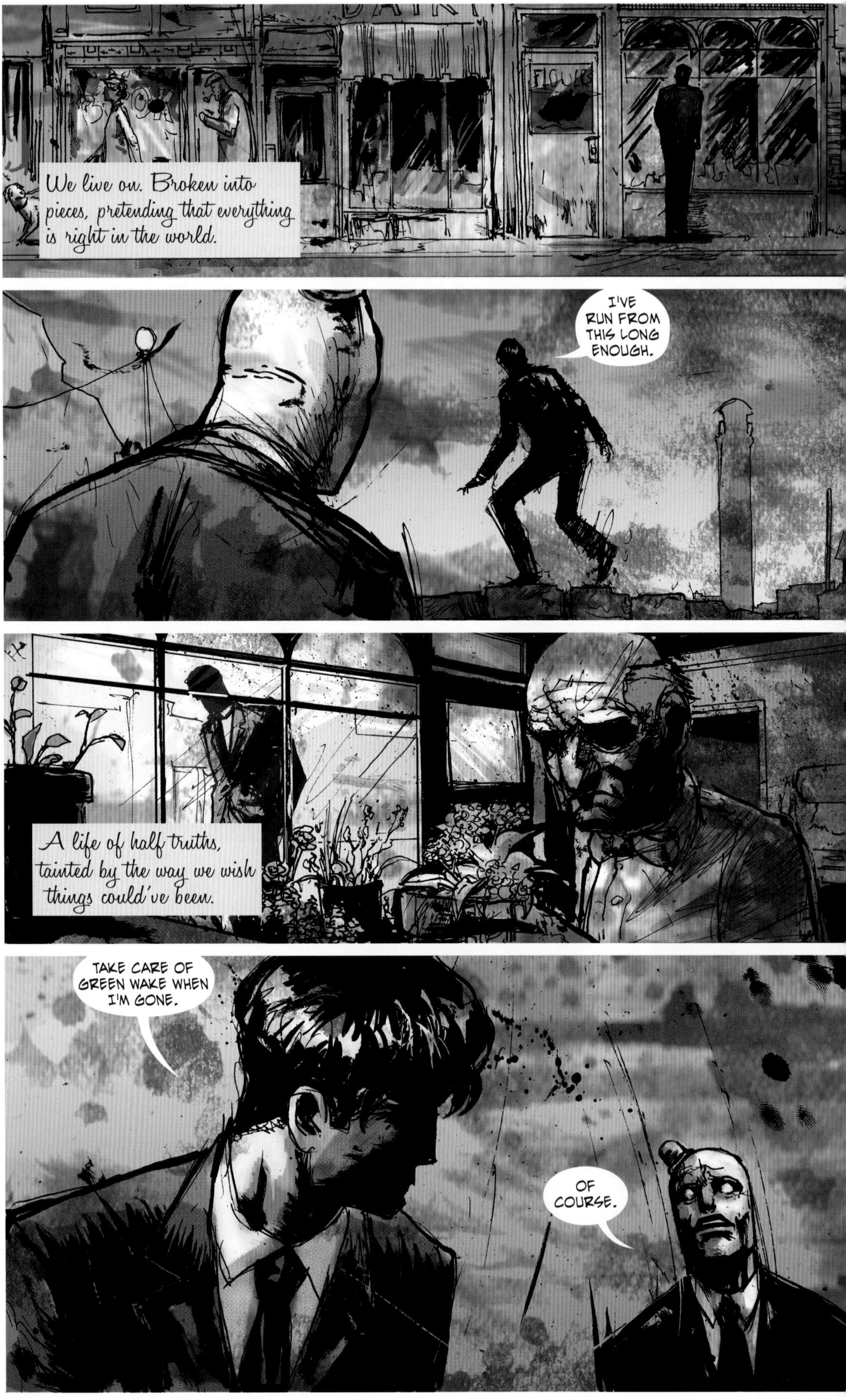
We live on. Broken into pieces, pretending that everything is right in the world.
I'VE RUN FROM THIS LONG ENOUGH.
A life of half truths, tainted by the way we wish things could've been.
TAKE CARE OF GREEN WAKE WHEN I'M GONE.
OF COURSE.

If you're lucky, you don't forget.

ONE LAST THING. WHATEVER HAPPENED BEFORE... SOMETIMES IT'S OUT OF OUR HANDS. THE BEST WE CAN DO IS LEARN TO FORGIVE OURSELVES.

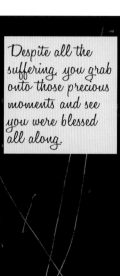

Despite all the suffering, you grab onto those precious moments and see you were blessed all along.

IT'S BEEN A PLEASURE.

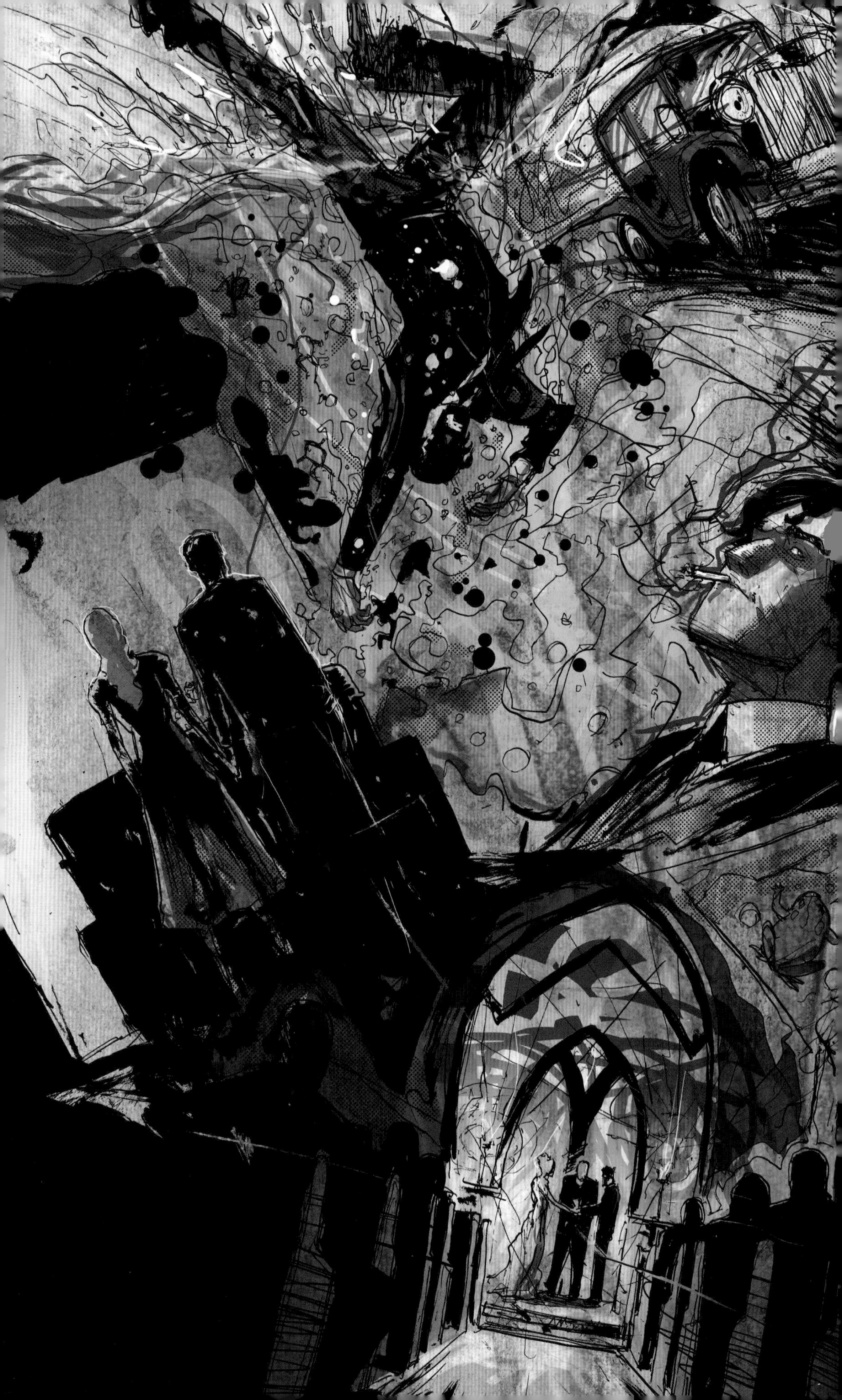

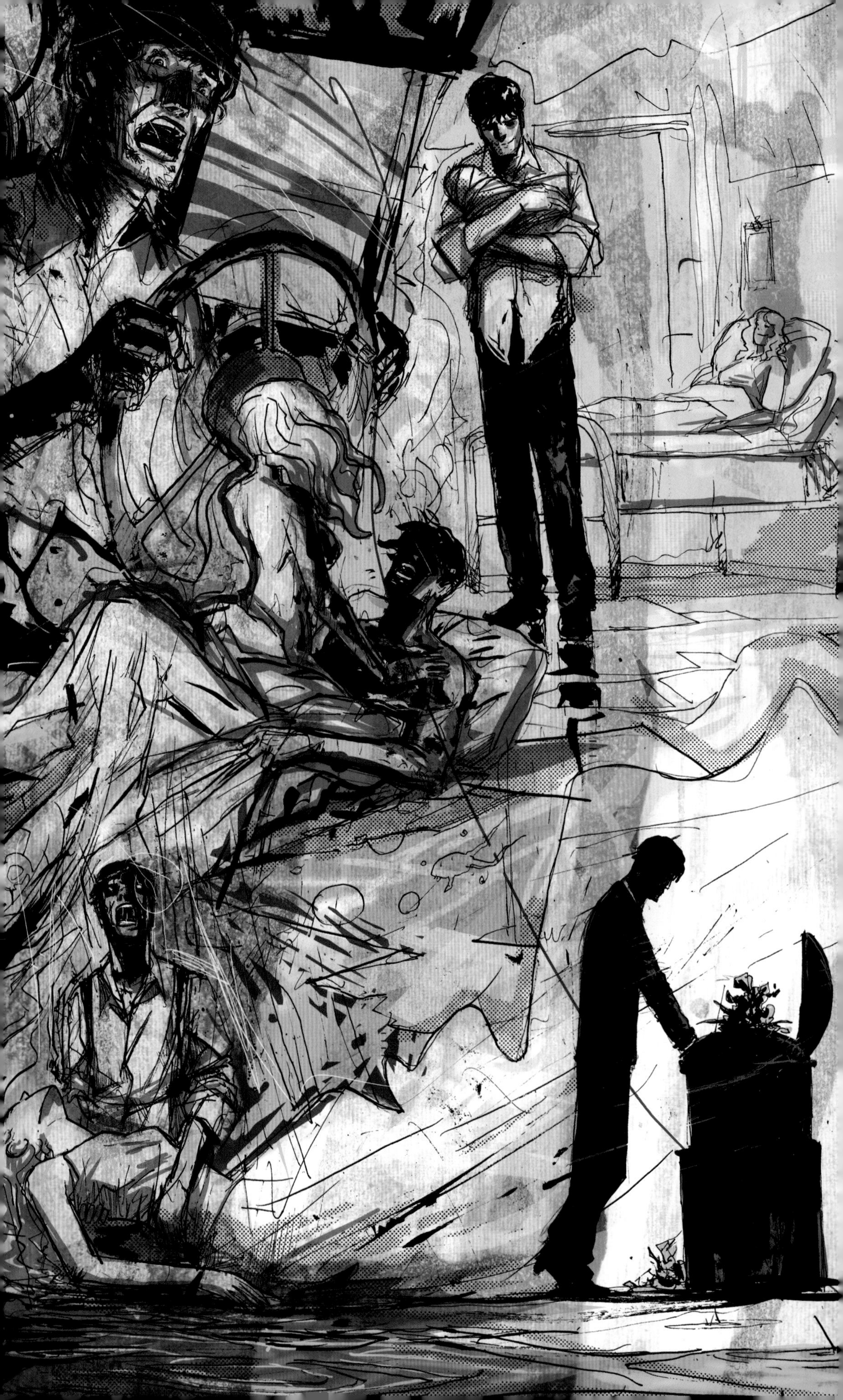

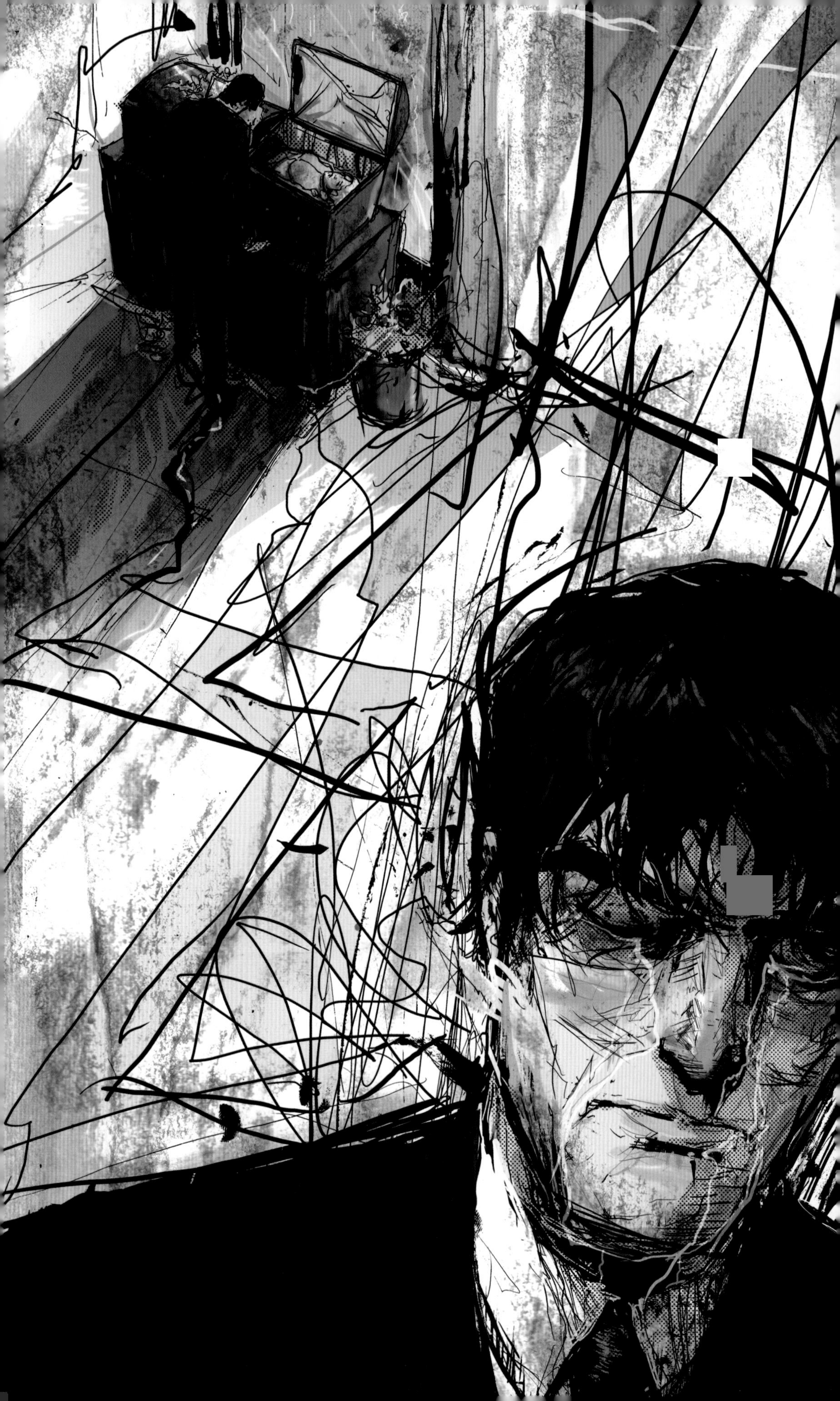

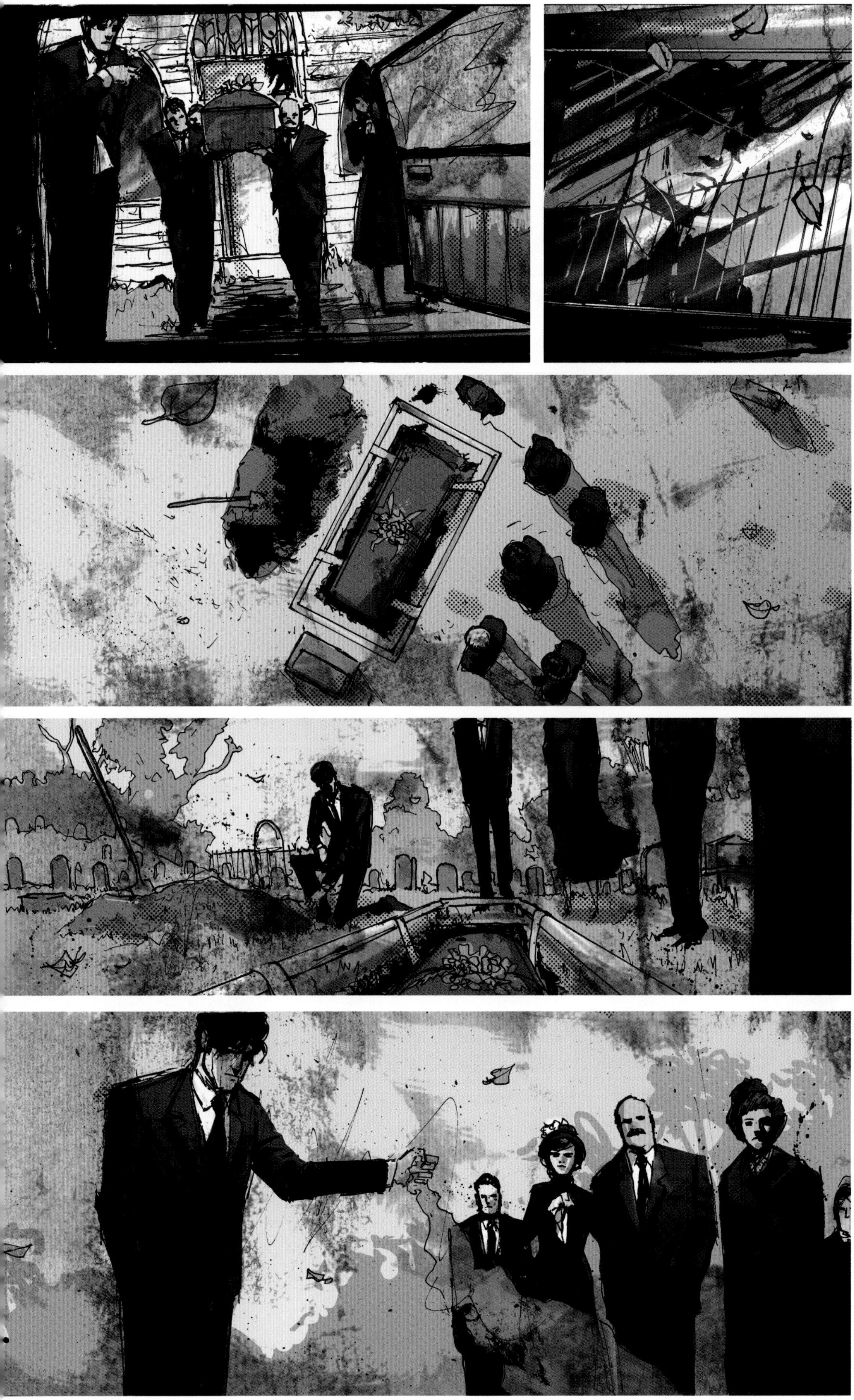

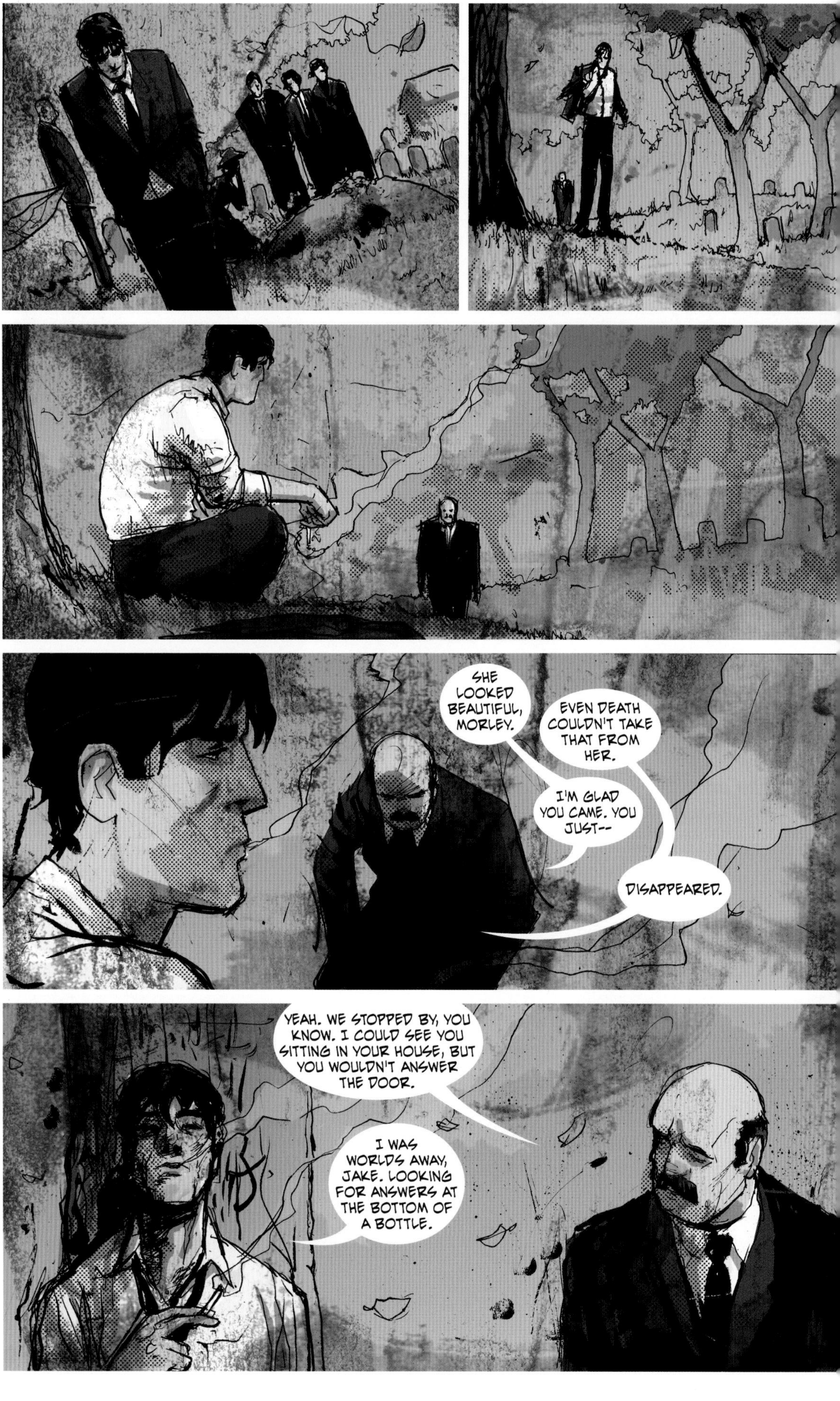
SHE LOOKED BEAUTIFUL, MORLEY.
EVEN DEATH COULDN'T TAKE THAT FROM HER.
I'M GLAD YOU CAME. YOU JUST--
DISAPPEARED.
YEAH. WE STOPPED BY, YOU KNOW. I COULD SEE YOU SITTING IN YOUR HOUSE, BUT YOU WOULDN'T ANSWER THE DOOR.
I WAS WORLDS AWAY, JAKE. LOOKING FOR ANSWERS AT THE BOTTOM OF A BOTTLE.

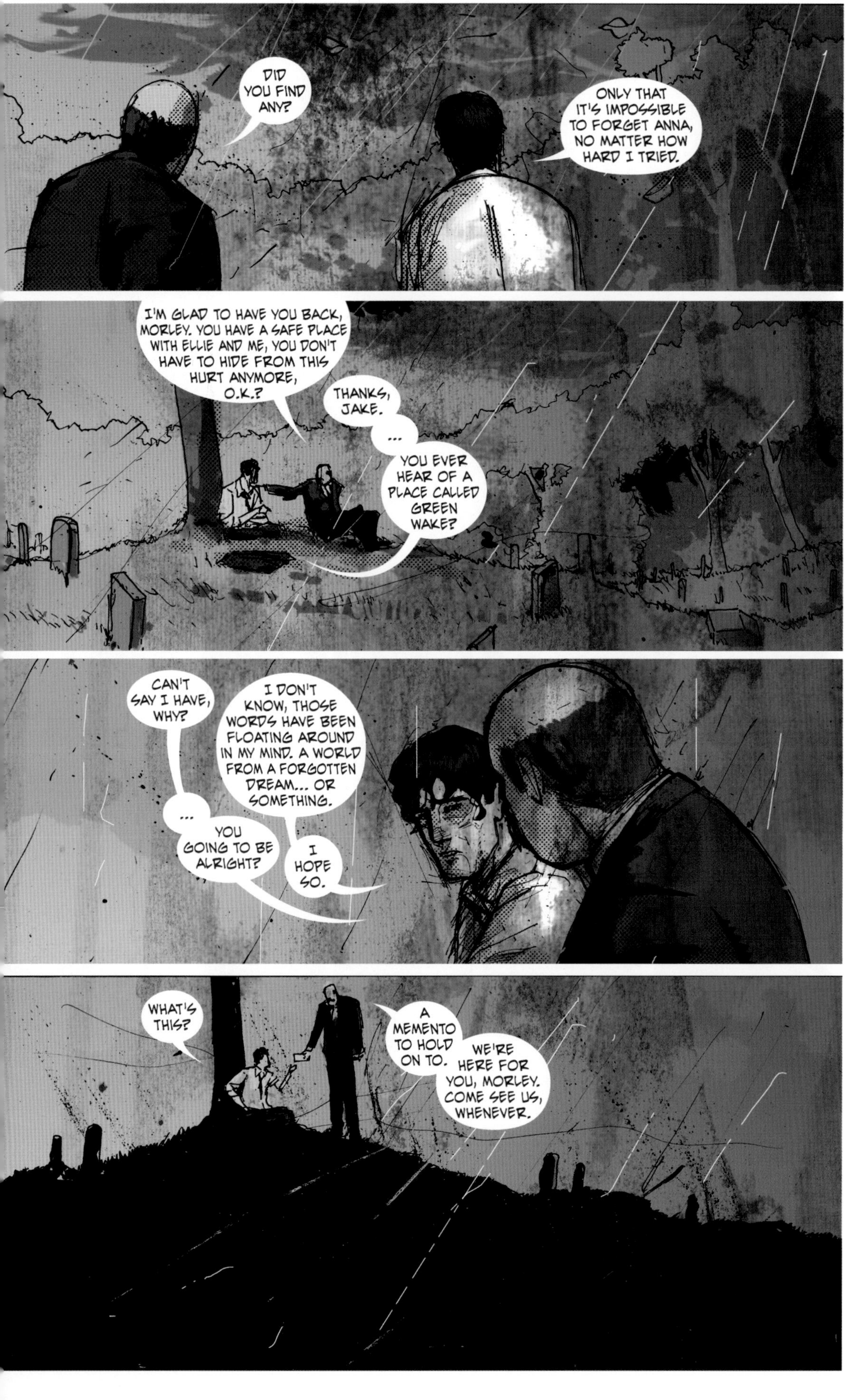
DID YOU FIND ANY?
ONLY THAT IT'S IMPOSSIBLE TO FORGET ANNA, NO MATTER HOW HARD I TRIED.
I'M GLAD TO HAVE YOU BACK, MORLEY. YOU HAVE A SAFE PLACE WITH ELLIE AND ME, YOU DON'T HAVE TO HIDE FROM THIS HURT ANYMORE, O.K.?
THANKS, JAKE.
...
YOU EVER HEAR OF A PLACE CALLED GREEN WAKE?
CAN'T SAY I HAVE, WHY?
I DON'T KNOW, THOSE WORDS HAVE BEEN FLOATING AROUND IN MY MIND. A WORLD FROM A FORGOTTEN DREAM... OR SOMETHING.
...
YOU GOING TO BE ALRIGHT?
I HOPE SO.
WHAT'S THIS?
A MEMENTO TO HOLD ON TO.
WE'RE HERE FOR YOU, MORLEY. COME SEE US, WHENEVER.

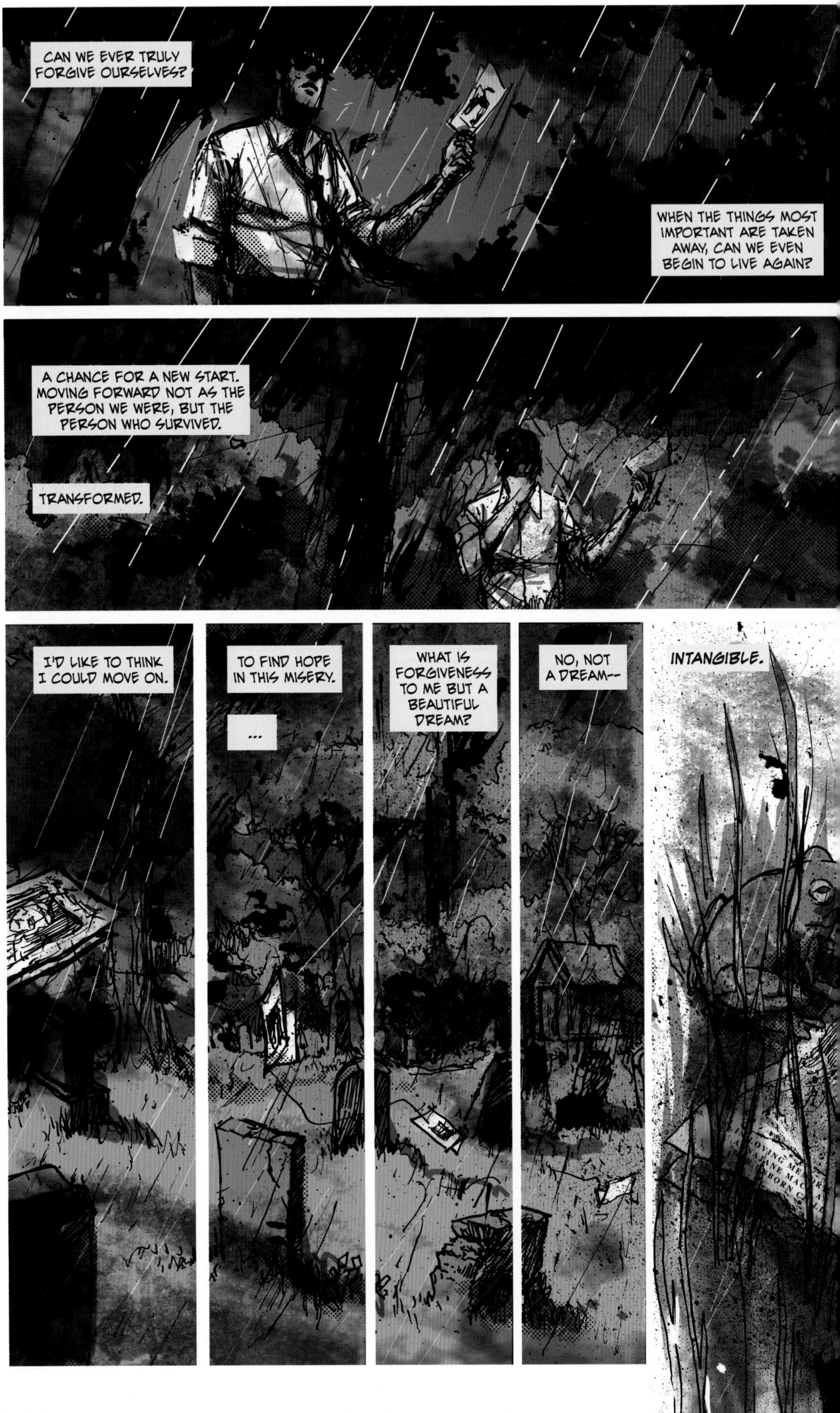
CAN WE EVER TRULY FORGIVE OURSELVES?
WHEN THE THINGS MOST IMPORTANT ARE TAKEN AWAY, CAN WE EVEN BEGIN TO LIVE AGAIN?
A CHANCE FOR A NEW START. MOVING FORWARD NOT AS THE PERSON WE WERE, BUT THE PERSON WHO SURVIVED.
TRANSFORMED.
I'D LIKE TO THINK I COULD MOVE ON.
TO FIND HOPE IN THIS MISERY.
...
WHAT IS FORGIVENESS TO ME BUT A BEAUTIFUL DREAM?
NO, NOT A DREAM--
INTANGIBLE.

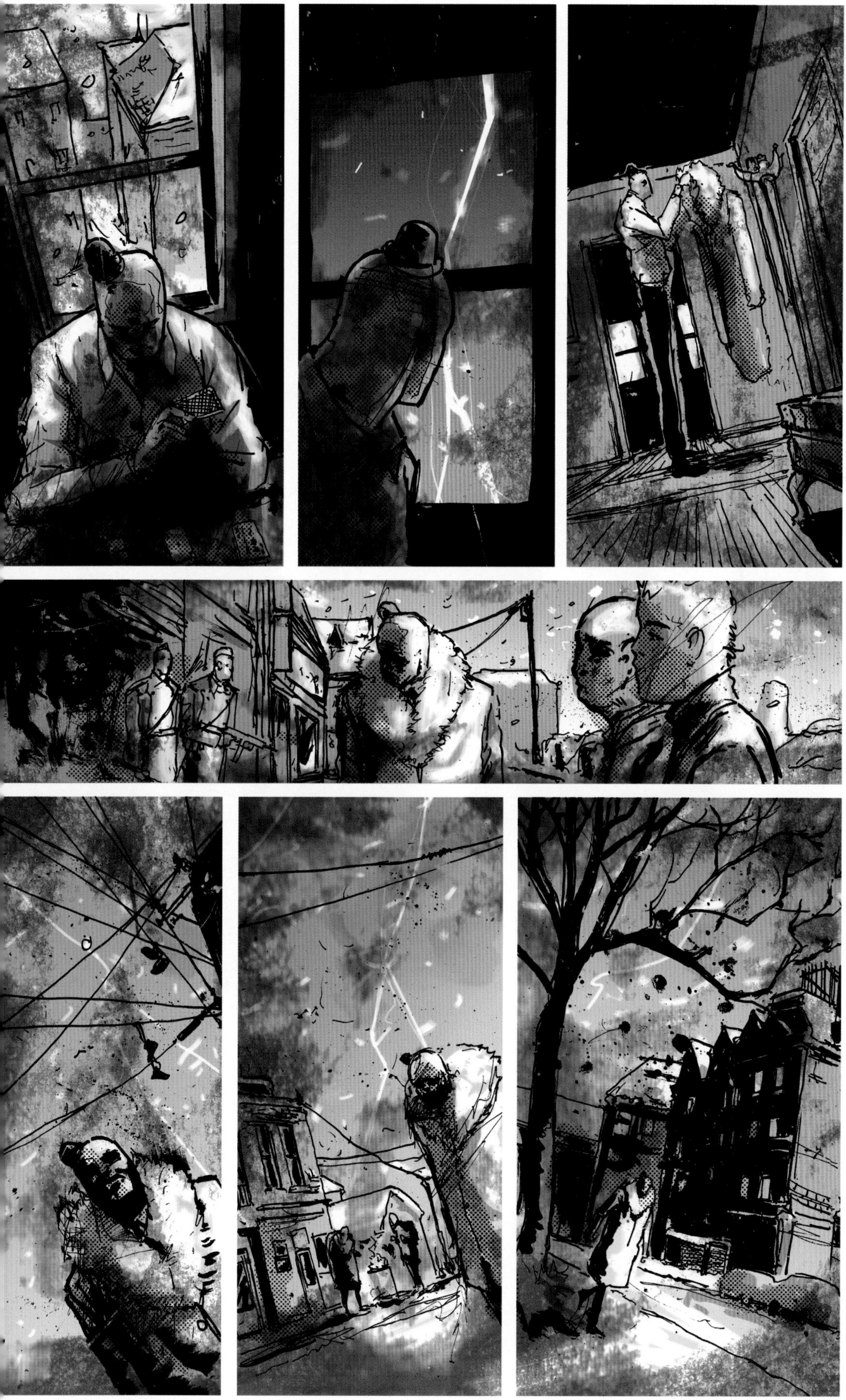

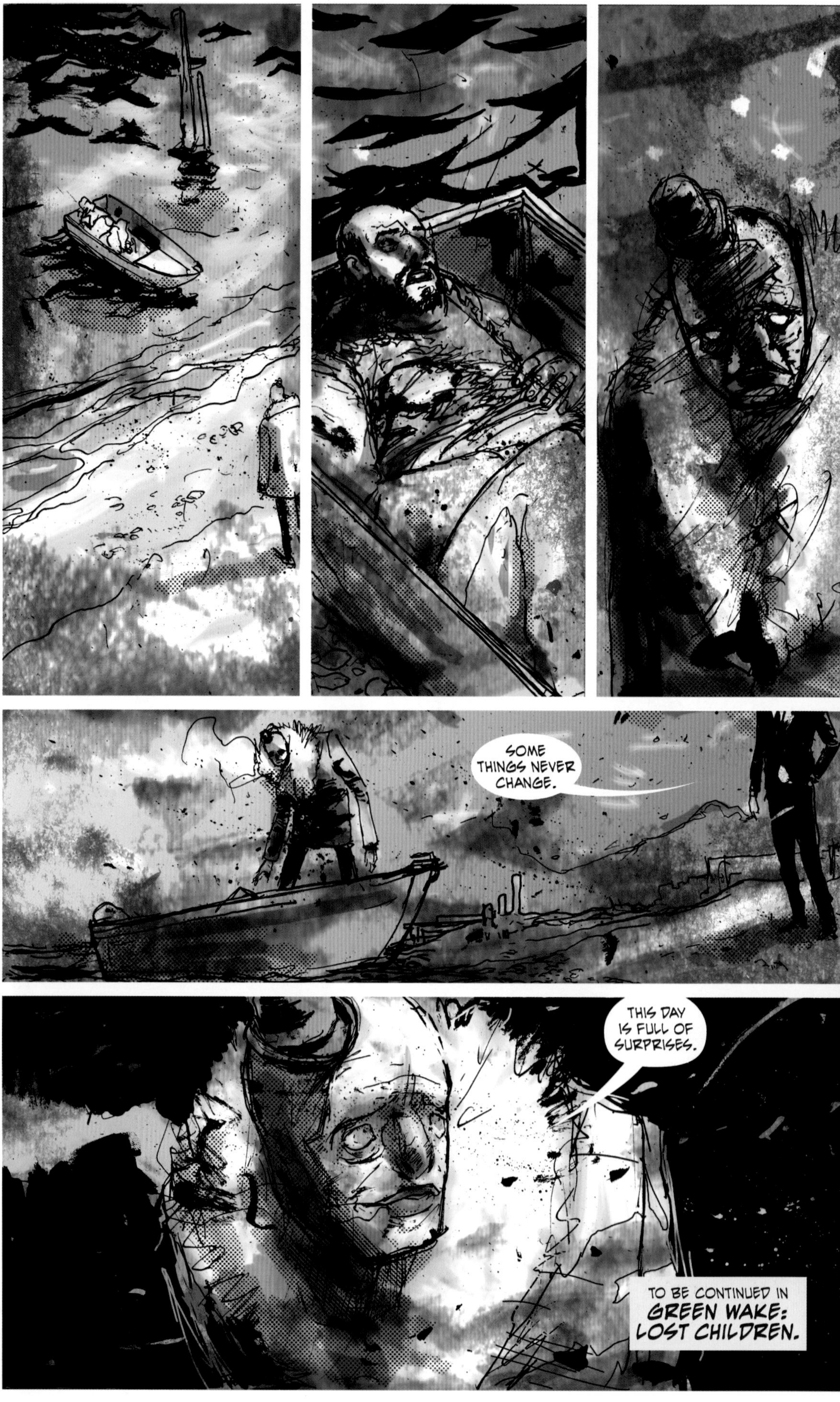
SOME THINGS NEVER CHANGE.
THIS DAY IS FULL OF SURPRISES.
TO BE CONTINUED IN GREEN WAKE: LOST CHILDREN.

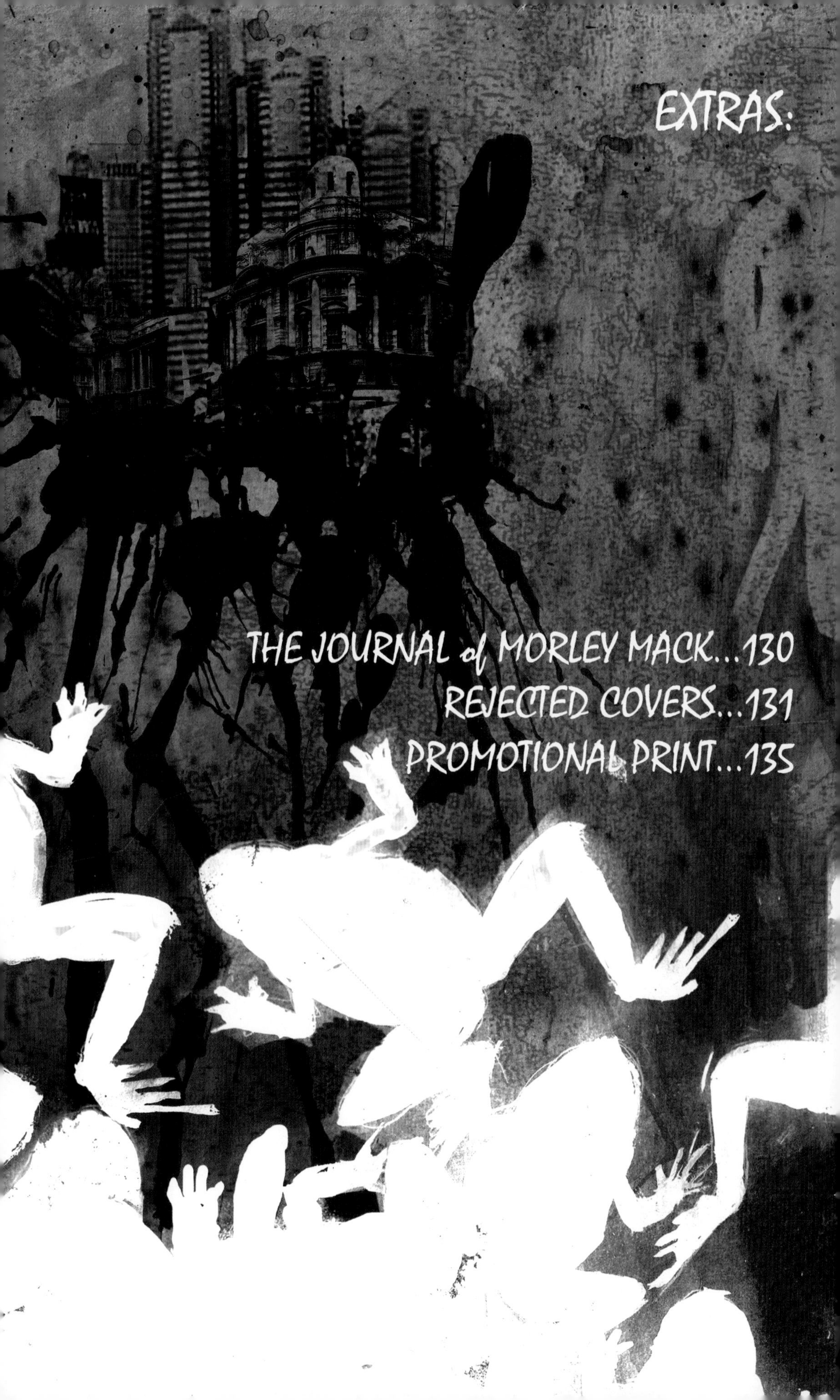

EXTRAS:

The Journal of Morley Mack (as featured on whatisgreenwake.blogspot.com)

Entry #1

"The river is a place I often find myself. It's quiet, but it seems like a thousand thoughts fill my head and I can hear the voices of everyone around me. Even in this place that is filled with residents, it's a ghost town. Green Wake is still a mystery, the people want desperately to be left alone, but I can see it in their eyes that they want to be connected with others. Still, no one leaves their homes.

I've yet to actually speak with anyone, though I've passed people here and there in the street. I'm curious how they, like me, ended up in this strange situation. Tomorrow I plan to introduce myself to someone, and I hope there is conversation to be had.

I can't stop thinking about you, Anna."

Entry #2

I can't tell how long I've been here, hours are difficult to count without any reference. I don't think the sun ever cracks through those clouds, or if it's just evening and the hours pass by slowly. It rains a lot, but there's never thunder. Never lightning. It just rains. Dark and dreary. In some ways, it takes me back to that night. Everything about it feels the same.

Today I was unable to meet anyone. I was ignored by everyone I approached, so I explored. Not long before the rain fell so heavy, I was shivering in my bones and needed shelter. I came across an old building, door unlocked. An old multi-room, multi-story house. Inside, I found a room and warmed up. I'm still here, writing this now. I can see the rain clearing, there's a balcony outside the room.

It's always quiet.

Entry #3

I've settled comfortably into what I'm going to call my temporary home. No one has caused a fuss, and I've been here for a few days now. Last night (night being indistinguishable from day, as previously noted), I decided to really take in the sights, get a feel for this strange old town. I walked for about an hour, the paths and cobbled roads winding this way and that. Nearly impossible to get your bearings.

Eventually, I came to what I assumed to be the edge of town. The tightly packed rows of zig-zag homes faded away and opened to a field, on the horizon a few husks of what I thought to be a farm perhaps. I continued and managed a photograph upon closer inspection.
It's Doug and Ellie's farm. I swear it, by every holy word ever uttered it is the farm, burned to the ground. The layout is exactly as I remember.

How long ago was it that we were there, Anna?

I tried to go further, but Green Wake was on the horizon. I suspected with no sun to guide me I was unable to orientate myself properly. I doubled back and continued that direction.
Green Wake was on the horizon.

I'm losing my mind.

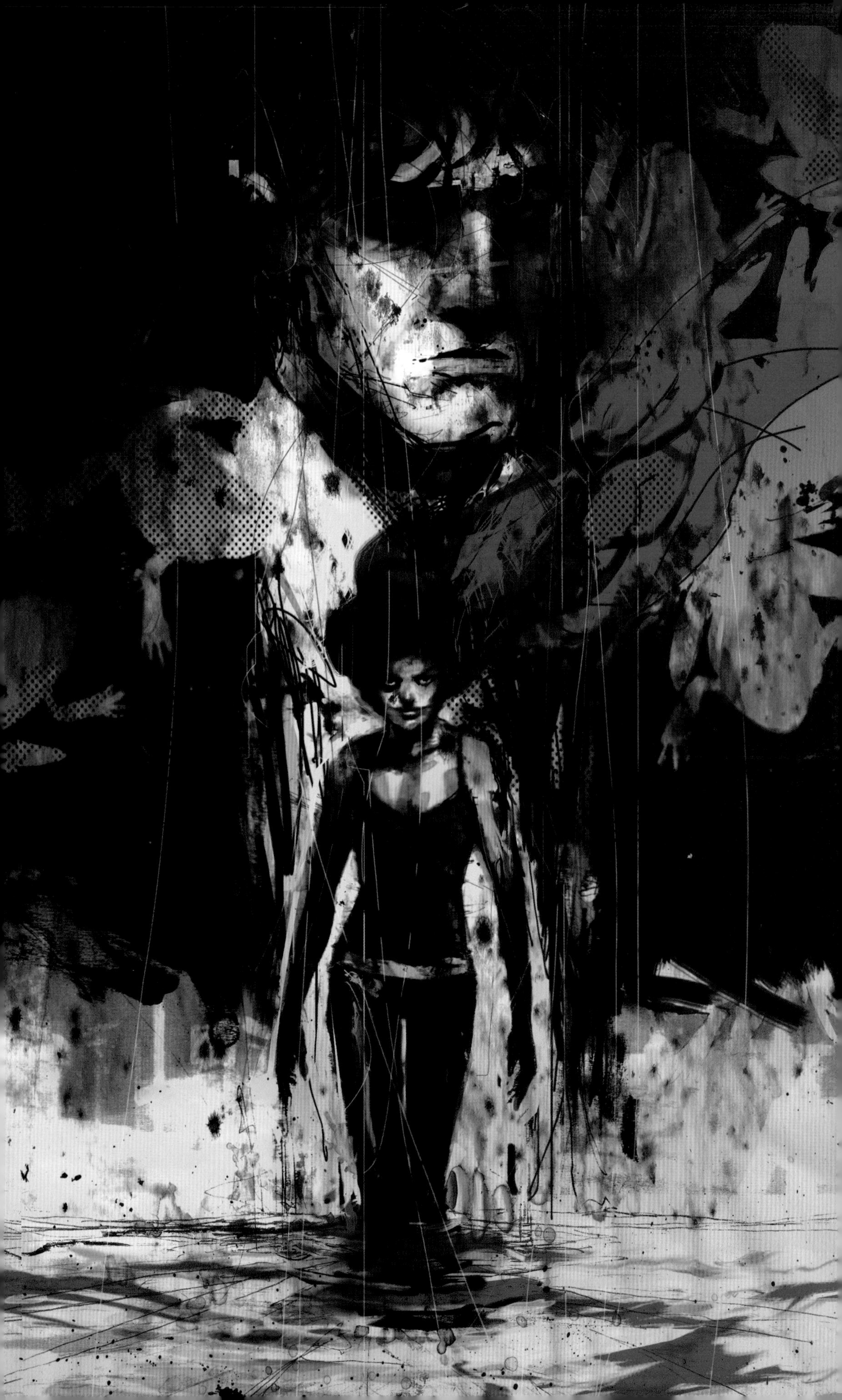

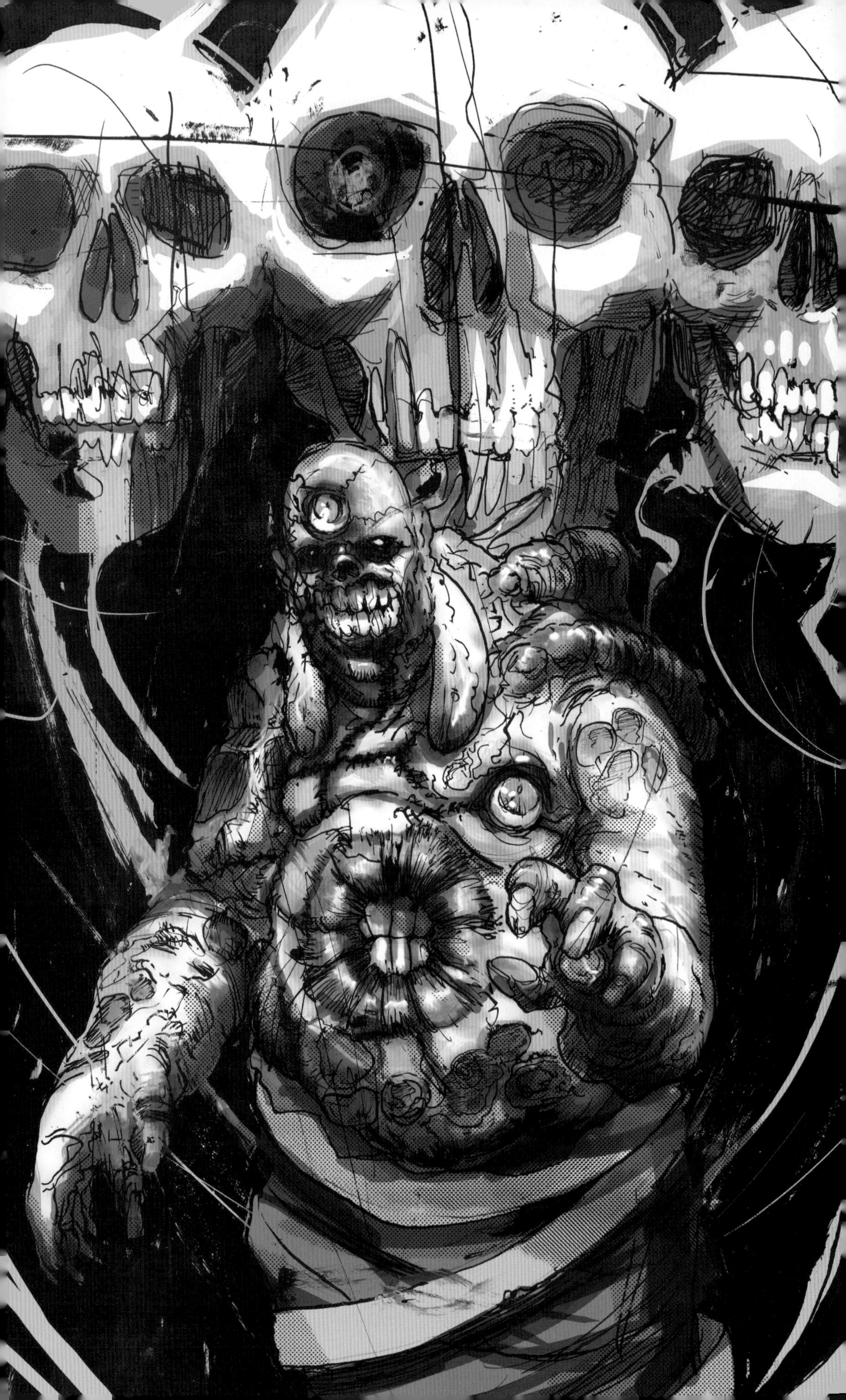

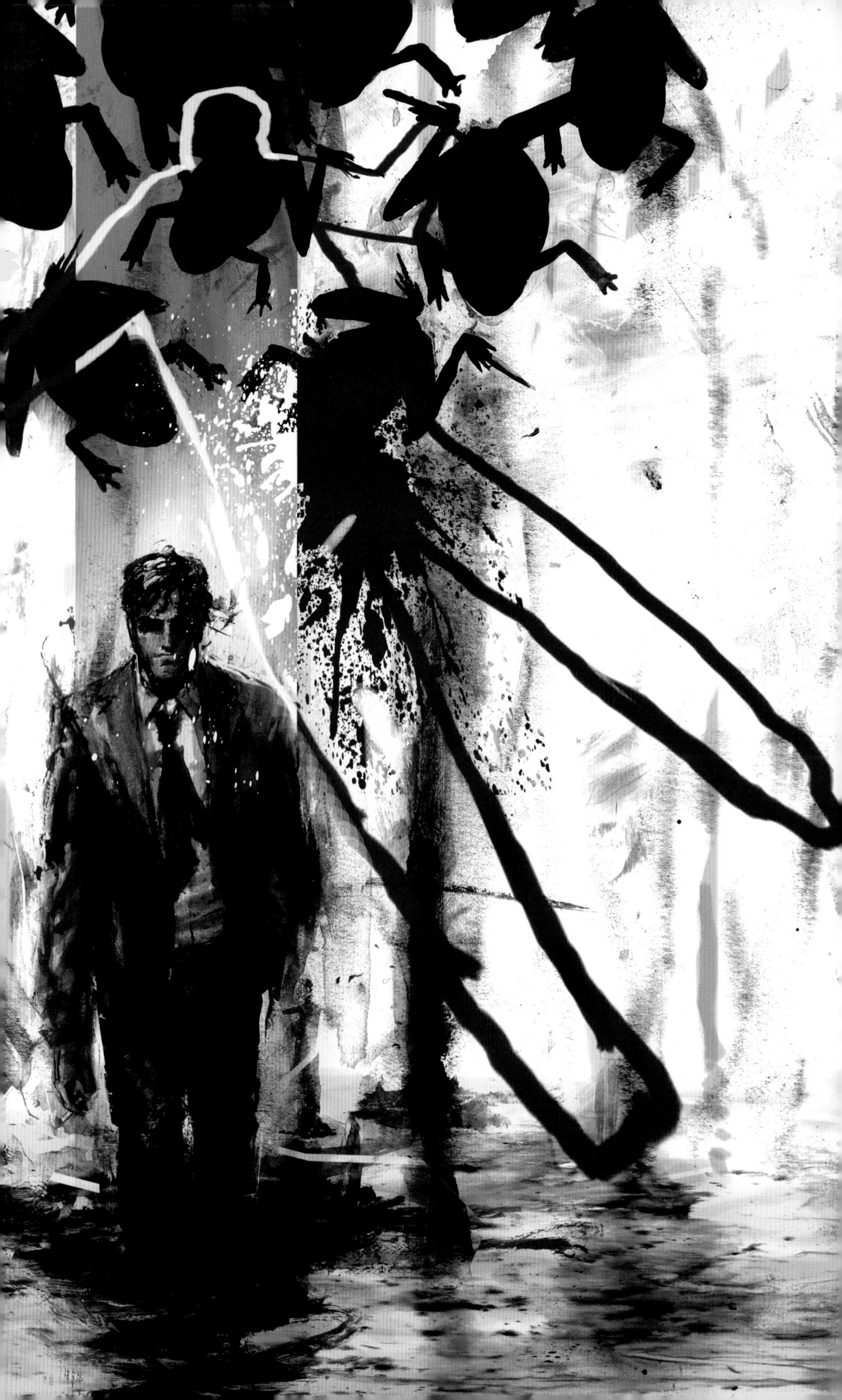

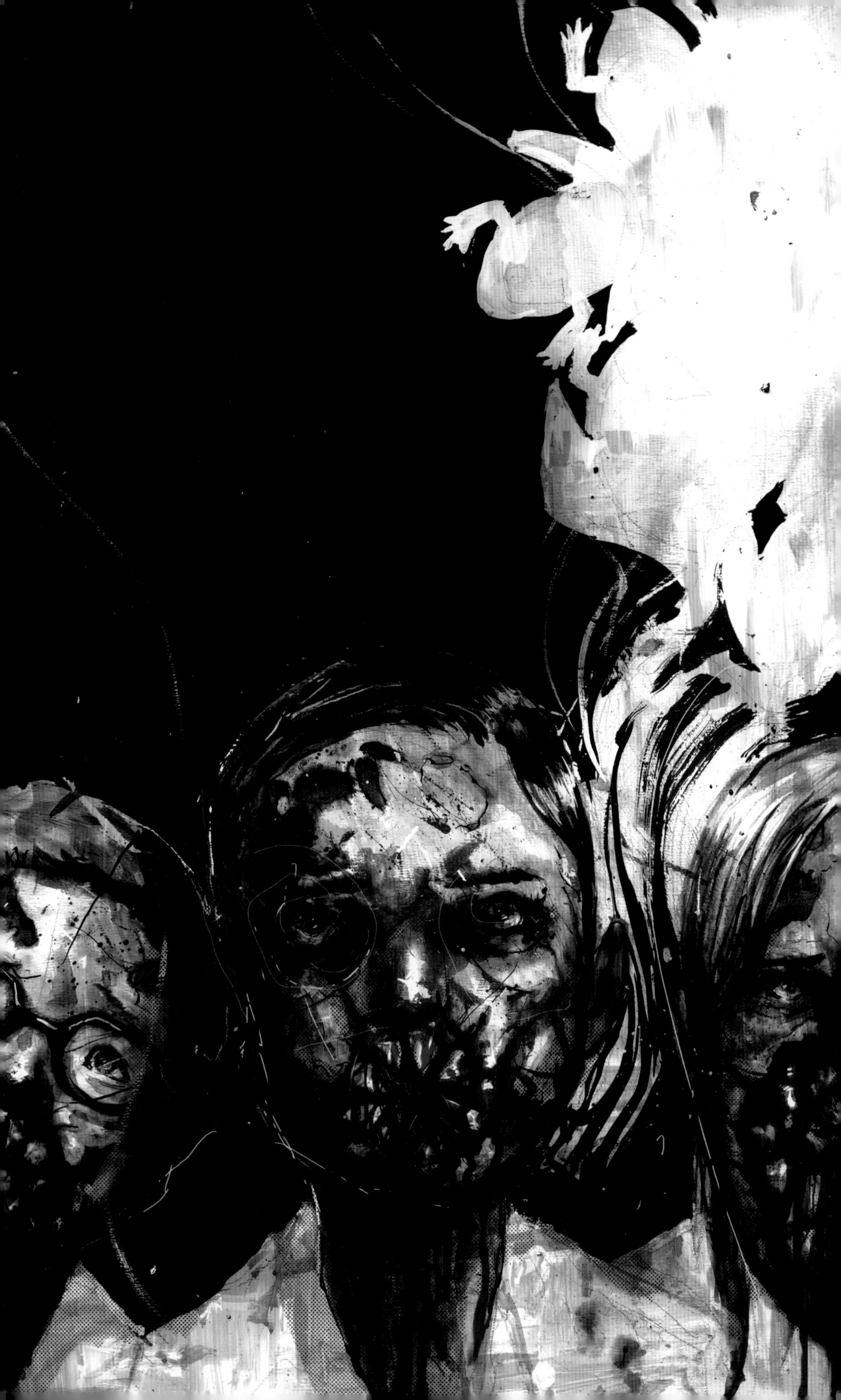

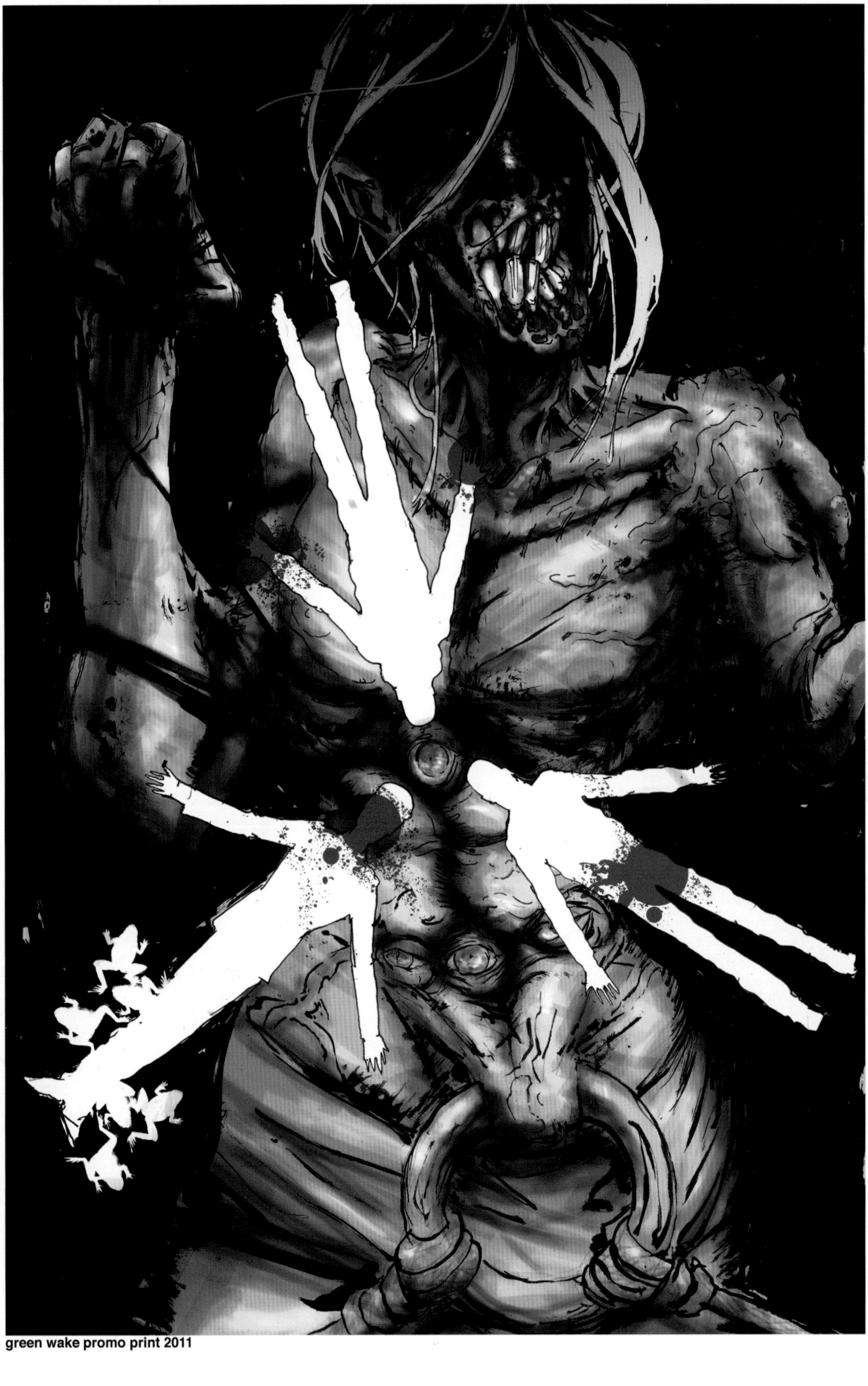

green wake promo print 2011